ILLUSTRATED ACTS IN GREEK

GlossaHouse Illustrated Biblical Texts

ILLUSTRATED ACTS IN GREEK

GlossaHouse Illustrated Biblical Texts

Fredrick J. Long

Matthew R. Peterson

GlossaHouse

Wilmore, KY

www.GlossaHouse.com

Illustrated Acts in Greek
Copyright © 2019 by GlossaHouse, LLC

GlossaHouse, LLC 110
Callis Circle
Wilmore, KY 40390

Bible. Acts. Greek (Tyndale Greek New Testament). 2017.
  Illustrated Acts in Greek : GlossaHouse Illustrated Biblical Texts / Fredrick J. Long, Matthew R. Peterson, [Keith Neely, illustrator].– Wilmore, KY : GlossaHouse, [©2019].
xviii, 140 pages : color illustrations ; 28 cm. – (Accessible Greek Resources and Online Studies
series. GlossaHouse Illustrated Biblical Texts. Bible)

Summary: The Greek text of the Acts of the Apostles is set within colorful illustrations to represent narration, dialogue, monologue, and scripture quotations, together with a new English version by GlossaHouse translators. Text in English and Koinē Greek.

Library of Congress Control Number: 2018911429

ISBN: 978-1942697763 (pb)

1. Bible. John – Cartoons and comics. I. Long, Fredrick J., 1966- II. Peterson, Matthew R.   III. Neely, Keith, 1943- IV. Title. IV. Series. V. Bible. Acts. English. 2019.

Cover Design by T. Michael W. Halcomb and Fredrick J. Long.
Book Design by Samuel T. Long, Fredrick J. Long, and Matthew R. Peterson
Illustration Design by Keith Neely

Dedicated to every student of the earliest church
aspiring to access the earliest narrative account
in the original Greek language.

AGROS

ACCESSIBLE GREEK RESOURCES AND ONLINE STUDIES

SERIES EDITORS

T. Michael W. Halcomb   Fredrick J. Long

GlossaHouse

Wilmore, KY

www.GlossaHouse.com

AGROS

The Greek word ἀγρός is a field where seeds are planted and growth occurs. It can also denote a small village or community that forms around such a field. The type of community envisioned here is one that attends to Holy Scripture, particularly one that encourages the use of biblical Greek. Accessible Greek Resources and Online Studies (AGROS) is a tiered curriculum suite featuring innovative readers, grammars, specialized studies, and other exegetical resources to encourage and foster the exegetical use of biblical Greek. The goal of AGROS is to facilitate the creation and publication of innovative and affordable print and digital resources for the exposition of Scripture within the context of the global church. The AGROS curriculum includes five tiers, and each tier is indicated on the book's cover: Tier 1 (Beginning I), Tier 2 (Beginning II), Tier 3 (Intermediate I), Tier 4 (Intermediate II), and Tier 5 (Advanced). There are also two resource tracks: Conversational and Translational. Both involve intensive study of morphology, grammar, syntax, and discourse features. The conversational track specifically values the spoken word, and the enhanced learning associated with speaking a language in actual conversation. The translational track values the written word, and encourages analytical study to aide in understanding and translating biblical Greek and other Greek literature. The two resource tracks complement one another and can be pursued independently or together.

GLOSSAHOUSE ILLUSTRATED BIBLICAL TEXTS

TABLE OF CONTENTS

INTRODUCTION

Illustrated Acts in Greek has been carefully designed from the initial editing of the Greek text, its translation, its textual layout, and choices made to best render intertextuality and intratextuality.

GREEK TEXT

The Greek text is from *The Greek New Testament, Produced at Tyndale House, Cambridge* under the oversight of editors Dirk Jongkind (St. Edmund's College, University of Cambridge) and Peter Williams (Tyndale House, Cambridge) with permissions from Crossway Publishing.

TRANSLATION

At the bottom of each page is the GlossaHouse English Version (GEV) prepared by Fredrick J. Long with some feedback from Matthew R. Peterson.[1] This translation freshly considered Greek word meanings in ancient context and is fairly literal; it attempts to preserve word order significance where this does not sound (too) unnatural in English. At the same time, the translation attempts to accurately represent important features of the Greek text reflecting prominence such as emphatic subject pronouns, double-negated sentences, rhetorical questions expecting "yes" or "no" responses, etc. Essentially, an attempt was made to represent every lexical unit/word in translation. Moreover, any English words supplied for idiomatic English translation that are not strictly found in the Greek text are placed inside of brackets. Such places attest to Greek idiom and ellipses. Then, too, where intensity of emotion was likely experienced in speech acts, such received an exclamation mark in translation. All of these features are intended for beginning students who may need help with Greek word meanings and understanding the significance of special constructions.

Some specific points of translation merit some discussion here: connectives, participles, and verbal aspect. First, some attempt was made to render connectives according to their basic "processing constraint" as recently studied and written about by Stephen H. Levinsohn, Steven E. Runge, Fredrick J. Long, and Christopher J. Fresch.[2] The conjunction καί was consistently translated "*and*" unless it is used in thematic addition constructions (*also, even*) in which cases it us translated right before the word it thematically adds. The conjunction Δέ presents more of a challenge since it marks +new development and this constraint may be translated variously into English idiom in context. Long suggests possible translations of "and, but, moreover, additionally" or possibly "well, … next."[3] Throughout Acts, δέ is typically rendered in one of these ways (except for "*and*") and very infrequently as "*then*," which then overlaps in translation with sentence initial τότε as found in 1:12; 4:8; 5:26 *et passim*. One also encounters the postpositive τέ quite often that marks +sameness; within discourse, τέ signifies that the next clause

---

[1] Cf. the basic translation philosophies as found in the introduction of T. Michael W. Halcomb and Fredrick J. Long, *Illustrated Mark in Greek*, GlossaHouse Illustrated Biblical Texts (Wilmore, KY: GlossaHouse, 2018) and idem, *Illustrated John in Greek*, GlossaHouse Illustrated Biblical Texts (Wilmore, KY: GlossaHouse, 2018)

[2] For a summary and bibliography, see Fredrick J. Long, *In Step with God's Word: Interpreting the New Testament with God's People*, GlossaHouse Hermeneutics & Translation 1 (Wilmore, KY: GlossaHouse, 2017), 120–25.

[3] Long, *Koine Greek Grammar: A Beginning-Intermediate Exegetical and Pragmatic Handbook*, Accessible Greek Resources and Online Studies (Wilmore, KY: GlossaHouse, 2015), 62, 65.

belongs in the same "scene" or mental representation as what preceded.[4] Throughout Acts, an attempt was made to translate τέ as "[and] at the same time, ..." to signify that the following clause belongs with the previous description.

Translating circumstantial participles, which are in fact unmarked for adverbial senses except possibly relative time,[5] represents an interesting exercise and challenge. It is somewhat conventional to render prepositioned aorist circumstantial participles as "time-prior" as in "<u>after doing</u> this or that...." or "<u>having done</u> this or that...." However, in this translation using "after" was avoided, being reserved for other constructions explicitly marking "after" such as μετά + acc. (5:37; 13:15; 18:1, etc.) or μετά with an infinitive (e.g., 10:41; 12:4, etc.). Thus, throughout one will find circumstantial participles translated quite minimally as in "coming..." or "saying these things ..." and occasionally marking time prior with aorist participles by using "having done...." In genitive absolute constructions which feature different agent(s) than the main verb, this minimal approach was not possible; so, fairly consistently genitive absolutes are introduced by "<u>with</u> so and so <u>doing</u> such and such...," and set off by commas. The reason for translating these circumstantial participles so minimally was to allow readers to more readily understand when Greek subordinating conjunctions were actually used (instead of participles) which are marked for adverbial meanings. Such subordinating conjunctions and constructions include ὡς ("as, when, while"), ὅτε ("when"), ἐν with the infinitive ("while"), etc. For example, consider these examples that illustrated some of these distinctions:

1:10 καὶ <u>ὡς</u> ἀτενίζοντες ἦσαν εἰς τὸν οὐρανὸν <u>πορευομένου αὐτοῦ</u>, καὶ ἰδοὺ ἄνδρες δύο παρειστήκεισαν αὐτοῖς ἐν ἐσθήσεσι λευκαῖς

1:10 And <u>as</u> [conjunction ὡς] they were gazing into heaven, <u>with him going away</u> [genitive absolute], also, behold, two men stood by them in white garments,

9:1–2a Ὁ δὲ Σαῦλος ἔτι <u>ἐμπνέων</u> ἀπειλῆς καὶ φόνου εἰς τοὺς μαθητὰς τοῦ κυρίου, <u>προσελθὼν</u> τῷ ἀρχιερεῖ, 2a ἠτήσατο παρ' αὐτοῦ ἐπιστολὰς εἰς Δαμασκὸν πρὸς τὰς συναγωγάς,

9:1–2a But Saul, still <u>breathing</u> [present circumstantial participle] threats and murder towards the disciples of the Lord, <u>having gone</u> [aorist circumstantial participle] to the high priest, 2a asked from him letters for Damascus to the synagogues,

Translating the participles in this minimal way, we think, helps to convey the action-packed events throughout Acts.

When translating indicative mood verbs an attempt was made to render the verbal aspect transparently. So, present tense verbs are often translated to reflect the incomplete and (implied) ongoingness of the action. Also, imperfect tense verbs are regularly translated with "was/were doing" and historic presents (somewhat rare) as simple English presents ("He says"). Likewise, this principle often applied to non-Indicative moods such that, if it were possible with reasonable English idiom, present tense infinitives and commands with imperfect aspect were translated to reflect such as in "be doing such and such...," "keep doing such and such...", or "continue to do such and such...." The examples below reflect these conventions:

---

[4] See the discussion and examples in Levinsohn, *Discourse Features of New Testament Greek: A Coursebook on the Information Structure of New Testament Greek*, 2nd ed. (Dallas: Summer Institute of Linguistics, 2000), 106–11.

[5] See the discussion in Long, *Koine Greek Grammar*, 326, 334–36

10:27–28a καὶ συνομιλῶν αὐτῷ <u>εἰσῆλθεν</u> καὶ εὑρίσκει συνεληλυθότας πολλούς, 28a ἔφη τε πρὸς αὐτούς·

10:27–28a And conversing with him, he <u>entered in</u> [aorist; perfective aspect] and finds [historic present] many having gathered together, 28a and at the same time he <u>was saying</u> [ἔφη parsed as imperfect tense] to them,

15:5 Ἐξανέστησαν δέ τινες τῶν ἀπὸ τῆς αἱρέσεως τῶν Φαρισαίων πεπιστευκότες, λέγοντες ὅτι δεῖ <u>περιτέμνειν</u> αὐτοὺς <u>παραγγέλλειν</u> τε τηρεῖν τὸν νόμον Μωϋσέως.

15:5 But some of the ones from the sect of the Pharisees who had believed rose up, saying this: "It is necessary <u>to be circumcising</u> them as well as <u>to be commanding</u> them <u>to continue keeping</u> the Law of Moses!" [each is a present tense infinitive]

Also, the form ἔφη, which may be parsed as imperfect or aorist, is translated always as imperfect since the aorist form εἶπεν was readily available for the author of Acts to use; thus, the change to ἔφη seemed to denote a difference of some kind that the original audience would have heard.

TEXT LAYOUT

Elements of Speech Arrangement

We have striven to preserve core elements of speech on the same line. For example, articles are kept on the same line as their associated nouns. Conjunctions that begin a new thought also generally appear on the same line as the thoughts that they begin.

There are some instances in which this approach could not be adhered to perfectly due to the constraints of working with images originally tied to an English text. Some longer words have been hyphenated to fit within the available space. For these cases the words are broken following a prefix or verbal stem to minimize confusion.

Verse Ranges & Numbers

For your reference the verse range covered by a page is provided at the top left of each even-numbered page and at the top right of each odd-numbered page. Verse numbers within narration and speech are presented in bold, orange text. Chapter numbers are only provided for the first verse of the chapter. Partial verses (e.g., 4a, 4b) are designated only when a verse has been broken up across images on different vertical levels of the page or across two different pages, in which case this will also be marked in the verse range at the top of the page.

Narration Boxes, Speech Bubbles, etc.

As a narrative text, Acts contains several different forms of communication. Much of the text is split between Luke's narration and direct speech by characters in the book. Our effort with this work has been to employ several visual indications for different forms of communication in order to aid the reader much like in a comic book. The types of communication and their associated elements are as follows:

ELEMENT TYPE	"FORM" OF TEXT
Tan Box with Justified Text	Narration
Speech Bubble with Centered Text	Direct Speech by a Character
Speech Bubble with Centered Text and Multiple Direction Tails	Direct Speech by Multiple Characters
Centered Text Directly on Background Image	Direct Speech of a Divine Character
'Scroll' Box with Centered Text	Direct Quotation from Old Testament
'Scroll' Incorporated into the Background Image with Centered Text	Written Letter of Correspondence (Page 71—Acts 15:23–29; Page 118—Acts 23:26–30)
Bolded, Italicized Text	Recalled Divine Speech from Earlier in the Book within a Character's Speech
Bolded Text	Quotation of Extra-Biblical Literature (Page 86—Acts 17:28)

Ambiguity in Rendering Choices

Some instances exist in which there is ambiguity as to how to properly render a text. One key case is Acts 14:22 (page 67) which reads:

ἐπιστηρίζοντες τὰς ψυχὰς τῶν μαθητῶν, παρακαλοῦντες ἐμμένειν τῇ πίστει καὶ ὅτι διὰ πολλῶν θλίψεων δεῖ ἡμᾶς εἰσελθεῖν εἰς τὴν βασιλείαν τοῦ θεοῦ.

The text occurs in a narration section covering the work of Paul and Barnabas with the churches in Lystra, Iconium, and Antioch. The full verse is rendered as narration in the KJV and ESV. In the NIV, NKJV, and NRSV the last third is provided as speech. The presence of a ὅτι conjunction followed by a first-person plural pronoun (ἡμᾶς) can be taken as an indication of speech, which we have adopted in the illustrated text.

As with all instances of ambiguity and formatting decisions in general, such decisions involve a degree of interpretation; we welcome you, as the reader, to arrive at your own determination when consulting the Greek text via other modern critical Greek editions or translations.

'Omitted Verses' in Greek vs English

Readers who primarily use the KJV or NKJV translations for their devotional reading or do not have access to a modern critical Greek text may notice several instances where verses are 'omitted' in this text. These verses that appear in the Textus Receptus only occur in certain manuscripts and have not been included in the Greek texts upon which more recent English translations such as the NIV and NRSV are based. Some English versions that omit these verses will often include a footnote indicating the removed text. Due to space limitations we have placed an asterisk (*) next to the following verse's number to indicate when this occurs.

The following verse numbers (and associated text) are omitted:

8:37 (page 33)   15:34 (page 72)   24:7 (page 120)   28:29 (page 140)

A special case occurs at Acts 19:40 (page 98) where most English translations split the text into two texts, making the chapter end with verse 41. Modern critical Greek editions do not divide the text but instead preserve it within a single verse. As no text is omitted in this section, the asterisk has been placed at the numbering for verse 40.

RENDERING INTERTEXTUALITY AND INTRATEXTUALITY

Intertextuality

Within Acts, Luke engages with the Old Testament in a variety of ways including direct quotation, allusion, and summary. These different uses have required interpretation on our part in deciding when to incorporate the 'Scroll' background designated for uses of the Old Testament. We have opted to provide these backgrounds for clear direct quotations that form significant arguments within the speech of characters or when Luke has signaled that an Old Testament text was being read. They are not used for allusions to or summaries of Old Testament events.

Examples of this approach can be seen throughout the book, but are especially prominent in the major speeches by Peter, Stephen, and Paul. Stephen's speech in 7:2–53 (pages 20–26) serves as a good review:

Page 20	7:2–3a summarizes God's appearance to Abraham and therefore *does not* receive a background.
	7:3b is a direct quotation of God's command in Genesis 12:1 and therefore has received a scroll background.
Page 21	7:6b–7 is a direct quotation of God's promise to Abraham in Genesis 15 and receives a scroll background. The remainder of the page contains summaries of related events which *do not* receive it.
Page 22	This page contains only summary of Old Testament events. None of this text is given a scroll background.
Page 23	7:26–28 contain the discussion between Moses and an Israelite over his killing of an Egyptian in Exodus 2. Because this discussion does not form a significant part of Stephen's argument it has not been given a scroll background.
	7:32 is direct speech by God to Moses from the burning bush in Exodus 3 and therefore has been given a scroll background.
Page 24	7:33–34 continues God's speech to Moses from Exodus 3 and has received a scroll background.
	7:35 is a repetition of the Israelite's charge against Moses in Exodus 2 and has not received a scroll background.
	7:37 quotes from Moses in Deuteronomy 18:15 where he states that God would send another prophet. This theme is significant in the context of Stephen's speech and has therefore received a scroll background.

Page 25	7:40 refers to the demand by the crowd that Aaron fashion an idol and has not received a scroll background.
	7:42–43 cites from a prophetic denunciation in Amos 5:25–27 and therefore has received a scroll background.
Page 26	7:49–50 form a closing statement that cites from Isaiah 66. It has been given a scroll background.

During his Areopagus speech in Athens (17:22–31) Paul appeals to the words of two Greek philosophers as part of his argument. These non-biblical texts are nevertheless citations. They have been rendered in plain **bold** text to indicate that he is engaging in a sort of proof-texting.

Intratextuality

The major speeches in Acts present interesting challenges for readers hoping to discern thematic links across the book. This is especially so when a speech incorporates words spoken by different characters at an earlier point in the wider narrative of Luke-Acts. In an effort to make these links more easily recognizable, we have rendered instances of recalled divine/supernatural speech in ***bold italicized*** text, as in the following cases:

Peter's Speech Recalling the Conversion of Cornelius (11:5–17)	
Page 47	11:7 and 9 recall God's direct speech to Peter in his vision of the unclean foods in ch. 10. These have been rendered in bold italic text to distinguish them from Peter's own thought and words.
	11:8, however, is Peter's recollection of his own response to God. This *has not* been rendered differently from the remainder of the text.
	11:13–14 contain a recollection of the angel's words to Cornelius in ch. 10. This has been rendered in bold italic text.
Page 48	11:16 includes Peter's remembrance of the words of Jesus in 1:5. This has been rendered in bold italic text.

Paul's Defense Speech in Jerusalem (22:1–21)	
Page 110	22:7, 8, and 10 each contain remembered words of Jesus from Paul's Damascus Road encounter in ch. 9. These have been rendered in bold italic text to distinguish from Paul's own thoughts and remembered speech in the surrounding context.
Page 111	22:18 and 21 contain Paul's recollection of a subsequent encounter with Jesus while praying in the temple at Jerusalem. Although this is not mentioned earlier in the narrative of Acts, it has been rendered in bold italic text to distinguish Jesus's words from Paul's.

| **Paul's Defense Speech before Festus and Agrippa (26:1–29)** | |
| Page 127 | 26:14–18 contain remembered words of Jesus from Paul's Damascus Road encounter in ch. 9. These have been rendered in bold italic text to distinguish from Paul's own thoughts and remembered speech in the surrounding context. |

KOINE ERA PRONUNCIATION

Finally, we encourage students learning Greek to adopt a restored Koine Era Pronunciation (KEP).[6] On the next page is a comprehensive overview of KEP and below are the most essential differences when transitioning from Erasmian pronunciation to KEP.

Vowels and Vowel Pairs (Monophthongs and Diphthongs)

ε = "eh" as in "b<u>e</u>t" (**not** "ah" or "[h]ay" [long "aaa"])
αι = "eh" as in "b<u>e</u>t" (**not** "eye/ I").
Thus, ε = αι in KEP. So, καί = "keh"

η = "ay" (long a) sound **not** "eh"

ι = "ee" sound
ει = "ee" sound

υ = "eew" as in ewe or au <u>jus</u> (French)
οι = "eew" as in ewe or au <u>jus</u> (French)

ο and ω are both long "o" sounds.

υ after α, ε, η is a "v" sound. Thus,
αυ = av (as in <u>av</u>ocado),
ευ = ev (<u>ev</u>ery),
ηυ = ay-v (as in "s<u>av</u>e")

Consonants

γ before ε, ει, ι = "y" sound as in "<u>y</u>et"
γ before other vowels = "gh" as in "<u>gh</u>ost"
δ = soft "th" or "dh" sound (**not** a hard "d" sound) as in "<u>th</u>e"

Consonant Pairs

γγ = "ng" sound (with the second gamma as in "get"); so, ἄγγελος = "an-ge-lohs"
γκ = "nk" sound as in "du<u>nk</u>"
γχ = "nkh sound as in "a<u>nkh</u>"
γξ = "nks" sound as in "tha<u>nks</u>"
ντ = "nd" sound; so -ονται is pronounced "own-deh"
μβ = "mv" sound as in "Hu<u>mv</u>ee"

---

[6] See Halcomb and Long, *Illustrated Mark*, ix and Long, *Koine Greek Grammar*, ch. 2.

OVERVIEW OF KOINE ERA PRONUNCIATION (KEP)

ALPHABET			
Letters	*Transliteration Value*	*Pronunciation (Approx. English Value/Sound)*	*Examples of Greek Words Transliterated*
Α, α	A, a	ah – tor<u>ah</u>	λαμβάνω <u>l</u>am<u>v</u>anō
Β, β	V, v	v – <u>v</u>et	λαμβάνω lam<u>v</u>anō
Γ, γ	Y, y – before ε, ι, ει Gh, gh – before other vowels	y – <u>y</u>et gh – <u>gh</u>ost (but a bit softer)	ἅγιος a-<u>yi</u>ōs ἀγαθός a<u>gh</u>athōs
Δ, δ	Dh, dh or Th, th	dh – <u>th</u>e (no good English equivalent) th – <u>th</u>e	διά <u>dh</u>ia, <u>th</u>ia
Ε, ε	E, e	eh – mikv<u>eh</u>	σέ, s<u>eh</u>
Ζ, ζ	Z, z	z – <u>z</u>oo	ζῷον, <u>z</u>ōōn
Η, η	Ā, ā	āy – p<u>ay</u>	μή, m<u>āy</u>
Θ, ϑ	Th, th	th – <u>th</u>ink	θεός, <u>th</u>eh-ōs
Ι, ι	I, i Y, y (in Hebrew names in Greek)	ee – b<u>ee</u>t y – <u>y</u>es (often will begin words)	τίς, t<u>ee</u>s Ἰησοῦς <u>Y</u>āy-sous
Κ, κ	K, k	k – <u>k</u>ey	καί, <u>k</u>eh
Λ, λ	L, l	l – <u>l</u>eg	λέγω, <u>l</u>egō
Μ, μ	M, m	m – <u>m</u>ad	μέν, <u>m</u>ehn
Ν, ν	N, n	n – <u>n</u>o	νῦν, <u>n</u>eew<u>n</u>
Ξ, ξ	Ks, ks	ks – boo<u>ks</u>	ξένος, <u>ks</u>enōs
Ο, ο	Ō, ō	o – g<u>o</u>	πρός, pr<u>ō</u>s
Π, π	P, p	p – <u>p</u>eek	παῖς, <u>p</u>ehs
Ρ, ρ	R, r	r – <u>r</u>im (trill/roll)	ῥίζα, <u>r</u>iza
Σ, σ, ς	S, s	s – <u>s</u>it	σοῦ, <u>s</u>ou
Τ, τ	T, t	t – <u>t</u>ip	τίς, <u>t</u>ees
Υ, υ	Y, y V, v – in diphthongs following α, ε, η (i.e. αυ, ευ, ηυ)	eew – au jus (cf. οι) av – <u>av</u>ocado (αυ) ev – <u>ev</u>ery (ευ) āv – <u>āv</u>ery (ηυ)	κύριος, <u>ky</u>r-iōs For examples, see diphthongs at right.
Φ, φ	F, f (or Ph, ph)	f – <u>f</u>it	φάγε, <u>fa</u>-yeh
Χ, χ	Kh, kh (or X, x)	kh – bac<u>kh</u>oe (guttural)	χάρις <u>kh</u>aris
Ψ, ψ	Ps, ps	ps – <u>ps</u>alm	ψώρα, <u>ps</u>ōra
Ω, ω	Ō, ō	o – g<u>o</u>	ᾠόν, <u>ōō</u>n

VOWEL PAIRS		
Letters	*Transliteration Value*	*Pronunciation (Approx. English Value/Sound)*
αι	ai	ai (= eh) – s<u>ai</u>d
αυ	af, av (before β, δ, γ, λ, μ, ν, ρ, ζ)	av – <u>av</u>ocado af – w<u>af</u>t
ει	ei	ee – b<u>ee</u>t
ευ	ef, ev (before β, δ, γ, λ, μ, ν, ρ, ζ)	ev – <u>ev</u>ery ef – <u>l</u>eft
ηυ	āf, āv (before β, δ, γ, λ, μ, ν, ρ, ζ)	āv – <u>āv</u>ery āf – s<u>āf</u>e
οι	oi	like "eew" in "jus" of French "au jus"
ου	ou	ou – c<u>ou</u>p
υι	ui	iy – ter<u>iy</u>aki

CONSONANT PAIRS		
γγ	ng	ng – ha<u>ng</u>
γκ	nk	nk – du<u>nk</u>
γχ	nkh	nkh – a<u>nkh</u>
γξ	nks	nks – tha<u>nks</u>
μβ	mv	mv – hu<u>mv</u>ee
ντ	nt	nt – a<u>nt</u>, or nd – a<u>nd</u>

Note: While the rough breathing mark is denoted in writing (e.g., Ἡ, ἡ), there is no "rough breathing" sound (the voiced "h" in "ha" or "help") articulated in the Koine Era Pronunciation. This is because aspiration (rough breathing) had fallen out of use hundreds of years prior to the Koine-Hellenistic era. In spite of this fact, Erasmian pronunciation continues to use rough breathing.

ΠΡΑΞΕΙΣ ΑΠΟΣΤΟΛΩΝ
The Acts of the Apostles

Acts
Chapter
1

1:1 Τὸν μὲν πρῶτον λόγον ἐποιησάμην περὶ πάντων, ὦ Θεόφιλε, ὧν ἤρξατο ὁ Ἰησοῦς ποιεῖν τε καὶ διδάσκειν 2 ἄχρι ἧς ἡμέρας ἐντειλάμενος τοῖς ἀποστόλοις διὰ πνεύματος ἁγίου οὓς ἐξελέξατο ἀνελήμφθη. 3 οἷς καὶ παρέστησεν ἑαυτὸν ζῶντα μετὰ τὸ παθεῖν αὐτὸν ἐν πολλοῖς τεκμηρίοις, δι᾽ ἡμερῶν τεσσεράκοντα ὀπτανόμενος αὐτοῖς

καὶ λέγων τὰ περὶ τῆς βασιλείας τοῦ θεοῦ.

4a καὶ συναλιζόμενος παρήγγειλεν αὐτοῖς ἀπὸ Ἱεροσολύμων μὴ χωρίζεσθαι, ἀλλὰ περιμένειν

4b τὴν ἐπαγγελίαν τοῦ πατρὸς ἣν ἠκούσατέ μου· 5 ὅτι Ἰωάννης μὲν ἐβάπτισεν ὕδατι, ὑμεῖς δὲ ἐν πνεύματι βαπτισθήσεσθε ἁγίῳ οὐ μετὰ πολλὰς ταύτας ἡμέρας.

6 Οἱ μὲν οὖν συνελθόντες ἠρώτων αὐτὸν λέγοντες·

κύριε, εἰ ἐν τῷ χρόνῳ τούτῳ ἀποκαθιστάνεις τὴν βασιλείαν τῷ Ἰσραήλ;

7 εἶπεν δὲ πρὸς αὐτούς·

οὐχ ὑμῶν ἐστιν γνῶναι χρόνους ἢ καιροὺς οὓς ὁ πατὴρ ἔθετο ἐν τῇ ἰδίᾳ ἐξουσίᾳ,

8 ἀλλὰ λήμψεσθε δύναμιν ἐπελθόντος τοῦ ἁγίου πνεύματος ἐφ᾽ ὑμᾶς καὶ ἔσεσθέ μου μάρτυρες ἔν τε Ἱερουσαλὴμ καὶ ἐν πάσῃ τῇ Ἰουδαίᾳ καὶ Σαμαρείᾳ καὶ ἕως ἐσχάτου τῆς γῆς.

9 καὶ ταῦτα εἰπὼν βλεπόντων αὐτῶν ἐπήρθη καὶ νεφέλη ὑπέλαβεν αὐτὸν ἀπὸ τῶν ὀφθαλμῶν αὐτῶν. 10 καὶ ὡς ἀτενίζοντες ἦσαν εἰς τὸν οὐρανὸν πορευομένου αὐτοῦ, καὶ ἰδοὺ ἄνδρες δύο παρειστήκεισαν αὐτοῖς ἐν ἐσθήσεσι λευκαῖς,

1:1 The former treatise indeed I made concerning all, O Theophilus, that Jesus began both to do and to teach, 2 until the day on which, having given commandment through the Holy Spirit to the apostles whom he had chosen, he was received up; 3 to whom he also presented himself alive after his passion by many proofs, appearing to them over forty days and speaking about the things concerning the kingdom of God. 4 And, eating together, he charged them not to depart from Jerusalem, but to wait for "the promise of the Father, which, [as he said,] you heard from me; 5 for John indeed baptized with water; but you will be baptized in the Holy Spirit not after these many days." 6 So then, they, having come together, asked him saying, "Lord, are you at this time restoring the kingdom to Israel?" 7 But he said to them, "It is not for you to know times or seasons that the Father set within His own authority. 8 Rather, you will receive power when the Holy Spirit comes upon you; and you will be my witnesses in Jerusalem and in all Judea and Samaria, and as far as the end of the earth." 9 And having said these things, with them looking, he was taken up; and a cloud received him out of their sight. 10 And as they were gazing into heaven, with him going away, also, behold, two men stood by them in white garments,

11 οἳ καὶ εἶπαν· ἄνδρες Γαλιλαῖοι, τί ἑστήκατε βλέποντες εἰς τὸν οὐρανόν; οὗτος ὁ Ἰησοῦς ὁ ἀναλημφθεὶς ἀφ' ὑμῶν εἰς τὸν οὐρανὸν οὕτως ἐλεύσεται ὃν τρόπον ἐθεάσασθε αὐτὸν πορευόμενον εἰς τὸν οὐρανόν.

12 Τότε ὑπέστρεψαν εἰς Ἰερουσαλὴμ ἀπὸ ὄρους τοῦ καλουμένου Ἐλαιῶνος, ὅ ἐστιν ἐγγὺς Ἰερουσαλὴμ σαββάτου ἔχον ὁδόν. **13a** καὶ ὅτε εἰσῆλθον, εἰς τὸ ὑπερῷον ἀνέβησαν οὗ ἦσαν καταμένοντες,

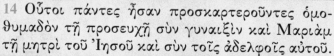

13b ὅ τε Πέτρος καὶ Ἰωάννης καὶ Ἰάκωβος καὶ Ἀνδρέας, Φίλιππος καὶ Θωμᾶς, Βαρθολομαῖος καὶ Μαθθαῖος, Ἰάκωβος Ἀλφαίου καὶ Σίμων ὁ ζηλωτὴς καὶ Ἰούδας Ἰακώβου.

14 Οὗτοι πάντες ἦσαν προσκαρτεροῦντες ὁμοθυμαδὸν τῇ προσευχῇ σὺν γυναιξὶν καὶ Μαριὰμ τῇ μητρὶ τοῦ Ἰησοῦ καὶ σὺν τοῖς ἀδελφοῖς αὐτοῦ.

15 Καὶ ἐν ταῖς ἡμέραις ταύταις ἀναστὰς Πέτρος ἐν μέσῳ τῶν ἀδελφῶν εἶπεν· ἦν τε ὄχλος ὀνομάτων ἐπὶ τὸ αὐτὸ ὡς ἑκατὸν εἴκοσι·

16 ἄνδρες ἀδελφοί, ἔδει πληρωθῆναι τὴν γραφὴν ἣν προεῖπεν τὸ πνεῦμα τὸ ἅγιον διὰ στόματος Δαυεὶδ περὶ Ἰούδα τοῦ γενομένου ὁδηγοῦ τοῖς συλλαβοῦσιν Ἰησοῦν· **17** ὅτι κατηριθμημένος ἦν ἐν ἡμῖν καὶ ἔλαχεν τὸν κλῆρον τῆς διακονίας ταύτης.

18 οὗτος μὲν οὖν ἐκτήσατο χωρίον ἐκ μισθοῦ τῆς ἀδικίας, καὶ πρηνὴς γενόμενος ἐλάκησεν μέσος καὶ ἐξεχύθη πάντα τὰ σπλάγχνα αὐτοῦ,

19 καὶ γνωστὸν ἐγένετο πᾶσι τοῖς κατοικοῦσιν Ἰερουσαλήμ, ὥστε κληθῆναι τὸ χωρίον ἐκεῖνο τῇ ἰδίᾳ διαλέκτῳ αὐτῶν Ἀχελδαμάχ τουτέστιν χωρίον αἵματος.

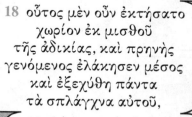

11 who also said, "Galilean Men, why do you stand looking into heaven? This Jesus, taken up from you into heaven, will thus come in like manner as you beheld him going into heaven!" 12 Then they returned into Jerusalem from the mount called Olivet which is near to Jerusalem, a Sabbath day's journey away. 13 And when they entered, they went up into the upper room where they were staying; Peter and John and James and Andrew, Philip and Thomas, Bartholomew and Matthew, James the son of Alphaeus, and Simon the Zealot, and Judas the son of James. 14 These all were continuing steadfastly with one accord in prayer with the women and Mary, the mother of Jesus, and with his brothers. 15 And in these days, standing up in the middle of the brothers, Peter said (at the same time, there was a crowd of names altogether, about a hundred and twenty), 16 "Fellow brothers, it was necessary for the Scripture to be fulfilled that the Holy Spirit spoke earlier by the mouth of David concerning Judas who became a guide to the ones who took Jesus: 17 'For he was numbered among us and received his portion in this ministry.' 18 So then, this man obtained a field with the reward of his iniquity; and falling headlong, he burst open in the middle and all his bowels gushed out. 19 And it became known to all inhabiting Jerusalem so that in their language that field is called Akeldama, that is, Field of Blood.

20 γέγραπται γὰρ ἐν βίβλῳ ψαλμῶν·

γενηθήτω ἡ ἔπαυλις αὐτοῦ ἔρημος καὶ μὴ ἔστω ὁ κατοικῶν ἐν αὐτῇ,

20 καὶ

τὴν ἐπισκοπὴν αὐτοῦ λαβέτω ἕτερος.

21 δεῖ οὖν τῶν συνελθόντων ἡμῖν ἀνδρῶν ἐν παντὶ χρόνῳ ᾧ εἰσῆλθεν καὶ ἐξῆλθεν ἐφ' ἡμᾶς ὁ κύριος Ἰησοῦς, 22 ἀρξάμενος ἀπὸ τοῦ βαπτίσματος Ἰωάννου ἕως τῆς ἡμέρας ἧς ἀνελήμφθη ἀφ' ἡμῶν, μάρτυρα τῆς ἀναστάσεως αὐτοῦ σὺν ἡμῖν γενέσθαι ἕνα τούτων.

23 καὶ ἔστησαν δύο, Ἰωσὴφ τὸν καλούμενον Βαρσαββᾶν ὃς ἐπεκλήθη Ἰοῦστος

καὶ Ματθίαν.

24 καὶ προσευξάμενοι εἶπαν·

σὺ κύριε καρδιογνῶστα πάντων, ἀνάδειξον ὃν ἐξελέξω ἐκ τούτων τῶν δύο ἕνα 25 λαβεῖν τὸν τόπον τῆς διακονίας ταύτης καὶ ἀποστολῆς ἀφ' ἧς παρέβη Ἰούδας πορευθῆναι εἰς τὸν τόπον τὸν ἴδιον.

26 καὶ ἔδωκαν κλήρους αὐτοῖς

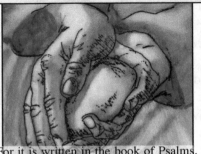

καὶ ἔπεσεν ὁ κλῆρος ἐπὶ Ματθίαν καὶ συνκατεψηφίσθη μετὰ τῶν ἕνδεκα ἀποστόλων.

20 For it is written in the book of Psalms, 'Let his habitation be made desolate, And let no man dwell within it'; and, 'His office let another take.' 21 Therefore, it is necessary from the men accompanying us during the entire time that the Lord Jesus went in and went out among us, 22 beginning from the baptism of John until the day that he was taken up from us, that one of these men become a witness with us of his resurrection." 23 And they put forward two, Joseph called Barsabbas, who was surnamed Justus, and Matthias. 24 And praying they said, "You, Lord, Knower of the hearts of all people, show which one you chose from these two 25 to take the place in this ministry and apostleship from which Judas fell away to go into his own place." 26 And they gave lots for them; and the lot fell upon Matthias and he was counted with the eleven apostles.

2:1 Καὶ ἐν τῷ συνπληροῦσθαι τὴν ἡμέραν τῆς πεντηκοστῆς ἦσαν πάντες ὁμοῦ ἐπὶ τὸ αὐτό. 2 καὶ ἐγένετο ἄφνω ἐκ τοῦ οὐρανοῦ ἦχος ὥσπερ φερομένης πνοῆς βιαίας καὶ ἐπλήρωσεν ὅλον τὸν οἶκον οὗ ἦσαν καθήμενοι 3 καὶ ὤφθησαν αὐτοῖς διαμεριζόμεναι γλῶσσαι ὡσεὶ πυρὸς

Κεφ. Β´

καὶ ἐκάθισεν ἐφ' ἕνα ἕκαστον αὐτῶν 4 καὶ ἐπλήσθησαν πάντες πνεύματος ἁγίου καὶ ἤρξαντο λαλεῖν ἑτέραις γλώσσαις καθὼς τὸ πνεῦμα ἐδίδου ἀποφθέγγεσθαι αὐτοῖς.

5 Ἦσαν δὲ ἐν Ἰερουσαλὴμ κατοικοῦντες Ἰουδαῖοι, ἄνδρες εὐλαβεῖς ἀπὸ παντὸς ἔθνους τῶν ὑπὸ τὸν οὐρανόν. 6 γενομένης δὲ τῆς φωνῆς ταύτης συνῆλθε τὸ πλῆθος καὶ συνεχύθη, ὅτι ἤκουον εἷς ἕκαστος τῇ ἰδίᾳ διαλέκτῳ λαλούντων αὐτῶν. 7 ἐξίσταντο δὲ πάντες καὶ ἐθαύμαζον λέγοντες·

8 καὶ πῶς ἡμεῖς ἀκούομεν ἕκαστος τῇ ἰδίᾳ διαλέκτῳ ἡμῶν ἐν ᾗ ἐγεννήθημεν,

οὐχ ἰδοὺ πάντες οὗτοί εἰσιν οἱ λαλοῦντες Γαλιλαῖοι;

9 Πάρθοι καὶ Μῆδοι καὶ Ἐλαμεῖται καὶ οἱ κατοικοῦντες τὴν Μεσοποταμίαν, Ἰουδαίαν τε καὶ Καππαδοκίαν, Πόντον καὶ τὴν Ἀσίαν, 10 Φρυγίαν τε καὶ Παμφυλίαν, Αἴγυπτον καὶ τὰ μέρη τῆς Λιβύης τῆς κατὰ Κυρήνην καὶ οἱ ἐπιδημοῦντες Ῥωμαῖοι, 11 Ἰουδαῖοί τε καὶ προσήλυτοι, Κρῆτες καὶ Ἄραβες, ἀκούομεν λαλούντων αὐτῶν ταῖς ἡμετέραις γλώσσαις τὰ μεγαλεῖα τοῦ θεοῦ;

12 Ἐξίσταντο δὲ πάντες καὶ διηπόρουν ἄλλος πρὸς ἄλλον λέγοντες·

τί θέλει τοῦτο εἶναι;

13 ἕτεροι δὲ διαχλευάζοντες ἔλεγον ὅτι

γλεύκους μεμεστωμένοι εἰσίν.

14 Σταθεὶς δὲ ὁ Πέτρος σὺν τοῖς ἕνδεκα ἐπῆρεν τὴν φωνὴν αὐτοῦ καὶ ἀπεφθέγξατο αὐτοῖς·

ἄνδρες Ἰουδαῖοι καὶ οἱ κατοικοῦντες Ἰερουσαλὴμ πάντες, τοῦτο ὑμῖν γνωστὸν ἔστω καὶ ἐνωτίσασθε τὰ ῥήματά μου. 15 οὐ γὰρ ὡς ὑμεῖς ὑπολαμβάνετε οὗτοι μεθύουσιν, ἔστιν γὰρ ὥρα τρίτη τῆς ἡμέρας,

2:1 And while the day of Pentecost was being completed, they were all together in one place. 2 And suddenly there came from heaven a sound just like the rushing of a mighty wind and it filled all the house where they were sitting. 3 And there appeared to them tongues being distributed like from fire; and it sat upon each one of them. 4 And they were all filled with the Holy Spirit and began to speak with other tongues just as the Spirit was giving them to declare. 5 Now Judeans were inhabiting in Jerusalem, devout men from every nation of the ones under heaven. 6 And, with this sound having occurred, the multitude came together and were confused, because each one was hearing them speaking in their own dialect. 7 And they all were continually amazed and were marveling, saying, "Behold, are not all these who are speaking Galileans? (Yes!) 8 And how are we ourselves hearing, each one in our own dialect in which we were born—9 Parthians and Medes and Elamites, and the ones inhabiting Mesopotamia; Judaea as well as Cappadocia, Pontus and Asia; 10 Phrygia as well as Pamphylia, Egypt and the parts of Libya around Cyrene, and the sojourners from Rome; 11 Judeans as well as proselytes, Cretans and Arabians—how are we hearing them speaking in our own dialects the mighty works of God?" 12 And they all were continually amazed and were thoroughly remaining perplexed, saying one to another, "What does this mean?!" 13 But others, mocking, were saying this: "They are filled with new wine!" 14 But Peter, standing up with the eleven, lifted up his voice and declared to them, "Judean Men and all dwelling in Jerusalem, let this be known to you and give ear to my words. 15 For it is not as you suppose [that] these people are drunk, for it is the third hour of the day;

16 ἀλλὰ τοῦτό ἐστιν τὸ εἰρημένον διὰ τοῦ προφήτου Ἰωήλ·

καὶ ἔσται ἐν ταῖς ἐσχάταις ἡμέραις, λέγει ὁ θεός, ἐκχεῶ ἀπὸ τοῦ πνεύματός μου ἐπὶ πᾶσαν σάρκα καὶ προφητεύσουσιν οἱ υἱοὶ ὑμῶν καὶ αἱ θυγατέρες ὑμῶν, καὶ οἱ νεανίσκοι ὑμῶν ὁράσεις ὄψονται καὶ οἱ πρεσβύτεροι ὑμῶν ἐνυπνίοις ἐνυπνιασθήσονται. 18 καὶ γε ἐπὶ τοὺς δούλους μου καὶ ἐπὶ τὰς δούλας μου ἐν ταῖς ἡμέραις ἐκείναις ἐκχεῶ ἀπὸ τοῦ πνεύματός μου καὶ προφητεύσουσιν. 19 καὶ δώσω τέρατα ἐν τῷ οὐρανῷ ἄνω καὶ σημεῖα ἐπὶ τῆς γῆς κάτω, αἷμα καὶ πῦρ καὶ ἀτμίδα καπνοῦ. 20 ὁ ἥλιος μεταστραφήσεται εἰς σκότος καὶ ἡ σελήνη εἰς αἷμα, πρὶν ἐλθεῖν ἡμέραν κυρίου τὴν μεγάλην καὶ ἐπιφανῆ. 21 καὶ ἔσται, πᾶς ὃς ἂν ἐπικαλέσηται τὸ ὄνομα κυρίου σωθήσεται

22 Ἄνδρες Ἰσραηλεῖται, ἀκούσατε τοὺς λόγους τούτους· Ἰησοῦν τὸν Ναζωραῖον, ἄνδρα ἀποδε-δειγμένον ἀπὸ τοῦ θεοῦ εἰς ὑμᾶς δυνάμεσι καὶ τέρασι καὶ σημείοις οἷς ἐποίησεν δι' αὐτοῦ ὁ θεὸς ἐν μέσῳ ὑμῶν, καθὼς αὐτοὶ οἴδατε, 23 τοῦτον τῇ ὡρισμένῃ βουλῇ καὶ προγνώσει τοῦ θεοῦ ἔκδοτον

διὰ χειρὸς ἀνόμων προσπήξαντες ἀνείλατε, 24 ὃν ὁ θεὸς ἀνέστησεν λύσας τὰς ὠδῖνας τοῦ θανάτου, καθότι οὐκ ἦν δυνατὸν κρατεῖσθαι αὐτὸν ὑπ' αὐτοῦ. 25 Δαυεὶδ γὰρ λέγει εἰς αὐτόν·

προορώμην τὸν κύριον ἐνώπιόν μου διὰ παντός, ὅτι ἐκ δεξιῶν μου ἐστὶν ἵνα μὴ σαλευθῶ· 26 διὰ τοῦτο ηὐφράνθη ἡ καρδία μου καὶ ἠγαλλιάσατο ἡ γλῶσσά μου, ἔτι δὲ καὶ ἡ σάρξ μου κατασκηνώσει ἐπ' ἐλπίδι. 27 ὅτι οὐκ ἐνκαταλείψεις τὴν ψυχήν μου εἰς ᾅδην, οὐδὲ δώσεις τὸν ὅσιόν σου ἰδεῖν διαφθοράν. 28 ἐγνώρισάς μοι ὁδοὺς ζωῆς, πληρώσεις με εὐφροσύνης μετὰ τοῦ προσώπου σου.

29 Ἄνδρες ἀδελφοί, ἐξὸν εἰπεῖν μετὰ παρρησίας πρὸς ὑμᾶς περὶ τοῦ πατριάρχου Δαυεὶδ ὅτι καὶ ἐτελεύτησεν καὶ ἐτάφη καὶ τὸ μνῆμα αὐτοῦ ἐστιν ἐν ἡμῖν ἄχρι τῆς ἡμέρας ταύτης. 30 προφήτης οὖν ὑπάρχων καὶ εἰδὼς ὅτι ὅρκῳ ὤμοσεν αὐτῷ ὁ θεὸς ἐκ καρποῦ τῆς ὀσφύος αὐτοῦ καθίσαι ἐπὶ τὸν θρόνον αὐτοῦ, 31 προϊδὼν ἐλάλησεν περὶ τῆς ἀναστάσεως τοῦ χριστοῦ ὅτι οὔτε ἐνκατελείφθη εἰς ᾅδου οὔτε ἡ σὰρξ αὐτοῦ εἶδεν διαφθοράν.

32 τοῦτον τὸν Ἰησοῦν ἀνέστησεν ὁ θεός, οὗ πάντες ἡμεῖς ἐσμεν μάρτυρες. 33 τῇ δεξιᾷ οὖν τοῦ θεοῦ ὑψωθεὶς τήν τε ἐπαγγελίαν τοῦ πνεύματος τοῦ ἁγίου λαβὼν παρὰ τοῦ πατρὸς ἐξέχεεν τοῦτο ὃ ὑμεῖς βλέπετε καὶ ἀκούετε. 34 οὐ γὰρ Δαυεὶδ ἀνέβη εἰς τοὺς οὐρανούς, λέγει δὲ αὐτός·

εἶπεν ὁ κύριος τῷ κυρίῳ μου· κάθου ἐκ δεξιῶν μου, 35 ἕως ἂν θῶ τοὺς ἐχθρούς σου ὑποπόδιον τῶν ποδῶν σου. 36 ἀσφαλῶς οὖν γινωσκέτω πᾶς οἶκος Ἰσραὴλ ὅτι καὶ κύριον αὐτὸν καὶ χριστὸν ὁ θεὸς ἐποίησεν, τοῦτον τὸν Ἰησοῦν ὃν ὑμεῖς ἐσταυρώσατε.

16 but this is what has been spoken through the prophet Joel: 17 And it will be in the last days, says God, I will pour out from My Spirit upon all flesh; And your sons and your daughters will prophesy, and your young men will see visions, and your old men will dream dreams. 18 And indeed on My male servants and on My female servants in those days will I pour out from My Spirit and they will prophesy. 19 And I will show wonders in the heaven above and signs on the earth beneath—blood and fire and vapor of smoke. 20 The sun will be turned into darkness and the moon into blood, before the day of the Lord comes, the great and manifest [day]. 21 And it will be, everyone, whoever calls on the name of the Lord, will be saved.' 22 Israelite men, hear these words: Jesus of Nazareth, a man approved from God to you by mighty works and wonders and signs that God did by him in your midst, just as you yourselves know, 23 him, being delivered up by the determined counsel and foreknowledge of God, you, by the hand of lawless men crucifying, slayed, 24 whom God raised up, having loosed the pangs of death, because it was not possible that he should be held by it. 25 For David says concerning him, 'I saw the Lord always before my face; for he is on my right hand, that I should not be moved; 26 on account of this, my heart was glad and my tongue rejoiced; moreover, even still my flesh will dwell in hope. 27 Because you will not leave my soul in Hades, nor will you give your Holy One to see corruption. 28 You made known to me the ways of life; you will make me full of gladness with your countenance.' 29 Fellow brothers, it is right to speak to you with frankness about the patriarch David, that he both died and was buried, and his tomb is with us to this day. 30 Therefore, being a prophet and knowing that God had sworn with an oath to him, that [someone] from the fruit of his loins He would set one upon his throne, 31 he foreseeing [this] spoke of the resurrection of the Christ that neither was he left in Hades nor did his flesh see corruption. 32 This Jesus did God raise up, whose witnesses we all are. 33 Therefore, at the right hand of God being exalted and at the same time having received from the Father the promise of the Holy Spirit, he has poured forth this that you see and hear. 34 For David did not ascend into the heavens, but he himself says, 'The Lord said to my Lord, 'Sit at my right hand, 35 until I make your enemies the footstool of your feet.'' 36 Assuredly, therefore, let all the house of Israel know that God has made him both Lord and Christ, this Jesus whom you yourselves crucified!"

37 Ἀκούσαντες δὲ κατενύγησαν τὴν καρδίαν, εἶπόν τε πρὸς τὸν Πέτρον καὶ τοὺς λοιποὺς ἀποστόλους·

τί ποιήσωμεν, ἄνδρες ἀδελφοί;

38 Πέτρος δὲ πρὸς αὐτούς·

μετανοήσατε φησὶν καὶ βαπτισθήτω ἕκαστος ὑμῶν ἐπὶ τῷ ὀνόματι Ἰησοῦ χριστοῦ εἰς ἄφεσιν τῶν ἁμαρτιῶν ὑμῶν καὶ λήμψεσθε τὴν δωρεὰν τοῦ ἁγίου πνεύματος· 39 ὑμῖν γάρ ἐστιν ἡ ἐπαγγελία καὶ τοῖς τέκνοις ὑμῶν καὶ πᾶσι τοῖς εἰς μακράν, ὅσους ἂν προσκαλέσηται κύριος ὁ θεὸς ἡμῶν.

40 ἑτέροις τε λόγοις πλείοσιν διεμαρτύρατο καὶ παρεκάλει αὐτοὺς λέγων·

σώθητε ἀπὸ τῆς γενεᾶς τῆς σκολιᾶς ταύτης.

41 οἱ μὲν οὖν ἀποδεξάμενοι τὸν λόγον αὐτοῦ ἐβαπτίσθησαν

καὶ προσετέθησαν ἐν τῇ ἡμέρᾳ ἐκείνῃ ψυχαὶ ὡσεὶ τρισχίλιαι.

42 Ἦσαν δὲ προσκαρτεροῦντες τῇ διδαχῇ τῶν ἀποστόλων καὶ τῇ κοινωνίᾳ,

τῇ κλάσει τοῦ ἄρτου καὶ ταῖς προσευχαῖς

43 ἐγίνετο δὲ πάσῃ ψυχῇ φόβος, πολλά τε τέρατα καὶ σημεῖα διὰ τῶν ἀποστόλων ἐγίνετο.

44 πάντες δὲ οἱ πιστεύοντες ἦσαν ἐπὶ τὸ αὐτὸ καὶ εἶχον ἅπαντα κοινά, 45 καὶ τὰ κτήματα καὶ τὰς ὑπάρξεις ἐπίπρασκον καὶ διεμέριζον αὐτὰ πᾶσιν καθότι ἄν τις χρείαν εἶχεν· 46 καθ᾽ ἡμέραν τε προσκαρτεροῦντες ὁμοθυμαδὸν ἐν τῷ ἱερῷ, κλῶντές τε κατ᾽ οἶκον ἄρτον μετελάμβανον τροφῆς ἐν ἀγαλλιάσει καὶ ἀφελότητι καρδίας 47 αἰνοῦντες τὸν θεὸν καὶ ἔχοντες χάριν πρὸς ὅλον τὸν λαόν. ὁ δὲ κύριος προσετίθει τοὺς σωζομένους καθ᾽ ἡμέραν ἐπὶ τὸ αὐτό.

37 So, hearing, they were pricked in heart and said both to Peter and the rest of the apostles, "Brothers, what should we do?" 38 So, Peter to them, "Repent!" he said, "and be baptized, every one of you in the name of Jesus Christ for the deliverance from your sins; and you will receive the gift of the Holy Spirit! 39 For the promise is for you and for your children and for all who are far off, however many the Lord, our God, will call!" 40 And with many other words he testified and was exhorting them, saying, "Be saved from this crooked generation!" 41 So then, the ones who received his word were baptized and there were added in that day about three thousand souls. 42 And they were continuing steadfastly in the teaching of the apostles and in the fellowship, in the breaking of bread and in the prayers. 43 And reverence came upon every soul, and many wonders and signs were accomplished through the apostles. 44 And all who were believing were together and were holding all things in common; 45 and they were selling their possessions and belongings and were dividing them to all to the degree that anyone was ever having need. 46 And day by day, continuing steadfastly with one accord in the temple and breaking bread at home, they were receiving their food with gladness and singleness of heart, 47 praising God and having favor with the whole people. Moreover, each day the Lord was adding to the ones being saved in one accord.

Κεφ. Γ΄

3:1 Πέτρος δὲ καὶ Ἰωάννης ἀνέβαινον εἰς τὸ ἱερὸν ἐπὶ τὴν ὥραν τῆς προσευχῆς τὴν ἐνάτην. 2 καί τις ἀνὴρ χωλὸς ἐκ κοιλίας μητρὸς αὐτοῦ ὑπάρχων ἐβαστάζετο, ὃν ἐτίθουν καθ᾽ ἡμέραν πρὸς τὴν θύραν τοῦ ἱεροῦ τὴν λεγομένην ὡραίαν τοῦ αἰτεῖν ἐλεημοσύνην παρὰ τῶν εἰσπορευομένων εἰς τὸ ἱερόν. 3 ὃς ἰδὼν Πέτρον καὶ Ἰωάννην μέλλοντας εἰσιέναι εἰς τὸ ἱερὸν ἠρώτα ἐλεημοσύνην λαβεῖν. 4 ἀτενίσας δὲ Πέτρος εἰς αὐτὸν σὺν τῷ Ἰωάννῃ εἶπεν·

βλέψον εἰς ἡμᾶς.

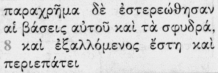
5 ὁ δὲ ἐπεῖχεν αὐτοῖς προσδοκῶν τι παρ᾽ αὐτῶν λαβεῖν.

6 Εἶπεν δὲ Πέτρος·

ἀργύριον καὶ χρυσίον οὐχ ὑπάρχει μοι· ὃ δὲ ἔχω, τοῦτό σοι δίδωμι. ἐν τῷ ὀνόματι Ἰησοῦ χριστοῦ τοῦ Ναζωραίου ἔγειρε καὶ περιπάτει.

7 καὶ πιάσας αὐτὸν τῆς δεξιᾶς χειρὸς ἤγειρεν αὐτόν.

παραχρῆμα δὲ ἐστερεώθησαν αἱ βάσεις αὐτοῦ καὶ τὰ σφυδρά, 8 καὶ ἐξαλλόμενος ἔστη καὶ περιεπάτει

καὶ εἰσῆλθεν σὺν αὐτοῖς εἰς τὸ ἱερὸν περιπατῶν καὶ ἁλλόμενος καὶ αἰνῶν τὸν θεόν. 9 Καὶ εἶδεν πᾶς ὁ λαὸς αὐτὸν περιπατοῦντα καὶ αἰνοῦντα τὸν θεόν. 10 ἐπεγίνωσκον δὲ αὐτὸν ὅτι αὐτὸς ἦν ὁ πρὸς τὴν ἐλεημοσύνην καθήμενος ἐπὶ τῇ ὡραίᾳ πύλῃ τοῦ ἱεροῦ, καὶ ἐπλήσθησαν θάμβους καὶ ἐκστάσεως ἐπὶ τῷ συμβεβηκότι αὐτῷ.

11 κρατοῦντος δὲ αὐτοῦ τὸν Πέτρον καὶ τὸν Ἰωάννην συνέδραμεν πᾶς ὁ λαὸς πρὸς αὐτοὺς ἐπὶ τῇ στοᾷ τῇ καλουμένῃ Σολομῶντος ἔκθαμβοι. 12 ἰδὼν δὲ ὁ Πέτρος ἀπεκρίνατο πρὸς τὸν λαόν·

ἄνδρες Ἰσραηλεῖται, τί θαυμάζετε ἐπὶ τούτῳ, ἢ ἡμῖν τί ἀτενίζετε ὡς ἰδίᾳ δυνάμει ἢ εὐσεβείᾳ πεποιηκόσιν τοῦ περιπατεῖν αὐτόν; 13 ὁ θεὸς Ἀβραὰμ καὶ Ἰσαὰκ καὶ Ἰακώβ, ὁ θεὸς τῶν πατέρων ἡμῶν, ἐδόξασεν τὸν παῖδα αὐτοῦ Ἰησοῦν ὃν ὑμεῖς μὲν παρεδώκατε καὶ ἠρνήσασθε κατὰ πρόσωπον Πιλάτου κρίναντος ἐκείνου ἀπολύειν·

3:1 Now Peter and John were going up into the temple at the ninth hour of prayer. 2 And a certain man who was lame from his mother's womb was being carried along, whom they laid daily at the door of the temple, which is called Beautiful, to be asking for alms from the ones entering into the temple; 3 who, seeing Peter and John about to go into the temple, was asking to receive alms. 4 And Peter, staring at him, with John said, "Look at us!" 5 And he was holding out to them, expecting to receive something from them. 6 But Peter said, "Silver and gold have I none; but that which I have, this I give to you. In the name of Jesus Christ of Nazareth, get up and walk!" 7 And, taking him by the right hand, he raised him up; and immediately his feet and his ankles were strengthened. 8 And leaping up he stood and was walking around and entered with them into the temple, walking and leaping about and praising God. 9 And all the people saw him walking about and praising God. 10 Moreover, they were recognizing him—that he himself was the one sitting for alms at the Beautiful Gate of the temple, and they were filled with wonder and amazement at what had happened to him. 11 And, with him holding onto Peter and John, all the people ran together to them in the porch called Solomon's, greatly astonished. 12 Then, seeing this, Peter responded to the people, "Israelite men, why are you marveling at this or staring at us as if by our own power or godliness we have produced his walking about?! 13 The God of Abraham, and of Isaac, and of Jacob, the God of our fathers, glorified his Servant Jesus, whom you yourselves indeed delivered up and denied before the face of Pilate who had determined to release him!

14 But you yourselves denied the Holy and Righteous One and asked for a murderer to be granted to you, 15 and moreover killed the Prince of life, whom God raised from the dead, whose witnesses we ourselves are. 16 And on the basis of faith in His name was this person whom you behold and know made strong—His name and the faith which is through Him gave him this perfect soundness in the presence of all of you. 17 And now, brothers, I know that you acted in ignorance, just as also your rulers. 18 But the things which God announced ahead of time by the mouth of all the Prophets, that his Christ should suffer, he thus fulfilled. 19 Repent, therefore, and turn again, in order that your sins would be blotted out, 20 so that there may come seasons of refreshing from the presence of the Lord and that he may send the One having been appointed for you, Christ Jesus, 21 whom heaven indeed needs to receive until the times of the restoration of all things about which God spoke through the mouth of His holy Prophets from of old. 22 Moses indeed said this: 'A prophet for you the Lord your God will raise up from among your brothers like me. Listen to him in all things, however much he speaks to you!' 23 And it will be [that] every soul, whoever does not listen to that prophet, will be utterly destroyed from among the people. 24 Moreover, also all the Prophets from Samuel and the ones after, as many as spoke, even announced these days. 25 You yourselves are sons of the Prophets and of the covenant which God made with your fathers, saying to Abraham, 'And in your seed will all the families of the earth be blessed.' 26 To you, first, God raising up his Servant sent Him to bless you as each of you turns away from your evil ways."

Κεφ. Δ΄

4:1 Λαλούντων δὲ αὐτῶν πρὸς τὸν λαὸν ἐπέστησαν αὐτοῖς οἱ ἱερεῖς καὶ ὁ στρατηγὸς τοῦ ἱεροῦ καὶ οἱ Σαδδουκαῖοι, 2 διαπονούμενοι διὰ τὸ διδάσκειν αὐτοὺς τὸν λαὸν καὶ καταγγέλλειν ἐν τῷ Ἰησοῦ τὴν ἀνάστασιν τὴν ἐκ νεκρῶν·

3 καὶ ἐπέβαλον αὐτοῖς τὰς χεῖρας καὶ ἔθεντο εἰς τήρησιν εἰς τὴν αὔριον· ἦν γὰρ ἑσπέρα ἤδη. 4 πολλοὶ δὲ τῶν ἀκουσάντων τὸν λόγον ἐπίστευσαν· καὶ ἐγενήθη ὁ ἀριθμὸς τῶν ἀνδρῶν ὡς χιλιάδες πέντε.

5 Ἐγένετο δὲ ἐπὶ τὴν αὔριον συναχθῆναι αὐτῶν τοὺς ἄρχοντας καὶ τοὺς πρεσβυτέρους καὶ τοὺς γραμματεῖς ἐν Ἰερουσαλὴμ

6 καὶ Ἄννας ὁ ἀρχιερεὺς καὶ Καϊάφας καὶ Ἰωάννης καὶ Ἀλέξανδρος καὶ ὅσοι ἦσαν ἐκ γένους ἀρχιερατικοῦ,

4:1 Then, with them speaking to the people, the priests and the captain of the temple and the Sadducees came upon them, 2 being annoyed because they were teaching the people and proclaiming in Jesus the resurrection from the dead. 3 And they laid hands on them and put them in custody for the next day; for it was already evening. 4 But many of the ones hearing the Word believed; and the number of the men came to about five thousand. 5 And it happened on the next day that their rulers and elders and scribes were gathered together in Jerusalem 6 and Annas the high priest and Caiaphas and John and Alexander were there, and as many as were from high-priestly descent.

7 And, having set them in the middle, they inquired, "By what sort of power or in sort of what name did you yourselves do this?" 8 Then Peter, filled with the Holy Spirit, said to them, "You rulers of the people and elders, 9 if we ourselves this day are being examined for a good deed for a sick person, by which this person has been made whole, 10 let it be known to you all and to all the people of Israel that in the name of Jesus Christ, the Nazarene, whom you yourselves crucified, whom God raised from the dead, in Him this person stands here before you whole. 11 This One is 'the stone rejected by you the builders, the One made into the head of the corner.' 12 And there is salvation in no single other person; for neither is there any other name under heaven that has been given among people by which it is necessary to be saved!" 13 And, seeing the boldness of Peter and John and perceiving that they were uneducated and laymen, they were marveling and at the same time they were recognizing them that they had been with Jesus, 14 and at the same time seeing the person who was healed standing with them, they were having nothing to contradict it. 15 But, commanding them to go aside out of the council, they were conferring among one another 16 saying, "What should we do to these persons? For indeed that a notable sign has been done through them is manifest to all inhabiting Jerusalem and we are not able to deny it; 17 but in order that it be no further distributed among the people,

17b ἀπειλησώμεθα αὐτοῖς μηκέτι λαλεῖν ἐπὶ τῷ ὀνόματι τούτῳ μηδενὶ ἀνθρώπων.

18 καὶ καλέσαντες αὐτοὺς παρήγγειλαν τὸ καθόλου μὴ φθέγγεσθαι μηδὲ διδάσκειν ἐπὶ τῷ ὀνόματι τοῦ Ἰησοῦ. 19 Ὁ δὲ Πέτρος καὶ Ἰωάννης ἀποκριθέντες εἶπον πρὸς αὐτούς·

εἰ δίκαιόν ἐστιν ἐνώπιον τοῦ θεοῦ ὑμῶν ἀκούειν μᾶλλον ἢ τοῦ θεοῦ, κρίνατε.

20 οὐ δυνάμεθα γὰρ ἡμεῖς ἃ εἴδαμεν καὶ ἠκούσαμεν μὴ λαλεῖν.

21 οἱ δὲ προσαπειλησάμενοι ἀπέλυσαν αὐτοὺς μηδὲν εὑρίσκοντες τὸ πῶς κολάσωνται αὐτούς, διὰ τὸν λαόν, ὅτι πάντες ἐδόξαζον τὸν θεὸν ἐπὶ τῷ γεγονότι. 22 ἐτῶν γὰρ ἦν πλειόνων τεσσεράκοντα ὁ ἄνθρωπος ἐφ' ὃν ἐγεγόνει τὸ σημεῖον τοῦτο τῆς ἰάσεως.

23 Ἀπολυθέντες δὲ ἦλθον πρὸς τοὺς ἰδίους καὶ ἀπήγγειλαν ὅσα πρὸς αὐτοὺς οἱ ἀρχιερεῖς καὶ οἱ πρεσβύτεροι εἶπαν. 24 οἱ δὲ ἀκούσαντες ὁμοθυμαδὸν ἦραν φωνὴν πρὸς τὸν θεὸν καὶ εἶπαν·

δέσποτα, σὺ ὁ ποιήσας τὸν οὐρανὸν καὶ τὴν γῆν καὶ τὴν θάλασσαν καὶ πάντα τὰ ἐν αὐτοῖς, 25 ὁ τοῦ πατρὸς ἡμῶν διὰ πνεύματος ἁγίου στόματος Δαυεὶδ παιδός σου εἰπών·

ἵνα τί ἐφρύαξαν ἔθνη καὶ λαοὶ ἐμελέτησαν κενά; 26 παρέστησαν οἱ βασιλεῖς τῆς γῆς καὶ οἱ ἄρχοντες συνήχθησαν ἐπὶ τὸ αὐτὸ κατὰ τοῦ κυρίου καὶ κατὰ τοῦ χριστοῦ αὐτοῦ.

17b let us threaten them to no longer be speaking in this name to any single person of the people." 18 And, calling them, they commanded [them] not to speak at all nor to teach in the name of Jesus. 19 But Peter and John, answering back, said to them, "Whether it is right in the sight of God to listen to you rather than to God, you judge. 20 For we ourselves are not able but to be speaking about what things we saw and heard." 21 However, they, having made more threats, released them finding no way how they could punish them because of the people, because they all were glorifying God for what had happened. 22 For the person was more than forty years old for whom this sign of healing had happened. 23 So, being released, they went to their own people and reported as much as the chief priests and the elders said to them. 24 Moreover, they, hearing, lifted up their voice to God with one accord and said, "O Lord, you are the One who made the heaven and the earth and the sea and everything in them, 25 the One who out of the mouth of our father David, your servant, through the Holy Spirit said, 'For what reason did the nations rage and the peoples care about vain things? 26 The kings of the earth set themselves in array and the rulers were gathered together in one accord against the Lord and against his Anointed One.'

27 Συνήχθησαν γὰρ ἐπ' ἀληθείας ἐν τῇ πόλει ταύτῃ ἐπὶ τὸν ἅγιον παῖδά σου, Ἰησοῦν ὃν ἔχρισας, Ἡρώδης τε καὶ Πόντιος Πιλᾶτος σὺν ἔθνεσιν καὶ λαοῖς Ἰσραήλ 28 ποιῆσαι ὅσα ἡ χείρ σου καὶ ἡ βουλή σου προώρισεν γενέσθαι. 29 καὶ τὰ νῦν, κύριε, ἔπιδε ἐπὶ τὰς ἀπειλὰς αὐτῶν καὶ δὸς τοῖς δούλοις σου μετὰ παρρησίας πάσης λαλεῖν τὸν λόγον σου

30 ἐν τῷ τὴν χεῖρά σου ἐκτείνειν σε εἰς ἴασιν καὶ σημεῖα καὶ τέρατα γίνεσθαι διὰ τοῦ ὀνόματος τοῦ ἁγίου παιδός σου Ἰησοῦ.

31 καὶ δεηθέντων αὐτῶν ἐσαλεύθη ὁ τόπος ἐν ᾧ ἦσαν συνηγμένοι, καὶ ἐπλήσθησαν ἅπαντες τοῦ ἁγίου πνεύματος καὶ ἐλάλουν τὸν λόγον τοῦ θεοῦ μετὰ παρρησίας.

32 Τοῦ δὲ πλήθους τῶν πιστευσάντων ἦν καρδία καὶ ψυχὴ μία· καὶ οὐδὲ εἷς τί τῶν ὑπαρχόντων αὐτῷ ἔλεγεν ἴδιον εἶναι, ἀλλ' ἦν αὐτοῖς ἅπαντα κοινά. 33 καὶ δυνάμει μεγάλῃ ἀπεδίδουν τὸ μαρτύριον οἱ ἀπόστολοι τῆς ἀναστάσεως τοῦ κυρίου Ἰησοῦ, χάρις τε μεγάλη ἦν ἐπὶ πάντας αὐτούς. 34 οὐδὲ γὰρ ἐνδεής τις ἦν ἐν αὐτοῖς· ὅσοι γὰρ κτήτορες χωρίων ἢ οἰκιῶν ὑπῆρχον πωλοῦντες ἔφερον τὰς τιμὰς τῶν πιπρασκομένων

35 καὶ ἐτίθουν παρὰ τοὺς πόδας τῶν ἀποστόλων, διεδίδετο δὲ ἑκάστῳ καθότι ἄν τις χρείαν εἶχεν. 36 Ἰωσὴφ δὲ ὁ ἐπικληθεὶς Βαρνάβας ἀπὸ τῶν ἀποστόλων ὅ ἐστιν μεθερμηνευόμενον υἱὸς παρακλήσεως, Λευίτης, Κύπριος τῷ γένει, 37 ὑπάρχοντος αὐτῷ ἀγροῦ, πωλήσας ἤνεγκεν τὸ χρῆμα καὶ ἔθηκεν παρὰ τοὺς πόδας τῶν ἀποστόλων.

5:1 Ἀνὴρ δέ τις Ἀνανίας ὀνόματι σὺν Σαπφείρᾳ τῇ γυναικὶ αὐτοῦ ἐπώλησεν κτῆμα 2 καὶ ἐνοσφίσατο ἀπὸ τῆς τιμῆς, συνειδυίης καὶ τῆς γυναικός, καὶ ἐνέγκας μέρος τι παρὰ τοὺς πόδας τῶν ἀποστόλων ἔθηκεν.

Κεφ. Ε΄

27 For in truth they were gathered together in this city against your holy Servant, Jesus whom you anointed—Herod and Pontius Pilate with the nations and the peoples of Israel—28 to do as much as your hand and your council decided beforehand to happen. 29 And regarding the present events, Lord, look upon their threats and grant to your servants to be speaking your Word with all boldness 30 while you keep stretching forth your hand for healing and signs and wonders keep occurring through the name of your holy Servant, Jesus." 31 And, with them praying, the place in which they were gathered together was shaken; and all of them were filled with the Holy Spirit and were speaking the Word of God with boldness. 32 Moreover, the multitude of the ones who believed were of one heart and soul; also, moreover, no one was saying anything belonging to him was his own; but all things were common among them. 33 And with great power the apostles were giving witness of the resurrection of the Lord Jesus, and at the same time great favor was upon them all. 34 For neither was there anyone in need among them; for as many as were owners of lands or houses, by selling them, were bringing the value of the things being sold 35 and were setting it at the feet of the apostles; moreover, it was being distributed to each person to the degree that anyone was having a need. 36 Moreover, Joseph, the one called Barnabas from the apostles (which is, being interpreted, 'Son of Encouragement'), a Levite, a man of Cyprus by race, 37 with a field belonging to him, selling it brought the money and set it at the feet of the apostles. 5:1 But a certain man, Ananias by name, with Sapphira his wife sold a property 2 and put aside for himself [some] of its value, his wife also knowing, and, having brought a certain portion, set it at the feet of the apostles.

3 Εἶπεν δὲ ὁ Πέτρος·

Ἀνανία, διὰ τί ἐπλήρωσεν ὁ σατανᾶς τὴν καρδίαν σου ψεύσασθαί σε τὸ πνεῦμα τὸ ἅγιον καὶ νοσφίσασθαι ἀπὸ τῆς τιμῆς τοῦ χωρίου;

4 οὐχὶ μένον σοὶ ἔμενεν καὶ πραθὲν ἐν τῇ σῇ ἐξουσίᾳ ὑπῆρχεν; τί ὅτι ἔθου ἐν τῇ καρδίᾳ σου τὸ πρᾶγμα τοῦτο;

οὐκ ἐψεύσω ἀνθρώποις ἀλλὰ τῷ θεῷ.

5 ἀκούων δὲ ὁ Ἀνανίας τοὺς λόγους τούτους πεσὼν ἐξέψυξεν. καὶ ἐγένετο φόβος μέγας ἐπὶ πάντας τοὺς ἀκούοντας·

6 ἀναστάντες δὲ οἱ νεώτεροι συνέστειλαν αὐτὸν καὶ ἐξενέγκαντες ἔθαψαν.

7 ἐγένετο δὲ ὡς ὡρῶν τριῶν διάστημα καὶ ἡ γυνὴ αὐτοῦ μὴ εἰδυῖα τὸ γεγονὸς εἰσῆλθεν 8 ἀπεκρίθη δὲ πρὸς αὐτὴν Πέτρος·

εἰπέ μοι, εἰ τοσούτου τὸ χωρίον ἀπέδοσθε;

ἡ δὲ εἶπεν· ναὶ τοσούτου.

3 But Peter said, "Ananias, for what reason did Satan fill your heart that you would lie to the Holy Spirit and put aside for yourself [some] of the value of the land? 4 Was it not, while remaining, remaining your own and, after being sold, being in fact in your power? (Yes!) Why is it that you held this matter in your heart? You have not lied to people, but to God!" 5 So, [while] hearing these words, Ananias, falling down, died. And a great fear came upon all the ones hearing [about it]. 6 And the young men arising wrapped him up and carrying him out they buried him. 7 Moreover, there was an interval of about three hours and his wife, not knowing what had happened, entered. 8 And Peter responded to her, "Tell me, did you sell the land for this much?" And she said, "Yes, for this much."

9 ὁ δὲ Πέτρος πρὸς αὐτήν·

τί ὅτι συνεφωνήθη ὑμῖν πειράσαι τὸ πνεῦμα κυρίου;

ἰδοὺ οἱ πόδες τῶν θαψάντων τὸν ἄνδρα σου ἐπὶ τῇ θύρᾳ καὶ ἐξοίσουσίν σε.

10 ἔπεσεν δὲ παραχρῆμα πρὸς τοὺς πόδας αὐτοῦ καὶ ἐξέψυξεν·

εἰσελθόντες δὲ οἱ νεανίσκοι εὗρον αὐτὴν νεκράν, καὶ ἐξενέγκαντες ἔθαψαν πρὸς τὸν ἄνδρα αὐτῆς· 11 καὶ ἐγένετο φόβος μέγας ἐφ' ὅλην τὴν ἐκκλησίαν καὶ ἐπὶ πάντας τοὺς ἀκού-οντας ταῦτα.

12 Διὰ δὲ τῶν χειρῶν τῶν ἀποστόλων ἐγίνετο σημεῖα καὶ τέρατα πολλὰ ἐν τῷ λαῷ·

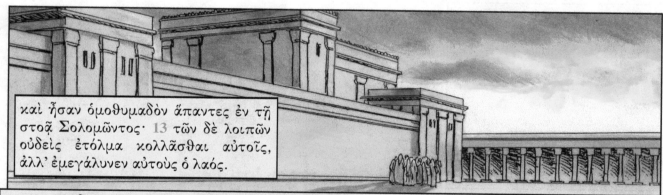

καὶ ἦσαν ὁμοθυμαδὸν ἅπαντες ἐν τῇ στοᾷ Σολομῶντος· 13 τῶν δὲ λοιπῶν οὐδεὶς ἐτόλμα κολλᾶσθαι αὐτοῖς, ἀλλ' ἐμεγάλυνεν αὐτοὺς ὁ λαός.

14 μᾶλλον δὲ προσετίθεντο πιστεύοντες τῷ κυρίῳ, πλήθη ἀνδρῶν τε καὶ γυναικῶν, 15 ὥστε καὶ εἰς τὰς πλατείας ἐκφέρειν τοὺς ἀσθενεῖς καὶ τιθέναι ἐπὶ κλιναρίων καὶ κραβάττων, ἵνα ἐρχομένου Πέτρου κἂν ἡ σκιὰ ἐπισκιάσῃ τινὶ αὐτῶν. 16 συνήρχετο δὲ καὶ τὸ πλῆθος τῶν πέριξ πόλεων Ἰερουσαλὴμ φέροντες ἀσθενεῖς καὶ ὀχλουμένους ὑπὸ πνευμάτων ἀκαθάρτων, οἵτινες ἐθεραπεύοντο ἅπαντες.

9 But Peter [said] to her, "Why is it that it was agreeable to you [two] to test the Spirit of the Lord? Behold, the feet of the ones who buried your husband are at the door and they will carry you out!" 10 Then she fell down immediately at his feet and expired. So, entering, the young men found her dead and carrying her out they buried her with her husband. 11 And great fear came upon the whole church and upon all the ones hearing these things. 12 Moreover, through the hands of the apostles many signs and wonders were happening among the people; and all of them were with one purpose in Solomon's porch. 13 But no one of the rest were daring to join them, yet the people were speaking highly of them. 14 But rather, they were being added [by] believing in the Lord—multitudes both of men and women—15 with the result that even into the streets they were carrying out the sick and setting them on beds and couches, in order that, with Peter coming, even his shadow would possibly fall upon some of them. 16 Moreover, the multitudes were also coming together from the cities round about Jerusalem bringing the sick and the ones being tormented by unclean spirits, all of whom were being healed.

17 Ἀναστὰς δὲ ὁ ἀρχι-ερεὺς καὶ πάντες οἱ σὺν αὐτῷ, ἡ οὖσα αἵρεσις τῶν Σαδδουκαίων, ἐπλήσθησαν ζήλου

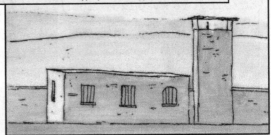

18 καὶ ἐπέβαλον τὰς χεῖρας ἐπὶ τοὺς ἀποστόλους καὶ ἔθεντο αὐτοὺς ἐν τηρήσει δημοσίᾳ.

19 Ἄγγελος δὲ κυρίου διὰ νυκτὸς ἤνοιξε τὰς θύρας τῆς φυλακῆς, ἐξαγαγών τε αὐτοὺς εἶπεν·

20 πορεύεσθε καὶ σταθέντες λαλεῖτε ἐν τῷ ἱερῷ τῷ λαῷ πάντα τὰ ῥήματα τῆς ζωῆς ταύτης.

21 ἀκούσαντες δὲ εἰσῆλθον ὑπὸ τὸν ὄρθρον εἰς τὸ ἱερὸν καὶ ἐδίδασκον.

21 Παραγενόμενος δὲ ὁ ἀρχι-ερεὺς καὶ οἱ σὺν αὐτῷ συνεκάλεσαν τὸ συνέδριον καὶ πᾶσαν τὴν γερουσίαν τῶν υἱῶν Ἰσραὴλ καὶ ἀπέστειλαν εἰς τὸ δεσμωτήριον ἀχθῆναι αὐτούς. 22 οἱ δὲ παραγενόμενοι ὑπηρέται οὐχ εὗρον αὐτοὺς ἐν τῇ φυλακῇ. ἀναστρέψαντες δὲ ἀπήγγειλαν 23 λέγοντες ὅτι

τὸ δεσμωτήριον εὕρομεν κεκλεισμένον ἐν πάσῃ ἀσφαλείᾳ καὶ τοὺς φύλακας ἑστῶτας ἐπὶ τῶν θυρῶν, ἀνοίξαντες δὲ ἔσω οὐδένα εὕρομεν.

24 ὡς δὲ ἤκουσαν τοὺς λόγους τούτους ὅ τε στρατηγὸς τοῦ ἱεροῦ καὶ οἱ ἀρχιερεῖς, διηπόρουν περὶ αὐτῶν, τί ἂν γένοιτο τοῦτο. 25 παραγενόμενος δέ τις ἀπ-ήγγειλεν αὐτοῖς ὅτι

ἰδοὺ οἱ ἄνδρες οὓς ἔθεσθε ἐν τῇ φυλακῇ, εἰσὶν ἐν τῷ ἱερῷ ἑστῶτες καὶ διδάσκοντες τὸν λαόν.

26 Τότε ἀπελθὼν ὁ στρατηγὸς σὺν τοῖς ὑπηρέταις ἦγεν αὐτοὺς οὐ μετὰ βίας, ἐφοβοῦντο γὰρ τὸν λαὸν μὴ λιθασθῶσιν. 27 Ἀγαγόντες δὲ αὐτοὺς ἔστησαν ἐν τῷ συνεδρίῳ. καὶ ἐπηρώτησεν αὐτοὺς ὁ ἀρχιερεὺς

17 But the high priest, arising, and all the ones with him (which is the sect of the Sadducees) were filled with jealousy 18 and they laid hands on the apostles and put them into public prison. 19 But an angel of the Lord by night opened the prison doors, and having led them out said, 20 "Go, and standing speak in the temple to the people all the matters of this life." 21 So, hearing, they entered into the temple about daybreak and were teaching. But the high priest, arriving, and the ones with him, called together the Sanhedrin and all the council of the sons of Israel and sent to the prison-house that they be brought. 22 But the officers who went did not find them in the prison. So, returning, they reported, 23 saying this: "We found the prison-house closed up in all safety and the keepers standing at the doors, but, after opening, we found no one inside." 24 So, when both the captain of the temple and the chief priests heard these words, they were greatly perplexed about them, whatever would become of this. 25 And someone, having arrived, reported to them this: "Behold, the men whom you put in the prison are in the temple standing and teaching the people!" 26 Then, departing, the captain with the officers were bringing them not with force, for they were fearing the people, that they would be stoned. 27 And, having brought them, they set them among the Sanhedrin. And the high priest asked them,

28 λέγων·

παραγγελίᾳ παρηγγείλαμεν ὑμῖν μὴ διδάσκειν ἐπὶ τῷ ὀνόματι τούτῳ.

καὶ ἰδοὺ πεπληρώκατε τὴν Ἰερουσαλὴμ τῆς διδαχῆς ὑμῶν καὶ βούλεσθε ἐπαγαγεῖν ἐφ' ἡμᾶς τὸ αἷμα τοῦ ἀνθρώπου τούτου.

29 Ἀποκριθεὶς δὲ Πέτρος καὶ οἱ ἀπόστολοι εἶπαν·

πειθαρχεῖν δεῖ θεῷ μᾶλλον ἢ ἀνθρώποις. 30 ὁ θεὸς τῶν πατέρων ἡμῶν ἤγειρεν Ἰησοῦν ὃν ὑμεῖς διεχειρίσασθε κρεμάσαντες ἐπὶ ξύλου· 31 τοῦτον ὁ θεὸς ἀρχηγὸν καὶ σωτῆρα ὕψωσεν τῇ δεξιᾷ αὐτοῦ δοῦναι μετάνοιαν τῷ Ἰσραὴλ καὶ ἄφεσιν ἁμαρτιῶν. 32 καὶ ἡμεῖς ἐσμεν μάρτυρες τῶν ῥημάτων τούτων καὶ τὸ πνεῦμα τὸ ἅγιον ὃ ἔδωκεν ὁ θεὸς τοῖς πειθαρχοῦσιν αὐτῷ.

33 οἱ δὲ ἀκούσαντες διεπρίοντο καὶ ἐβούλοντο ἀνελεῖν αὐτούς.

34 Ἀναστὰς δέ τις ἐν τῷ συνεδρίῳ Φαρισαῖος ὀνόματι Γαμαλιήλ, νομοδιδάσκαλος τίμιος παντὶ τῷ λαῷ, ἐκέλευσεν ἔξω βραχὺ τοὺς ἀνθρώπους ποιῆσαι,

35 εἶπέν τε πρὸς αὐτούς·

ἄνδρες Ἰσραηλεῖται, προσέχετε ἑαυτοῖς ἐπὶ τοῖς ἀνθρώποις τούτοις τί μέλλετε πράσσειν. 36 πρὸ γὰρ τούτων τῶν ἡμερῶν ἀνέστη Θευδᾶς λέγων εἶναί τινα ἑαυτόν, ᾧ προσεκλίθη ἀνδρῶν ἀριθμὸς ὡς τετρακοσίων· ὃς ἀνῃρέθη, καὶ πάντες ὅσοι ἐπείθοντο αὐτῷ διελύθησαν καὶ ἐγένοντο εἰς οὐδέν.

28 saying, "By command we charged you not to be teaching in this name. And behold, you have filled Jerusalem with your teaching and you are intending to bring the blood of this person upon us!" 29 But answering back, Peter and the apostles said, "It is necessary to obey God rather than people. 30 The God of our fathers raised up Jesus, whom you yourselves killed, hanging him on a tree. 31 This One as Prince and Savior God exalted to his right hand to give repentance to Israel and deliverance from sins. 32 And we ourselves are witnesses of these matters, and [so is] the Holy Spirit whom God gave to the ones obeying him." 33 But they, hearing, were infuriated and were intending to kill them. 34 But a certain Pharisee in the Sanhedrin, Gamaliel by name, a teacher of the Law honored by all the people, commanded that the persons be put outside for a little while, 35 and he said to them, "Israelite men, take care for yourselves regarding these persons, what you are about to do! 36 For before these days Theudas rose up saying that he himself was somebody, to whom a number of men, about four hundred, joined; he was slain, and all, as many as were obeying him, were dispersed and they came to nothing.

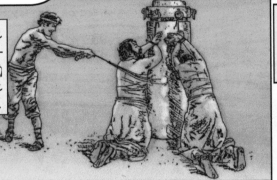

37 μετὰ τοῦτον ἀνέστη Ἰούδας ὁ Γαλιλαῖος ἐν ταῖς ἡμέραις τῆς ἀπογραφῆς καὶ ἀπέστησεν λαὸν ὀπίσω αὐτοῦ· κἀκεῖνος ἀπώλετο, καὶ πάντες ὅσοι ἐπείθοντο αὐτῷ διεσκορπίσθησαν. 38 καὶ τὰ νῦν λέγω ὑμῖν, ἀπόστητε ἀπὸ τῶν ἀνθρώπων τούτων καὶ ἄφετε αὐτούς, ὅτι ἐὰν ᾖ ἐξ ἀνθρώπων ἡ βουλὴ αὕτη ἢ τὸ ἔργον τοῦτο, καταλυθήσεται·

39 εἰ δὲ ἐκ θεοῦ ἐστιν, οὐ δυνήσεσθε καταλῦσαι αὐτούς, μή ποτε καὶ θεομάχοι εὑρεθῆτε.

ἐπείσθησαν δὲ αὐτῷ,

40 καὶ προσκαλεσάμενοι τοὺς ἀποστόλους δείραντες παρήγγειλαν μὴ λαλεῖν ἐπὶ τῷ ὀνόματι τοῦ Ἰησοῦ καὶ ἀπέλυσαν.

41 Οἱ μὲν οὖν ἐπορεύοντο χαίροντες ἀπὸ προσώπου τοῦ συνεδρίου, ὅτι κατηξιώθησαν ὑπὲρ τοῦ ὀνόματος ἀτιμασθῆναι·

42 πᾶσάν τε ἡμέραν ἐν τῷ ἱερῷ καὶ κατ' οἶκον οὐκ ἐπαύοντο διδάσκοντες καὶ εὐαγγελιζόμενοι τὸν χριστὸν Ἰησοῦν.

Κεφ. Ϛ´

6:1 Ἐν δὲ ταῖς ἡμέραις ταύταις πληθυνόντων τῶν μαθητῶν ἐγένετο γογγυσμὸς τῶν Ἑλληνιστῶν πρὸς τοὺς Ἑβραίους, ὅτι παρεθεωροῦντο ἐν τῇ διακονίᾳ τῇ καθημερινῇ αἱ χῆραι αὐτῶν.

37 After this man, Judas of Galilee rose up in the days of the census and moved people to revolt after him; and that one perished, and all, as many as were obeying him, were dispersed. 38 And with respect to the current events, I say to you, keep away from these persons and release them, because, if this plan or this work is from people, it will be overthrown; 39 but, if it is from God, you will not be able to overthrow them, even worse you may even be found to be fighting against God!" But with him they were persuaded. 40 And, having called the apostles, after scourging them, they charged that they not speak in the name of Jesus and they released them. 41 So then, they were going out rejoicing from the presence of the council, because they were counted worthy for the sake of the Name to be dishonored. 42 Also, every day in the temple and from house to house they were not ceasing from teaching and announcing the good news of the Christ, Jesus. 6:1 Now in these days, with the disciples multiplying, a complaint of the Hellenistic Judeans against the Hebrews occurred because their widows were being neglected in the daily serving.

2 προσκαλεσάμενοι δὲ οἱ δώδεκα τὸ πλῆθος τῶν μαθητῶν εἶπαν·

οὐκ ἀρεστόν ἐστιν ἡμᾶς καταλείψαντας τὸν λόγον τοῦ θεοῦ διακονεῖν τραπέζαις. 3 ἐπισκέψασθε οὖν, ἀδελφοί, ἄνδρας ἐξ ὑμῶν μαρτυρουμένους ἑπτὰ πλήρεις πνεύματος καὶ σοφίας οὓς καταστήσομεν ἐπὶ τῆς χρείας ταύτης· 4 ἡμεῖς δὲ τῇ προσευχῇ καὶ τῇ διακονίᾳ τοῦ λόγου προσκαρτερήσομεν.

5 καὶ ἤρεσεν ὁ λόγος ἐνώπιον παντὸς τοῦ πλήθους, καὶ ἐξελέξαντο Στέφανον, ἄνδρα πλήρης πίστεως καὶ πνεύματος ἁγίου, καὶ Φίλιππον καὶ Πρόχορον καὶ Νικάνορα καὶ Τίμωνα καὶ Παρμενᾶν καὶ Νικόλαον προσήλυτον Ἀντιοχέα,

6 οὓς ἔστησαν ἐνώπιον τῶν ἀποστόλων, καὶ προσευξάμενοι ἐπέθηκαν αὐτοῖς τὰς χεῖρας. 7 Καὶ ὁ λόγος τοῦ θεοῦ ηὔξανεν, καὶ ἐπληθύνετο ὁ ἀριθμὸς τῶν μαθητῶν ἐν Ἱερουσαλὴμ σφόδρα, πολύς τε ὄχλος τῶν ἱερέων ὑπήκουον τῇ πίστει.

8 Στέφανος δὲ πλήρης χάριτος καὶ δυνάμεως ἐποίει τέρατα καὶ σημεῖα μεγάλα ἐν τῷ λαῷ.

9 Ἀνέστησαν δέ τινες τῶν ἐκ τῆς συναγωγῆς τῆς λεγομένης Λιβερτίνων καὶ Κυρηναίων καὶ Ἀλεξανδρέων καὶ τῶν ἀπὸ Κιλικίας καὶ Ἀσίας, συνζητοῦντες τῷ Στεφάνῳ· 10 καὶ οὐκ ἴσχυον ἀντιστῆναι τῇ σοφίᾳ καὶ τῷ πνεύματι ᾧ ἐλάλει. 11 Τότε ὑπέβαλον ἄνδρας λέγοντας ὅτι

ἀκηκόαμεν αὐτοῦ λαλοῦντος ῥήματα βλάσφημα εἰς Μωϋσῆν καὶ τὸν θεόν·

2 And the twelve, having called together the multitude of the disciples, said, "It is not acceptable that we, abandoning the Word of God, would serve tables. 3 Therefore, brothers, select men from among you being well-attested, seven, full of the Spirit and of wisdom, whom we will appoint for this need. 4 But we ourselves will continue steadfastly in prayer and in the ministry of the Word." 5 And the speech was acceptable before all the multitude, and they chose Stephen, a man full of faith and of the Holy Spirit, and Philip and Prochorus and Nicanor and Timon and Parmenas and Nicolaus, a proselyte of Antioch, 6 whom they set before the apostles, and praying they laid hands upon them. 7 And the Word of God was increasing, and the number of the disciples in Jerusalem was being multiplied greatly, and at the same time a great company of the priests were obeying the faith. 8 Moreover, Stephen, full of grace and power, was performing great wonders and signs among the people. 9 But some of the ones from the synagogue called "Of the Freedmen" and from the Cyrenians and the Alexandrians and of the ones from Cilicia and Asia rose up, disputing with Stephen. 10 And they were not strong enough to oppose the wisdom and the Spirit by which he was speaking. 11 Then they induced men who were saying this: "We have heard him speaking blasphemous words against Moses and God!"

12 συνεκείνησάν τε τὸν λαὸν καὶ τοὺς πρεσβυτέρους καὶ τοὺς γραμματεῖς, καὶ ἐπιστάντες συνήρπασαν αὐτὸν καὶ ἤγαγον εἰς τὸ συνέδριον, 13 ἔστησάν τε μάρτυρας ψευδεῖς λέγοντας·

ὁ ἄνθρωπος οὗτος οὐ παύεται λαλῶν ῥήματα κατὰ τοῦ τόπου τοῦ ἁγίου καὶ τοῦ νόμου· 14 ἀκηκόαμεν γὰρ αὐτοῦ λέγοντος ὅτι Ἰησοῦς ὁ Ναζωραῖος οὗτος καταλύσει τὸν τόπον τοῦτον καὶ ἀλλάξει τὰ ἔθη ἃ παρέδωκεν ἡμῖν Μωϋσῆς.

15 καὶ ἀτενίσαντες εἰς αὐτὸν πάντες οἱ καθεζόμενοι ἐν τῷ συνεδρίῳ, εἶδον τὸ πρόσωπον αὐτοῦ ὡσεὶ πρόσωπον ἀγγέλου.

Κεφ. Ζ΄

7:1 Εἶπεν δὲ ὁ ἀρχιερεύς· εἰ ταῦτα οὕτως ἔχει;

2 ὁ δὲ ἔφη· ἄνδρες ἀδελφοὶ καὶ πατέρες, ἀκούσατε.

ὁ θεὸς τῆς δόξης ὤφθη τῷ πατρὶ ἡμῶν Ἀβραὰμ ὄντι ἐν τῇ Μεσοποταμίᾳ πρὶν ἢ κατοικῆσαι αὐτὸν ἐν Χαρράν, 3 καὶ εἶπεν πρὸς αὐτόν· ἔξελθε ἐκ τῆς γῆς σου καὶ ἐκ τῆς συγγενείας σου καὶ δεῦρο εἰς τὴν γῆν ἣν ἄν σοι δείξω.

12 At the same time, they stirred up the people and the elders and the scribes, and coming upon him in surprise they seized and brought him into the council, 13 and set up false witnesses who were saying, "This person does not cease speaking words against this holy place and the Law; 14 for we have heard him say this: 'This Jesus the Nazarene will destroy this place and will change the customs which Moses delivered to us'." 15 And, gazing at him, all the ones sitting in the council saw his face as if the face of an angel. 7:1 Then the high priest said, "Are these things so?" 2 And he said, "Men, brothers and fathers, listen! The God of glory appeared to our father Abraham being in Mesopotamia before even he dwelled in Haran, 3 and he said to him, 'Depart from your land and from your relatives and go into the land whichever I show to you.'

20

4 Τότε ἐξελθὼν ἐκ γῆς Χαλδαίων κατώκησεν ἐν Χαρράν· κἀκεῖθεν μετὰ τὸ ἀποθανεῖν τὸν πατέρα αὐτοῦ μετώκισεν αὐτὸν εἰς τὴν γῆν ταύτην εἰς ἣν ὑμεῖς νῦν κατοικεῖτε, 5 καὶ οὐκ ἔδωκεν αὐτῷ κληρονομίαν ἐν αὐτῇ οὐδὲ βῆμα ποδὸς

Haran

Mediterranean Sea

Sea of Galilee

Dead Sea

καὶ ἐπηγγείλατο δοῦναι αὐτῷ εἰς κατάσχεσιν αὐτὴν καὶ τῷ σπέρματι αὐτοῦ μετ' αὐτόν, οὐκ ὄντος αὐτῷ τέκνου. 6 ἐλάλησεν δὲ οὕτως ὁ θεός, ὅτι ἔσται τὸ σπέρμα αὐτοῦ πάροικον ἐν γῇ ἀλλοτρίᾳ καὶ δουλώσουσιν αὐτὸ καὶ κακώσουσιν ἔτη τετρακόσια.

καὶ τὸ ἔθνος ᾧ ἐὰν δουλεύσωσιν, κρινῶ ἐγώ, ὁ θεὸς εἶπεν, καὶ μετὰ ταῦτα ἐξελεύσονται καὶ λατρεύσουσίν μοι ἐν τῷ τόπῳ τούτῳ. 8 καὶ ἔδωκεν αὐτῷ διαθήκην περιτομῆς· καὶ οὕτως ἐγέννησεν τὸν Ἰσαὰκ καὶ περιέτεμεν αὐτὸν τῇ ἡμέρᾳ τῇ ὀγδόῃ, καὶ Ἰσαὰκ τὸν Ἰακώβ, καὶ Ἰακὼβ τοὺς δώδεκα πατριάρχας.

9 καὶ οἱ πατριάρχαι ζηλώσαντες τὸν Ἰωσὴφ ἀπέδοντο εἰς Αἴγυπτον· καὶ ἦν ὁ θεὸς μετ' αὐτοῦ 10 καὶ ἐξείλατο αὐτὸν ἐκ πασῶν τῶν θλίψεων αὐτοῦ καὶ ἔδωκεν αὐτῷ χάριν καὶ σοφίαν ἐναντίον Φαραὼ βασιλέως Αἰγύπτου καὶ κατέστησεν αὐτὸν ἡγούμενον ἐπ' Αἴγυπτον καὶ ὅλον τὸν οἶκον αὐτοῦ.

4 Then, having departed from the land of the Chaldeans, he dwelled in Haran; and from there, after his father died, [God] resettled him into this land into which you yourselves are now dwelling, 5 and he gave him no inheritance in it, not even a footstep, and promised to give it to him as a possession itself and to his seed after him, with no child existing to him. 6 Moreover, God spoke in this way, that his seed would be foreigners in a strange land and they would enslave them and would treat them badly for four hundred years. 7 'And the nation, whichever enslaves them, I myself will punish,' God said, 'and after these things they will come out and will worship me in this place.' 8 And he gave him a covenant of circumcision; and so [Abraham] begat Isaac and circumcised him on the eighth day, and Isaac Jacob, and Jacob the twelve patriarchs. 9 And the patriarchs, being jealous of Joseph, sold him into Egypt; and God was with him 10 and delivered him from all his afflictions and gave him favor and wisdom before Pharaoh king of Egypt and he made him governor over Egypt and his whole house.

11 ἦλθεν δὲ λιμὸς ἐφ' ὅλην τὴν Αἴγυπτον καὶ Χανάαν καὶ θλίψις μεγάλη καὶ οὐχ εὕρισκον χορτάσματα οἱ πατέρες ἡμῶν. 12 Ἀκούσας δὲ Ἰακὼβ ὄντα σιτία εἰς Αἴγυπτον ἐξαπέστειλεν τοὺς πατέρας ἡμῶν πρῶτον,

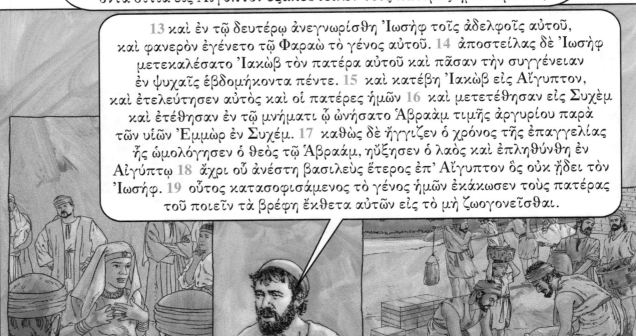

13 καὶ ἐν τῷ δευτέρῳ ἀνεγνωρίσθη Ἰωσὴφ τοῖς ἀδελφοῖς αὐτοῦ, καὶ φανερὸν ἐγένετο τῷ Φαραὼ τὸ γένος αὐτοῦ. 14 ἀποστείλας δὲ Ἰωσὴφ μετεκαλέσατο Ἰακὼβ τὸν πατέρα αὐτοῦ καὶ πᾶσαν τὴν συγγένειαν ἐν ψυχαῖς ἑβδομήκοντα πέντε. 15 καὶ κατέβη Ἰακὼβ εἰς Αἴγυπτον, καὶ ἐτελεύτησεν αὐτὸς καὶ οἱ πατέρες ἡμῶν 16 καὶ μετετέθησαν εἰς Συχὲμ καὶ ἐτέθησαν ἐν τῷ μνήματι ᾧ ὠνήσατο Ἀβραὰμ τιμῆς ἀργυρίου παρὰ τῶν υἱῶν Ἐμμὼρ ἐν Συχέμ. 17 καθὼς δὲ ἤγγιζεν ὁ χρόνος τῆς ἐπαγγελίας ἧς ὡμολόγησεν ὁ θεὸς τῷ Ἀβραάμ, ηὔξησεν ὁ λαὸς καὶ ἐπληθύνθη ἐν Αἰγύπτῳ 18 ἄχρι οὗ ἀνέστη βασιλεὺς ἕτερος ἐπ' Αἴγυπτον ὃς οὐκ ᾔδει τὸν Ἰωσήφ. 19 οὗτος κατασοφισάμενος τὸ γένος ἡμῶν ἐκάκωσεν τοὺς πατέρας τοῦ ποιεῖν τὰ βρέφη ἔκθετα αὐτῶν εἰς τὸ μὴ ζωογονεῖσθαι.

20 ἐν ᾧ καιρῷ ἐγεννήθη Μωϋσῆς καὶ ἦν ἀστεῖος τῷ θεῷ· ὃς ἀνετράφη μῆνας τρεῖς ἐν τῷ οἴκῳ τοῦ πατρός· 21 ἐκτεθέντος δὲ αὐτοῦ ἀνείλατο αὐτὸν ἡ θυγάτηρ Φαραὼ καὶ ἀνεθρέψατο αὐτὸν ἑαυτῇ εἰς υἱόν. 22 καὶ ἐπαιδεύθη Μωϋσῆς πάσῃ σοφίᾳ Αἰγυπτίων· ἦν δὲ δυνατὸς ἐν λόγοις καὶ ἔργοις αὐτοῦ.

11 Then, a famine came over the whole of Egypt and Canaan and [there was] great affliction and our fathers were finding no food. 12 But Jacob, hearing that grain was in Egypt, sent forth our fathers the first time, 13 and at the second time Joseph was made known to his brothers, and his family became apparent to Pharaoh. 14 Moreover, Joseph, sending, called for Jacob, his father, and all his kindred— seventy-five in [number of] souls. 15 And Jacob went down into Egypt, and he himself and our fathers died 16 and they were carried over to Shechem and laid in the tomb that Abraham bought for a price in silver from the sons of Hamor in Shechem. 17 But, just as the time of the promise was drawing near which God swore to Abraham, the people grew and were multiplied in Egypt 18 until another king arose over Egypt who did not know Joseph. 19 This one, dealing craftily with our race, mistreated our fathers so as to make their babes exposed in order that they would not live. 20 At which season, Moses was born and was handsome to God, who was nourished three months in his father's house. 21 Moreover, with him being cast out, Pharaoh's daughter took him up and nourished him for herself as a son. 22 And Moses was instructed in all the wisdom of the Egyptians; and he was powerful in his words and works.

23 ὡς δὲ ἐπληροῦτο αὐτῷ τεσσερακονταετὴς χρόνος, ἀνέβη ἐπὶ τὴν καρδίαν αὐτοῦ ἐπισκέψασθαι τοὺς ἀδελφοὺς αὐτοῦ τοὺς υἱοὺς Ἰσραήλ. 24 καὶ ἰδὼν τινὰ ἀδικούμενον ἠμύνατο καὶ ἐποίησεν ἐκδίκησιν τῷ καταπονουμένῳ πατάξας τὸν Αἰγύπτιον.

25 ἐνόμιζεν δὲ συνιέναι τοὺς ἀδελφοὺς αὐτοῦ ὅτι ὁ θεὸς διὰ χειρὸς αὐτοῦ δίδωσιν σωτηρίαν αὐτοῖς· οἱ δὲ οὐ συνῆκαν. 26 τῇ τε ἐπιούσῃ ἡμέρᾳ ὤφθη αὐτοῖς μαχομένοις καὶ συνήλλασσεν αὐτοὺς εἰς εἰρήνην εἰπών· ἄνδρες, ἀδελφοί ἐστε· ἵνα τί ἀδικεῖτε ἀλλήλους; 27 ὁ δὲ ἀδικῶν τὸν πλησίον ἀπώσατο αὐτὸν εἰπών· τίς σε κατέστησεν ἄρχοντα καὶ δικαστὴν ἐφ' ἡμῶν; 28 μὴ ἀνελεῖν με σὺ θέλεις ὃν τρόπον ἀνεῖλες ἐχθὲς τὸν Αἰγύπτιον;

29 ἔφυγεν δὲ Μωϋσῆς ἐν τῷ λόγῳ τούτῳ καὶ ἐγένετο πάροικος ἐν γῇ Μαδιάμ, οὗ ἐγέννησεν υἱοὺς δύο. 30 καὶ πληρωθέντων ἐτῶν τεσσεράκοντα ὤφθη αὐτῷ ἐν τῇ ἐρήμῳ τοῦ ὄρους Σινᾶ ἄγγελος ἐν φλογὶ πυρὸς βάτου.

31 ὁ δὲ Μωϋσῆς ἰδὼν ἐθαύμασεν τὸ ὅραμα· προσερχομένου δὲ αὐτοῦ κατανοῆσαι, ἐγένετο φωνὴ κυρίου·

32 ἐγὼ ὁ θεὸς τῶν πατέρων σου, ὁ θεὸς Ἀβραὰμ καὶ Ἰσαὰκ καὶ Ἰακώβ.

ἔντρομος δὲ γενόμενος Μωϋσῆς οὐκ ἐτόλμα κατανοῆσαι.

23 But as forty years' time was being fulfilled in him, it entered into his heart to visit his brothers, the children of Israel. 24 And, seeing someone being wronged, he defended and gave vengeance to the one being oppressed, striking down the Egyptian. 25 Moreover, he was supposing that his brothers understood that God through his hand was giving deliverance to them; but they did not understand. 26 And on the following day he appeared to them as they were fighting and he pushed them towards peace, saying, 'Men, you are brothers! For what purpose are you wronging one another?!' 27 But the one wronging his neighbor thrust him away, saying, 'Who made you a ruler and a judge over us?! 28 You yourself are not wanting to kill me in the manner that you killed the Egyptian yesterday, are you?!' (No!) 29 Then Moses fled at this word and became a sojourner in the land of Midian, where he begat two sons. 30 And, with forty years fulfilled, an angel appeared to him in the wilderness of Mount Sinai in a flame of fire in a bush. 31 Moreover, Moses, seeing wondered at the sight; and as he was drawing near to inspect it, the voice of the Lord came, 32 'I am the God of your fathers, the God of Abraham, and of Isaac, and of Jacob.' And, trembling, Moses was not daring to inspect it.

33 And the Lord said to him, 'Loosen the shoes from your feet; for the place upon which you stand is holy ground! 34 Looking, I saw the affliction of my people who are in Egypt and I heard their groaning; and I went down to deliver them; and now come, I will send you into Egypt.' 35 This Moses whom they refused, saying, 'Who made you a ruler and a judge?!'— this one God has sent as both ruler and deliverer with the hand of the angel who appeared to him in the bush. 36 This man led them out, performing wonders and signs in Egypt and in the Red Sea and in the wilderness for forty years. 37 This is the Moses who said to the children of Israel, 'A prophet God will raise up for you from your brothers, like me.' 38 This is the one who was in the assembly in the wilderness with the angel speaking to him at Mount Sinai and with our fathers, [the one] who received living oracles to give to us;

39 ᾧ οὐκ ἠθέλησαν ὑπήκοοι γενέσθαι οἱ πατέρες ἡμῶν, ἀλλὰ ἀπώσαντο καὶ ἐστράφησαν ἐν ταῖς καρδίαις αὐτῶν εἰς Αἴγυπτον, 40 εἰπόντες τῷ Ἀαρών· ποίησον ἡμῖν θεοὺς οἳ προπορεύσονται ἡμῶν· ὁ γὰρ Μωϋσῆς οὗτος ὃς ἐξήγαγεν ἡμᾶς ἐκ γῆς Αἰγύπτου, οὐκ οἴδαμεν τί ἐγένετο αὐτῷ.

41 καὶ ἐμοσχοποίησαν ἐν ταῖς ἡμέραις ἐκείναις καὶ ἀνήγαγον θυσίαν τῷ εἰδώλῳ καὶ εὐφραίνοντο ἐν τοῖς ἔργοις τῶν χειρῶν αὐτῶν.

42 ἔστρεψεν δὲ ὁ θεὸς καὶ παρέδωκεν αὐτοὺς λατρεύειν τῇ στρατιᾷ τοῦ οὐρανοῦ, καθὼς γέγραπται ἐν βίβλῳ τῶν προφητῶν·

μὴ σφάγια καὶ θυσίας προσηνέγκατέ μοι ἔτη τεσσεράκοντα ἐν τῇ ἐρήμῳ, οἶκος Ἰσραήλ; 43 καὶ ἀνελάβετε τὴν σκηνὴν τοῦ Μολὸχ καὶ τὸ ἄστρον τοῦ θεοῦ ὑμῶν Ῥεφάν, τοὺς τύπους οὓς ἐποιήσατε προσκυνεῖν αὐτοῖς· καὶ μετοικιῶ ὑμᾶς ἐπέκεινα Βαβυλῶνος.

44 Ἡ σκηνὴ τοῦ μαρτυρίου ἦν τοῖς πατράσιν ἡμῶν ἐν τῇ ἐρήμῳ, καθὼς διετάξατο ὁ λαλῶν τῷ Μωϋσῇ ποιῆσαι αὐτὴν κατὰ τὸν τύπον ὃν ἑωράκει·

39 to whom our fathers did not want to be obedient, but repudiated him and turned back in their hearts to Egypt, 40 saying to Aaron, 'Make for us gods that will go before us; for this Moses who led us forth out of the land of Egypt, we do not know what has happened to him!' 41 And they made a calf in those days and brought a sacrifice to the idol and were rejoicing in the works of their hands. 42 But God turned and handed them over to worship the host of heaven, just as it is written in the book of the Prophets; 'You did not offer to me slain beasts and sacrifices for forty years in the wilderness, O house of Israel, did you? (No!) 43 And you took up the tabernacle of Moloch and the star of your god Rephan, the figures which you made in order to worship them; and I will resettle you beyond Babylon.' 44 The tabernacle of the testimony was in the wilderness with our fathers, just as the One speaking to Moses appointed that he should make it according to the figure that he had seen;

45 ἦν καὶ εἰσήγαγον διαδεξάμενοι οἱ πατέρες ἡμῶν μετὰ Ἰησοῦ ἐν τῇ κατασχέσει τῶν ἐθνῶν, ὧν ἐξῶσεν ὁ θεὸς ἀπὸ προσώπου τῶν πατέρων ἡμῶν ἕως τῶν ἡμερῶν Δαυείδ· 46 ὃς εὗρεν χάριν ἐνώπιον τοῦ θεοῦ καὶ ᾐτήσατο εὑρεῖν σκήνωμα τῷ θεῷ Ἰακώβ.

47 Σολομὼν δὲ ᾠκοδόμησεν αὐτῷ οἶκον. 48 ἀλλ' οὐχ ὁ ὕψιστος ἐν χειροποιήτοις κατοικεῖ, καθὼς ὁ προφήτης λέγει·

49 ὁ οὐρανός μοι θρόνος, ἡ δὲ γῆ ὑποπόδιον τῶν ποδῶν μου· ποῖον οἶκον οἰκοδομήσετέ μοι; λέγει κύριος, ἢ τίς τόπος τῆς καταπαύσεώς μου; 50 οὐχὶ ἡ χείρ μου ἐποίησεν ταῦτα πάντα;

51 σκληροτράχηλοι καὶ ἀπερίτμητοι ταῖς καρδίαις ὑμῶν καὶ τοῖς ὠσίν, ὑμεῖς ἀεὶ τῷ πνεύματι τῷ ἁγίῳ ἀντιπίπτετε, ὡς οἱ πατέρες ὑμῶν καὶ ὑμεῖς· 52 τίνα τῶν προφητῶν οὐκ ἐδίωξαν οἱ πατέρες ὑμῶν; καὶ ἀπέκτειναν τοὺς προκαταγγείλαντας περὶ τῆς ἐλεύσεως τοῦ δικαίου, οὗ νῦν ὑμεῖς προδόται καὶ φονεῖς ἐγένεσθε·

53 οἵτινες ἐλάβετε τὸν νόμον εἰς διαταγὰς ἀγγέλων καὶ οὐκ ἐφυλάξατε.

45 which also our fathers entered into, in turn with Joshua, taking possession of the nations which God thrust out before the face of our fathers until the days of David; 46 who found favor in the sight of God and asked to find a dwelling place for the God of Jacob. 47 But Solomon built a house for him. 48 However, the Most High does not dwell in handmade temples just as the prophet says, 49 'The heaven is my throne, and the earth the footstool of my feet; what sort of house will you build for me?' says the Lord, 'Or what is the place of my rest? 50 Did not my hand make all these things? (Yes!)' 51 You are stiff-necked and uncircumcised in heart and ears! You yourselves always resist the Holy Spirit; as your fathers did, so do you! 52 Which of the Prophets did your fathers not persecute? And they killed the ones who announced ahead of time about the coming of the Righteous One, whose betrayers and murderers you yourselves now became! 53 You who received the Law as ordained by angels and did not kept it!"

54 Now, [while] hearing these things, they were being cut to their heart and were gnashing their teeth at him. 55 Moreover, being full of the Holy Spirit, looking up steadfastly into heaven, he saw the glory of God and Jesus standing on the right hand of God 56 and said, "Behold, I am seeing the heavens opened up and the Son of Man standing at the right hand of God!" 57 But, crying out with a loud voice, they stopped their ears and rushed with one purpose at him; 58 and, having cast him out of the city, they were stoning him. And the witnesses laid down their garments at the feet of a young man called Saul. 59 And they continued stoning Stephen as he was calling out and saying, "Lord Jesus, receive my spirit!"

60 θεὶς δὲ τὰ γόνατα ἔκραξεν φωνῇ μεγάλῃ·

κύριε, μὴ στήσῃς αὐτοῖς ταύτην τὴν ἁμαρτίαν.

καὶ τοῦτο εἰπὼν ἐκοιμήθη.

Κεφ. Η´

8:1 Σαῦλος δὲ ἦν συνευδοκῶν τῇ ἀναιρέσει αὐτοῦ.

Ἐγένετο δὲ ἐν ἐκείνῃ τῇ ἡμέρᾳ διωγμὸς μέγας ἐπὶ τὴν ἐκκλησίαν τὴν ἐν Ἱεροσολύμοις· πάντες δὲ διεσπάρησαν κατὰ τὰς χώρας τῆς Ἰουδαίας καὶ Σαμαρείας πλὴν τῶν ἀποστόλων. 2 Συνεκόμισαν δὲ τὸν Στέφανον ἄνδρες εὐλαβεῖς καὶ ἐποίησαν κοπετὸν μέγαν ἐπ᾽ αὐτῷ.

3 Σαῦλος δὲ ἐλυμαίνετο τὴν ἐκκλησίαν κατὰ τοὺς οἴκους εἰσπορευόμενος, σύρων τε ἄνδρας καὶ γυναῖκας παρεδίδου εἰς φυλακήν.

60 Then, slumping on his knees, he cried out with a loud voice, "Lord, do not hold this sin against them!" And, having said this, he fell asleep. 8:1 Now, Saul was consenting of his death. And on that day a great persecution occurred against the church in Jerusalem; and they all were dispersed throughout the regions of Judaea and Samaria, except the apostles. 2 And devout men buried Stephen and made great mourning over him. 3 Yet, Saul was persecuting the church going into house by house; at the same time dragging men and women, he was handing them over to prison.

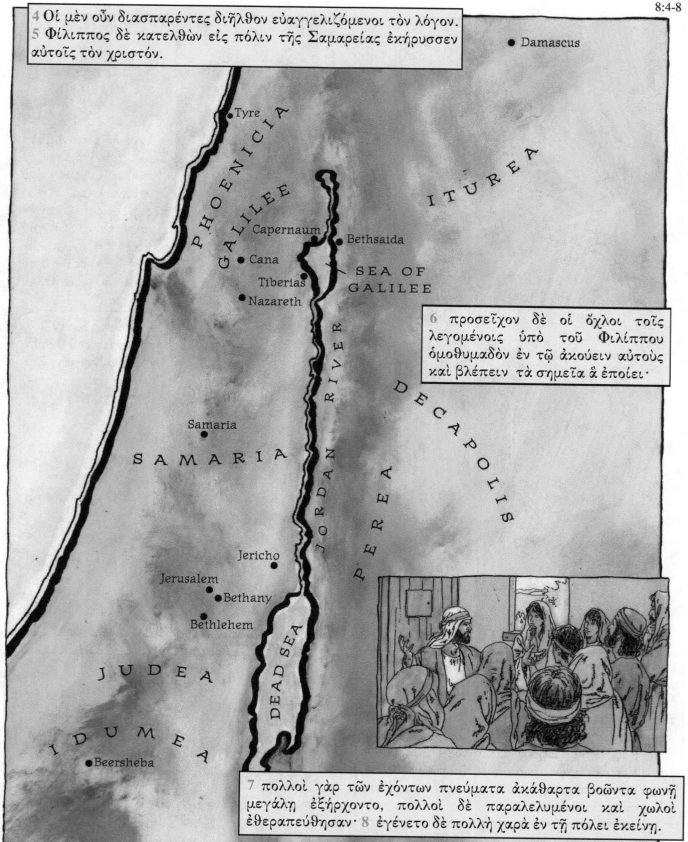

4 Οἱ μὲν οὖν διασπαρέντες διῆλθον εὐαγγελιζόμενοι τὸν λόγον. 5 Φίλιππος δὲ κατελθὼν εἰς πόλιν τῆς Σαμαρείας ἐκήρυσσεν αὐτοῖς τὸν χριστόν.

• Damascus

Tyre

PHOENICIA

GALILEE

ITUREA

Capernaum

• Bethsaida

• Cana

SEA OF GALILEE

Tiberias

• Nazareth

6 προσεῖχον δὲ οἱ ὄχλοι τοῖς λεγομένοις ὑπὸ τοῦ Φιλίππου ὁμοθυμαδὸν ἐν τῷ ἀκούειν αὐτοὺς καὶ βλέπειν τὰ σημεῖα ἃ ἐποίει·

DECAPOLIS

Samaria

SAMARIA

JORDAN RIVER

PEREA

Jericho

Jerusalem

• Bethany

Bethlehem

JUDEA

DEAD SEA

IDUMEA

• Beersheba

7 πολλοὶ γὰρ τῶν ἐχόντων πνεύματα ἀκάθαρτα βοῶντα φωνῇ μεγάλῃ ἐξήρχοντο, πολλοὶ δὲ παραλελυμένοι καὶ χωλοὶ ἐθεραπεύθησαν· 8 ἐγένετο δὲ πολλὴ χαρὰ ἐν τῇ πόλει ἐκείνῃ.

4 So then, the ones who were dispersed went throughout announcing the good news of the Word. 5 And Philip, having gone down to the city of Samaria, proclaimed to them the Christ. 6 And the crowds were following the words being spoken by Philip as they were hearing and seeing the signs that he was doing. 7 For many of the ones having unclean spirits, shouting with a loud voice, came out; and many being paralyzed and lame were healed. 8 And there was much joy in that city.

9 Ἀνὴρ δέ τις ὀνόματι Σίμων προϋπῆρχεν ἐν τῇ πόλει μαγεύων καὶ ἐξιστάνων τὸ ἔθνος τῆς Σαμαρείας λέγων εἶναί τινα ἑαυτὸν μέγαν· 10 ᾧ προσεῖχον πάντες ἀπὸ μικροῦ ἕως μεγάλου λέγοντες·

οὗτός ἐστιν ἡ δύναμις τοῦ θεοῦ ἡ καλουμένη μεγάλη.

11 προσεῖχον δὲ αὐτῷ διὰ τὸ ἱκανῷ χρόνῳ ταῖς μαγείαις ἐξεστακέναι αὐτούς· 12 ὅτε δὲ ἐπίστευσαν τῷ Φιλίππῳ εὐαγγελιζομένῳ περὶ τῆς βασιλείας τοῦ θεοῦ καὶ τοῦ ὀνόματος Ἰησοῦ χριστοῦ, ἐβαπτίζοντο ἄνδρες τε καὶ γυναῖκες. 13 ὁ δὲ Σίμων καὶ αὐτὸς ἐπίστευσεν, καὶ βαπτισθεὶς ἦν προσκαρτερῶν τῷ Φιλίππῳ, θεωρῶν τε σημεῖα καὶ δυνάμεις μεγάλας γινομένας ἐξίστατο.

9 But a certain man, Simon by name, had earlier lived in the city using sorcery and astonishing the people of Samaria, saying that he was himself some great person; 10 whom they all were following from the least to the greatest saying, "This person is what is called the great power of God!" 11 And they were following him because for a long time he had amazed them with his sorceries. 12 But when they believed Philip announcing the good news concerning the kingdom of God and the name of Jesus Christ, they were being baptized, both men and women. 13 Moreover, Simon also himself believed and, being baptized, was devoted to Philip, and at the same time seeing the signs and great miracles occurring, he continued being astonished.

14 Ἀκούσαντες δὲ οἱ ἐν Ἱεροσολύμοις ἀπόστολοι ὅτι δέδεκται ἡ Σαμάρεια τὸν λόγον τοῦ θεοῦ, ἀπέστειλαν πρὸς αὐτοὺς Πέτρον καὶ Ἰωάννην·

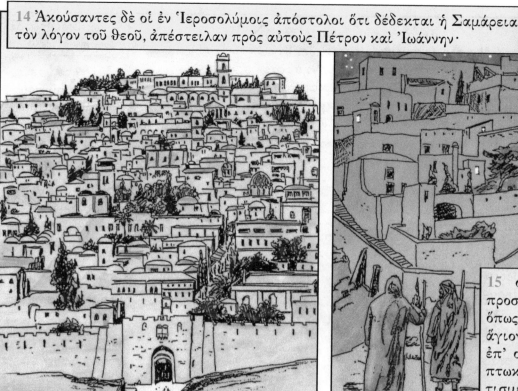

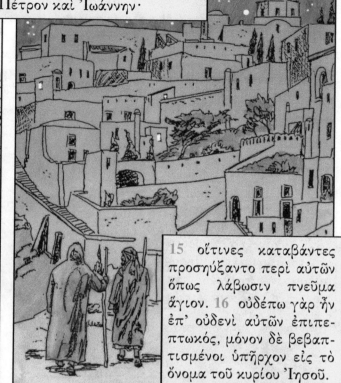

15 οἵτινες καταβάντες προσηύξαντο περὶ αὐτῶν ὅπως λάβωσιν πνεῦμα ἅγιον. 16 οὐδέπω γὰρ ἦν ἐπ' οὐδενὶ αὐτῶν ἐπιπεπτωκός, μόνον δὲ βεβαπτισμένοι ὑπῆρχον εἰς τὸ ὄνομα τοῦ κυρίου Ἰησοῦ.

17 τότε ἐπετίθεσαν τὰς χεῖρας ἐπ' αὐτούς, καὶ ἐλάμβανον πνεῦμα ἅγιον. 18 Ἰδὼν δὲ ὁ Σίμων ὅτι διὰ τῆς ἐπιθέσεως τῶν χειρῶν τῶν ἀποστόλων δίδοται τὸ πνεῦμα τὸ ἅγιον, προσήνεγκεν αὐτοῖς χρήματα 19 λέγων·

δότε κἀμοὶ τὴν ἐξουσίαν ταύτην, ἵνα ᾧ ἐὰν ἐπιθῶ τὰς χεῖρας λαμβάνῃ πνεῦμα ἅγιον.

Πέτρος δὲ εἶπεν πρὸς αὐτόν·

τὸ ἀργύριόν σου σὺν σοὶ εἴη εἰς ἀπώλειαν, ὅτι τὴν δωρεὰν τοῦ θεοῦ ἐνόμισας διὰ χρημάτων κτᾶσθαι. 21 οὐκ ἔστιν σοι μερὶς οὐδὲ κλῆρος ἐν τῷ λόγῳ τούτῳ· ἡ γὰρ καρδία σου οὐκ ἔστιν εὐθεῖα ἔναντι τοῦ θεοῦ.

14 Now, the apostles at Jerusalem, hearing that Samaria had received the Word of God, sent to them Peter and John, 15 who, going down, prayed for them in order that they would receive the Holy Spirit. 16 For it had not yet fallen upon a single one of them, but they only in fact had been baptized into the name of the Lord Jesus. 17 Then they laid their hands on them, and they began receiving the Holy Spirit. 18 Moreover, Simon, having seen that through the laying on of the apostles' hands the Holy Spirit was being given, he offered money to them, 19 saying, "Give also to me this power in order that on whomever I lay my hands they would receive the Holy Spirit!" 20 But Peter said to him, "May your silver go to destruction with you, because you thought to obtain the gift of God with money! 21 There is neither part nor lot for you in this matter! For your heart is not right before God.

22 μετανόησον οὖν ἀπὸ τῆς κακίας σου ταύτης καὶ δεήθητι τοῦ κυρίου, εἰ ἄρα ἀφεθήσεταί σοι ἡ ἐπίνοια τῆς καρδίας σου. 23 εἰς γὰρ χολὴν πικρίας καὶ σύνδεσμον ἀδικίας ὁρῶ σε ὄντα.

24 ἀποκριθεὶς δὲ ὁ Σίμων εἶπεν·

δεήθητε ὑμεῖς ὑπὲρ ἐμοῦ πρὸς τὸν κύριον, ὅπως μηδὲν ἐπέλθῃ ἐπ᾽ ἐμὲ ὧν εἰρήκατε.

25 οἱ μὲν οὖν διαμαρτυράμενοι καὶ λαλήσαντες τὸν λόγον τοῦ κυρίου ὑπέστρεφον εἰς Ἱεροσόλυμα, πολλάς τε κώμας τῶν Σαμαρειτῶν εὐηγγελίζοντο.

26 Ἄγγελος δὲ κυρίου ἐλάλησεν πρὸς Φίλιππον λέγων·

ἀνάστηθι καὶ πορεύου κατὰ μεσημβρίαν ἐπὶ τὴν ὁδὸν τὴν καταβαίνουσαν ἀπὸ Ἱερουσαλὴμ εἰς Γάζαν·

αὕτη ἐστὶν ἔρημος.

27 καὶ ἀναστὰς ἐπορεύθη·

καὶ ἰδοὺ ἀνὴρ Αἰθίοψ εὐνοῦχος δυνάστης Κανδάκης βασιλίσσης Αἰθιόπων, ὃς ἦν ἐπὶ πάσης τῆς γάζης αὐτῆς, ὃς ἐληλύθει προσκυνήσων εἰς Ἱερουσαλήμ,

28 ἦν τε ὑποστρέφων καὶ καθήμενος ἐπὶ τοῦ ἅρματος αὐτοῦ καὶ ἀνεγίνωσκεν τὸν προφήτην Ἡσαΐαν.

29 εἶπεν δὲ τὸ πνεῦμα τῷ Φιλίππῳ·

πρόσελθε καὶ κολλήθητι τῷ ἅρματι τούτῳ.

22 Repent, therefore, from this wickedness of yours and pray to the Lord, if perhaps the thought of your heart will be forgiven you. 23 For I am seeing that you are in the gall of bitterness and in the bond of iniquity." 24 But answering back, Simon said, "You yourselves pray for me to the Lord, in order that nothing of which you have spoken would come upon me!" 25 So then, the ones who had testified and had spoken the Word of the Lord returned to Jerusalem; and they were proclaiming the good news in many villages of the Samaritans. 26 But an angel of the Lord spoke to Philip, saying, "Arise and begin going toward the south to the way that goes down from Jerusalem to Gaza." (This road was desolate.) 27 And arising, he went. And behold, there was a man of Ethiopia, a eunuch of great authority under Candace, queen of the Ethiopians, who was over all her treasury, who had come in order to worship in Jerusalem; 28 and he was returning and sitting in his chariot and was reading the prophet Isaiah. 29 And the Spirit said to Philip, "Go near and join yourself to this chariot."

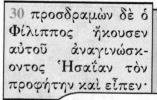
30 προσδραμὼν δὲ ὁ Φίλιππος ἤκουσεν αὐτοῦ ἀναγινώσκοντος Ἡσαΐαν τὸν προφήτην καὶ εἶπεν·

ἆρά γε γινώσκεις ἃ ἀναγινώσκεις;

31 ὁ δὲ εἶπεν·

πῶς γὰρ ἂν δυναίμην, ἐὰν μή τις ὁδηγήσει με;

παρεκάλεσέν τε τὸν Φίλιππον ἀναβάντα καθίσαι σὺν αὐτῷ.

32 ἡ δὲ περιοχὴ τῆς γραφῆς ἣν ἀνεγίνωσκεν ἦν αὕτη·

ὡς πρόβατον ἐπὶ σφαγὴν ἤχθη, καὶ ὡς ἀμνὸς ἐναντίον τοῦ κείραντος αὐτὸν ἄφωνος, οὕτως οὐκ ἀνοίγει τὸ στόμα αὐτοῦ. 33 ἐν τῇ ταπεινώσει ἡ κρίσις αὐτοῦ ἤρθη, τὴν γενεὰν αὐτοῦ τίς διηγήσεται; ὅτι αἴρεται ἀπὸ τῆς γῆς ἡ ζωὴ αὐτοῦ.

34 Ἀποκριθεὶς δὲ ὁ εὐνοῦχος τῷ Φιλίππῳ εἶπεν·

δέομαί σου, περὶ τίνος ὁ προφήτης λέγει τοῦτο; περὶ ἑαυτοῦ, ἢ περὶ ἑτέρου τινός;

ἰδοὺ ὕδωρ· τί κωλύει με βαπτισθῆναι;

35 ἀνοίξας δὲ ὁ Φίλιππος τὸ στόμα αὐτοῦ καὶ ἀρξάμενος ἀπὸ τῆς γραφῆς ταύτης εὐηγγελίσατο αὐτῷ τὸν Ἰησοῦν. 36 Ὡς δὲ ἐπορεύοντο κατὰ τὴν ὁδόν, ἦλθον ἐπί τι ὕδωρ καὶ φησὶν ὁ εὐνοῦχος·

38* καὶ ἐκέλευσεν στῆναι τὸ ἅρμα, καὶ κατέβησαν ἀμφότεροι εἰς τὸ ὕδωρ, ὅ τε Φίλιππος καὶ ὁ εὐνοῦχος, καὶ ἐβάπτισεν αὐτόν.

39 ὅτε δὲ ἀνέβησαν ἐκ τοῦ ὕδατος, πνεῦμα κυρίου ἥρπασεν τὸν Φίλιππον, καὶ οὐκ εἶδεν αὐτὸν οὐκέτι ὁ εὐνοῦχος· ἐπορεύετο γὰρ τὴν ὁδὸν αὐτοῦ χαίρων. 40 Φίλιππος δὲ εὑρέθη εἰς Ἄζωτον, καὶ διερχόμενος εὐηγγελίζετο τὰς πόλεις πάσας ἕως τοῦ ἐλθεῖν αὐτὸν εἰς Καισάρειαν.

30 And running forth, Philip heard him reading Isaiah the prophet and said, "So, are you actually understanding what you are reading?!" And he asked Philip, coming up, to sit with him. 31 And he said, "How would I be able, unless someone would guide me?!" And he asked Philip, coming up, to sit with him. 32 Now the passage of the Scripture which he was reading was this: "As a sheep he was led to the slaughter; And as a lamb before his shearer is silent, thus he does not open his mouth: 33 In his humiliation his judgment was taken away; His generation who will declare? For his life is taken from the earth." 34 And responding back, the eunuch said to Philip, "I beg of you, concerning whom is the prophet speaking this? Concerning himself, or concerning some other person?" 35 And Philip, opening his mouth and beginning from this Scripture, proclaimed to him the good news of Jesus. 36 And as they were going along the way, they came to some water and the eunuch says, "Behold water! What is preventing me to be baptized?" 38 And he commanded the chariot to stand still, and they both went down into the water, both Philip and the eunuch, and he baptized him. 39 And when they came up out of the water, the Spirit of the Lord snatched away Philip, and the eunuch did not see him any longer; for he continued going on his way rejoicing. 40 But Philip was found at Azotus, and, passing through, he was proclaiming the good news in all the cities until he came into Caesarea.

Κεφ. Θ´

9:1 Ὁ δὲ Σαῦλος ἔτι ἐμπνέων ἀπειλῆς καὶ φόνου εἰς τοὺς μαθητὰς τοῦ κυρίου, προσελθὼν τῷ ἀρχιερεῖ, 2 ᾐτήσατο παρ' αὐτοῦ ἐπιστολὰς εἰς Δαμασκὸν πρὸς τὰς συναγωγάς, ὅπως ἐάν τινας εὕρῃ τῆς ὁδοῦ ὄντας ἄνδρας τε καὶ γυναῖκας, δεδεμένους ἀγάγῃ εἰς Ἱερουσαλήμ.

3 ἐν δὲ τῷ πορεύεσθαι ἐγένετο αὐτὸν ἐγγίζειν τῇ Δαμασκῷ, ἐξέφνης τε αὐτὸν περιήστραψεν φῶς ἐκ τοῦ οὐρανοῦ·

4 καὶ πεσὼν ἐπὶ τὴν γῆν ἤκουσεν φωνὴν λέγουσαν αὐτῷ·

Σαοὺλ Σαούλ, τί με διώκεις;

5 εἶπεν δέ·

τίς εἶ, κύριε;

ὁ δέ·

ἐγώ εἰμι Ἰησοῦς ὃν σὺ διώκεις· 6 ἀλλὰ ἀνάστηθι καὶ εἴσελθε εἰς τὴν πόλιν, καὶ λαληθήσεταί σοι ὅ τί σε δεῖ ποιεῖν.

7 οἱ δὲ ἄνδρες οἱ συνοδεύοντες αὐτῷ ἱστήκεισαν ἐνεοί, ἀκούοντες μὲν τῆς φωνῆς, μηδένα δὲ θεωροῦντες. 8 ἠγέρθη δὲ Σαῦλος ἀπὸ τῆς γῆς, ἀνεῳγμένων δὲ τῶν ὀφθαλμῶν αὐτοῦ οὐδὲν ἔβλεπεν· χειραγωγοῦντες δὲ αὐτὸν εἰσήγαγον εἰς Δαμασκόν.

9:1 But Saul, still breathing threats and murder towards the disciples of the Lord, having gone to the high priest, 2 asked from him letters for Damascus to the synagogues, in order that, if he found some of the Way present, both men and women, he would bring them bound up to Jerusalem. 3 And while he was going, it happened that he was drawing near to Damascus; and suddenly a light out of heaven shone around him! 4 And, having fallen on the ground, he heard a voice saying to him, "Saul, Saul, why are you persecuting me?!" 5 And he said, "Who are you, Lord?" And he said, "I am Jesus whom you yourself are persecuting! 6 But arise and enter into the city, and it will be told to you what is necessary for you to do." 7 And the men journeying with him stood speechless, on the one hand, hearing the voice, but on the other hand, seeing no one. 8 Then Saul arose from the ground; but, with his eyes opened up he was seeing nothing; and leading him by hand they brought him into Damascus.

9 καὶ ἦν ἡμέρας τρεῖς μὴ βλέπων καὶ οὐκ ἔφαγεν οὐδὲ ἔπιεν.

10 Ἦν δέ τις μαθητὴς ἐν Δαμασκῷ ὀνόματι Ἀνανίας, καὶ εἶπεν πρὸς αὐτὸν ἐν ὁράματι ὁ κύριος·

Ἀνανία.

ὁ δὲ εἶπεν·

ἰδοὺ ἐγώ, κύριε.

11 ὁ δὲ κύριος πρὸς αὐτόν·

ἀναστὰς πορεύθητι ἐπὶ τὴν ῥύμην τὴν καλουμένην εὐθεῖαν καὶ ζήτησον ἐν οἰκίᾳ Ἰούδα Σαῦλον ὀνόματι Ταρσέα· ἰδοὺ γὰρ προσεύχεται 12 καὶ εἶδεν ἄνδρα ἐν ὁράματι Ἀνανίαν ὀνόματι εἰσελθόντα καὶ ἐπιθέντα αὐτῷ χεῖρας, ὅπως ἀναβλέψῃ.

13 Ἀπεκρίθη δὲ Ἀνανίας·

κύριε, ἤκουσα ἀπὸ πολλῶν περὶ τοῦ ἀνδρὸς τούτου, ὅσα κακὰ τοῖς ἁγίοις σου ἐποίησεν ἐν Ἰερουσαλήμ· 14 καὶ ὧδε ἔχει ἐξουσίαν παρὰ τῶν ἀρχιερέων δῆσαι πάντας τοὺς ἐπικαλουμένους τὸ ὄνομά σου.

15 Εἶπεν δὲ πρὸς αὐτὸν ὁ κύριος·

πορεύου, ὅτι σκεῦος ἐκλογῆς ἐστίν μοι οὗτος τοῦ βαστάσαι τὸ ὄνομά μου ἐνώπιον ἐθνῶν τε καὶ βασιλέων υἱῶν τε Ἰσραήλ. 16 ἐγὼ γὰρ ὑποδείξω αὐτῷ ὅσα δεῖ αὐτὸν ὑπὲρ τοῦ ὀνόματός μου παθεῖν.

17 Ἀπῆλθεν δὲ Ἀνανίας καὶ εἰσῆλθεν εἰς τὴν οἰκίαν,

καὶ ἐπιθεὶς ἐπ᾽ αὐτὸν τὰς χεῖρας εἶπεν·

Σαοὺλ ἀδελφέ, ὁ κύριος ἀπέσταλκέν με, Ἰησοῦς ὁ ὀφθείς σοι ἐν τῇ ὁδῷ ᾗ ἤρχου, ὅπως ἀναβλέψῃς καὶ πλησθῇς πνεύματος ἁγίου.

9 And for three days he was not seeing and he neither ate nor drank. 10 Now there was a certain disciple in Damascus, Ananias by name, and the Lord said to him in a vision, "Ananias." And he said, "Behold, I am here, Lord." 11 And the Lord said to him, "Arising, go to the street that is called Straight, and inquire in the house of Judas for Saul by name, a man of Tarsus; for behold, he is praying; 12 and in a vision he has seen a man, Ananias by name, coming in and laying hands upon him, in order that he would see again." 13 But Ananias answered back, "Lord, I heard from many about this man, how many evil things he did to your saints in Jerusalem; 14 and here he has authority from the chief priests to bind all the ones calling upon your name!" 15 But the Lord said to him, "Start going, because this person is a chosen vessel for me to bear my name before both the Gentiles and kings as well as the children of Israel. 16 For I myself will show him how many things it is necessary that he undergo for my name's sake." 17 So Ananias departed and entered into the house, and, laying his hands on him, he said, "Brother Saul, the Lord has sent me—Jesus, the one who appeared to you on the way in which you were coming in order that you would see again and be filled with the Holy Spirit."

18 καὶ εὐθέως ἀπέπεσαν αὐτοῦ ἀπὸ τῶν ὀφθαλμῶν ὡς λεπίδες, ἀνέβλεψέν τε καὶ ἀναστὰς ἐβαπτίσθη,

19 καὶ λαβὼν τροφὴν ἐνίσχυσεν.

Ἐγένετο δὲ μετὰ τῶν ἐν Δαμασκῷ μαθητῶν ἡμέρας τινάς·

20 καὶ εὐθέως ἐν ταῖς συναγωγαῖς ἐκήρυσσεν τὸν Ἰησοῦν, ὅτι

οὗτός ἐστιν ὁ υἱὸς τοῦ θεοῦ.

21 Ἐξίσταντο δὲ πάντες οἱ ἀκούοντες καὶ ἔλεγον·

οὐχ οὗτός ἐστιν ὁ πορθήσας ἐν Ἰερουσαλὴμ τοὺς ἐπικαλουμένους τὸ ὄνομα τοῦτο; καὶ ὧδε εἰς τοῦτο ἐληλύθει ἵνα δεδεμένους αὐτοὺς ἀγάγῃ ἐπὶ τοὺς ἀρχιερεῖς.

22 Σαῦλος δὲ μᾶλλον ἐνεδυναμοῦτο καὶ συνέχυνεν τοὺς Ἰουδαίους τοὺς κατοικοῦντας ἐν Δαμασκῷ, συμβιβάζων ὅτι οὗτός ἐστιν ὁ χριστός.

23 ὡς δὲ ἐπληροῦντο ἡμέραι ἱκαναί, συνεβουλεύσαντο οἱ Ἰουδαῖοι ἀνελεῖν αὐτόν· 24 ἐγνώσθη δὲ τῷ Σαύλῳ ἡ ἐπιβουλὴ αὐτῶν.

παρετηροῦντο δὲ καὶ τὰς πύλας ἡμέρας τε καὶ νυκτός, ὅπως αὐτὸν ἀνέλωσιν· 25 λαβόντες δὲ οἱ μαθηταὶ αὐτοῦ νυκτὸς διὰ τοῦ τείχους καθῆκαν αὐτὸν χαλάσαντες ἐν σπυρίδι.

18 And immediately there fell from his eyes something like scales, and at the same time he saw again and arising was baptized; 19 and, having taken food, he regained strength. Moreover, he was with the disciples in Damascus for some days. 20 And immediately in the synagogues he was preaching about Jesus this: "This one is the Son of God!" 21 And all hearing him were astonished and were saying, "Is this not the one who endeavored in Jerusalem to destroy the ones calling on this name? (Yes!) And for this purpose, he had come here in order that he would bring them bound up before the chief priests." 22 But Saul was increasing more in strength and confounding the Judeans dwelling in Damascus, proving that this One was the Christ. 23 And when a number of days were fulfilled, the Judeans took counsel together to kill him; 24 but their plot was known to Saul. Moreover, they were also watching the gates both day and night, in order that they would kill him; 25 but his disciples, having taken him by night, let him down through the wall lowering him in a basket.

26 Παραγενόμενος δὲ εἰς Ἰερουσαλὴμ ἐπείραζεν κολλᾶσθαι τοῖς μαθηταῖς· καὶ πάντες ἐφοβοῦντο αὐτὸν μὴ πιστεύοντες ὅτι ἐστὶν μαθητής.

27 Βαρνάβας δὲ ἐπιλαβόμενος αὐτὸν ἤγαγεν πρὸς τοὺς ἀποστόλους καὶ διηγήσατο αὐτοῖς πῶς ἐν τῇ ὁδῷ εἶδεν τὸν κύριον καὶ ὅτι ἐλάλησεν αὐτῷ καὶ πῶς ἐν Δαμασκῷ ἐπαρρησιάσατο ἐν τῷ ὀνόματι τοῦ Ἰησοῦ.

28 καὶ ἦν μετ' αὐτῶν εἰσπορευόμενος καὶ ἐκπορευόμενος εἰς Ἰερουσαλήμ, παρρησιαζόμενος ἐν τῷ ὀνόματι τοῦ κυρίου,

29 ἐλάλει τε καὶ συνεζήτει πρὸς τοὺς Ἑλληνιστάς· οἱ δὲ ἐπεχείρουν ἀνελεῖν αὐτόν.

30 ἐπιγνόντες δὲ οἱ ἀδελφοὶ κατήγαγον αὐτὸν εἰς Καισάρειαν καὶ ἐξαπέστειλαν αὐτὸν εἰς Ταρσόν.

31 Ἡ μὲν οὖν ἐκκλησία καθ' ὅλης τῆς Ἰουδαίας καὶ Γαλιλαίας καὶ Σαμαρείας εἶχεν εἰρήνην, οἰκοδομουμένη καὶ πορευομένη τῷ φόβῳ τοῦ κυρίου, καὶ τῇ παρακλήσει τοῦ ἁγίου πνεύματος ἐπληθύνετο.

26 And having arrived into Jerusalem, he was attempting to be associated with the disciples; and all were fearing him, not believing that he was a disciple. 27 But Barnabas, having received him, led him to the apostles and related to them how on the road he saw the Lord, and that He had spoken to him, and how in Damascus he boldly spoke in the name of Jesus. 28 And he was with them going into and going out of Jerusalem, speaking boldly in the name of the Lord, 29 and he was speaking and disputing with the Hellenistic Judeans; but they were trying to kill him. 30 And having learned this, the brothers brought him down to Caesarea and sent him forth to Tarsus. 31 So then, the church across the whole of Judaea and Galilee and Samaria was having peace, being built up and proceeding in the fear of the Lord, and in the encouragement of the Holy Spirit it was multiplied.

32 Ἐγένετο δὲ Πέτρον διερχόμενον διὰ πάντων κατελθεῖν καὶ πρὸς τοὺς ἁγίους τοὺς κατοικοῦντας Λύδδα.

33 εὗρεν δὲ ἐκεῖ ἄνθρωπόν τινα ὀνόματι Αἰνέαν ἐξ ἐτῶν ὀκτὼ κατακείμενον ἐπὶ κραβάττου ὃς ἦν παραλελυμένος.

34 καὶ εἶπεν αὐτῷ ὁ Πέτρος·

Αἰνέα, ἰᾶταί σε Ἰησοῦς χριστός·

ἀνάστηθι καὶ στρῶσον σεαυτῷ. καὶ εὐθέως ἀνέστη· 35 καὶ εἶδαν αὐτὸν πάντες οἱ κατοικοῦντες Λύδδα καὶ τὸν Σαρῶνα, οἵτινες ἐπέστρεψαν ἐπὶ τὸν κύριον.

36 Ἐν Ἰόππῃ δέ τις ἦν μαθήτρια ὀνόματι Ταβιθά, ἣ διερμηνευομένη λέγεται Δορκάς· αὕτη ἦν πλήρης ἔργων ἀγαθῶν καὶ ἐλεημοσυνῶν ὧν ἐποίει·

37 ἐγένετο δὲ ἐν ταῖς ἡμέραις ἐκείναις ἀσθενήσασαν αὐτὴν ἀποθανεῖν· λούσαντες δὲ ἔθηκαν αὐτὴν ἐν ὑπερῴῳ.

32 And it happened that Peter, going through all parts, came down also to the saints inhabiting Lydda. 33 And he found there a certain man, Aeneas by name, for eight years lying in bed, who was paralyzed. 34 And Peter said to him, "Aeneas, Jesus Christ heals you! Arise and make the bed for yourself." And immediately he arose. 35 And they saw him, all inhabiting Lydda and Sharon who turned to the Lord. 36 Now in Joppa there was a certain disciple, Tabitha by name, who is, being interpreted, called Dorcas; this woman was full of good works and charitable gifts, which she was [regularly] doing. 37 And it happened in those days that, having fallen sick, she died; and, having washed [her], they laid her in an upper chamber.

38

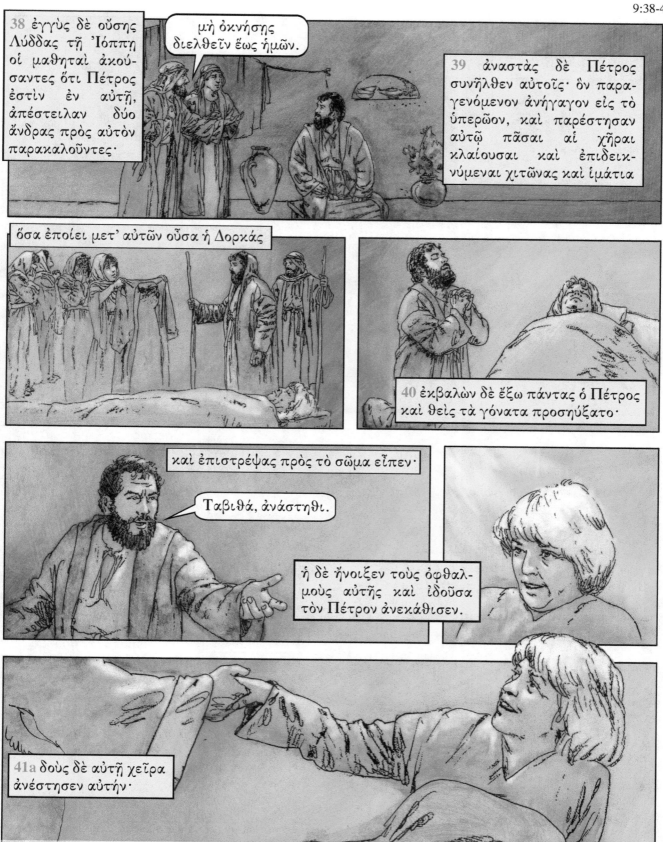

38 And, since Lydda was close to Joppa, the disciples having heard that Peter was in Lydda sent two men to him entreating, "Do not delay to come over to us!" 39 And arising, Peter went with them, whom arriving they led up into the upper chamber, and all the widows stood by him weeping and showing the coats and garments as many as Dorcas was making while being with them. 40 But, having cast them all outside and bowing his knees, Peter prayed; and turning to the body, he said, "Tabitha, arise!" And she opened her eyes; and, seeing Peter, she sat up. 41a And giving her a hand, he raised her up;

41b φωνήσας δὲ τοὺς ἁγίους καὶ τὰς χήρας παρέστησεν αὐτὴν ζῶσαν.

42 γνωστὸν δὲ ἐγένετο καθ᾽ ὅλης τῆς Ἰόππης, καὶ ἐπίστευσαν πολλοὶ ἐπὶ τὸν κύριον. 43 ἐγένετο δὲ αὐτὸν ἡμέρας ἱκανὰς μεῖναι ἐν Ἰόππῃ παρά τινι Σίμωνι βυρσεῖ.

Κεφ. Ι´

10:1 Ἀνὴρ δέ τις ἐν Καισαρείᾳ ὀνόματι Κορνήλιος, ἑκατοντάρχης ἐκ σπείρης τῆς καλουμένης Ἰταλικῆς,

2 εὐσεβὴς καὶ φοβούμενος τὸν θεὸν σὺν παντὶ τῷ οἴκῳ αὐτοῦ, ποιῶν ἐλεημοσύνας πολλὰς τῷ λαῷ καὶ δεόμενος τοῦ θεοῦ διὰ παντός· 3 εἶδεν ἐν ὁράματι φανερῶς ὡσεὶ περὶ ὥραν ἐνάτην τῆς ἡμέρας ἄγγελον τοῦ θεοῦ εἰσελθόντα πρὸς αὐτὸν καὶ εἰπόντα αὐτῷ·

εἶπεν δὲ αὐτῷ·

Κορνήλιε.

4 ὁ δὲ ἀτενίσας αὐτῷ καὶ ἔμφοβος γενόμενος εἶπεν·

τί ἐστιν, κύριε;

αἱ προσευχαί σου καὶ αἱ ἐλεημοσύναι σου ἀνέβησαν εἰς μνημόσυνον ἔμπροσθεν τοῦ θεοῦ. 5 καὶ νῦν πέμψον ἄνδρας εἰς Ἰόππην καὶ μετάπεμψαι Σίμωνά τινα ὃς ἐπικαλεῖται Πέτρος· 6 οὗτος ξενίζεται παρά τινι Σίμωνι βυρσεῖ, ᾧ ἐστιν οἰκία παρὰ θάλασσαν.

41b and calling the saints and widows, he presented her alive. 42 So it became known across the whole of Joppa, and many believed upon the Lord. 43 Moreover, it happened that he remained in Joppa a number of days with a certain Simon, a tanner. 10:1 Now a certain man in Caesarea, Cornelius by name, a centurion from the cohort called the Italian regiment, 2 a devout man and fearing God along with all his house, giving many charitable gifts to the people and praying to God always, 3 saw in a vision manifestly (just as it was about the ninth hour of the day) an angel of God entering to him and saying to him, "Cornelius." 4 And he, gazing at him and being terrified, said, "What is it, Lord?" And he said to him, "Your prayers and your charitable gifts went up as a memorial in the sight of God. 5 And now send men into Joppa and summon a certain Simon, who is surnamed Peter; 6 this man is being hosted by a certain Simon, a tanner, whose house is along the seaside."

7 Ὡς δὲ ἀπῆλθεν ὁ ἄγγελος ὁ λαλῶν αὐτῷ, φωνήσας δύο τῶν οἰκετῶν καὶ στρατιώτην εὐσεβῆ τῶν προσκαρτερούντων αὐτῷ, 8 καὶ ἐξηγησάμενος ἅπαντα αὐτοῖς, ἀπέστειλεν αὐτοὺς εἰς τὴν Ἰόππην.

9 Τῇ δὲ ἐπαύριον ὁδοιπορούντων ἐκείνων καὶ τῇ πόλει ἐγγιζόντων, ἀνέβη Πέτρος ἐπὶ τὸ δῶμα προσεύξασθαι περὶ ὥραν ἕκτην. 10 ἐγένετο δὲ πρόσπεινος, καὶ ἤθελεν γεύσασθαι. παρασκευαζόντων δὲ αὐτῶν ἐγένετο ἐπ' αὐτὸν ἔκστασις, 11 καὶ θεωρεῖ τὸν οὐρανὸν ἀνεῳγμένον καὶ καταβαῖνον σκεῦός τι ὡς ὀθόνην μεγάλην τέσσαρσιν ἀρχαῖς δεδεμένον καὶ καθιέμενον ἐπὶ τῆς γῆς·

12 ἐν ᾧ ὑπῆρχεν πάντα τὰ τετράποδα καὶ ἑρπετὰ τῆς γῆς καὶ πετεινὰ τοῦ οὐρανοῦ.

7 And when the angel that was speaking to him departed, he called two of his household-servants and a devout soldier who were devoted to him, 8 and, describing everything to them, he sent them to Joppa. 9 Now on the next day as these men were journeying and approaching the city, Peter went up on the housetop to pray at around the sixth hour (noon). 10 And he became hungry and was wanting to eat. But as they were preparing [it], a trance came upon him, 11 and he beholds heaven opened and some vessel descending to him like a great sheet bound by four corners and being let down to the ground, 12 in which were all the four-footed animals and reptiles of the earth and birds of the heaven.

13 καὶ ἐγένετο φωνὴ πρὸς αὐτόν·

ἀναστὰς Πέτρε, θῦσον καὶ φάγε.

14 ὁ δὲ Πέτρος εἶπεν·

μηδαμῶς, κύριε· ὅτι οὐδέποτε ἔφαγον πᾶν κοινὸν καὶ ἀκάθαρτον.

15 καὶ φωνὴ πάλιν ἐκ δευτέρου πρὸς αὐτόν·

ἃ ὁ θεὸς ἐκαθάρισεν, σὺ μὴ κοίνου.

16 τοῦτο δὲ ἐγένετο ἐπὶ τρίς, καὶ εὐθὺς ἀνελήμφθη τὸ σκεῦος εἰς τὸν οὐρανόν. 17 ὡς δὲ ἐν ἑαυτῷ διηπόρει ὁ Πέτρος τί ἂν εἴη τὸ ὅραμα ὃ εἶδεν, ἰδοὺ οἱ ἄνδρες οἱ ἀπεσταλμένοι ὑπὸ τοῦ Κορνηλίου διερωτήσαντες τὴν οἰκίαν τοῦ Σίμωνος, ἐπέστησαν ἐπὶ τὸν πυλῶνα·

18 καὶ φωνήσαντες ἐπυνθάνοντο

εἰ Σίμων ὁ ἐπικαλούμενος Πέτρος ἐνθάδε ξενίζεται.

19 Τοῦ δὲ Πέτρου διενθυμουμένου περὶ τοῦ ὁράματος εἶπεν τὸ πνεῦμα αὐτῷ·

ἰδοὺ ἄνδρες τρεῖς ζητοῦσίν σε· 20 ἀλλὰ ἀναστὰς κατάβηθι καὶ πορεύου σὺν αὐτοῖς μηδὲν διακρινόμενος, ὅτι ἐγὼ ἀπέσταλκα αὐτούς.

21 καταβὰς δὲ Πέτρος πρὸς τοὺς ἄνδρας εἶπεν·

ἰδοὺ ἐγώ εἰμι ὃν ζητεῖτε· τίς ἡ αἰτία δι' ἣν πάρεστε;

13 And a voice came to him, "Arising, Peter, kill and eat!" 14 But Peter said, "Certainly not, Lord! For never once did I eat anything common or unclean!" 15 And a voice again [came] the second time to him, "That which God made clean, you yourself must not declare unclean!" 16 And this occurred three times, and immediately the vessel was taken up into heaven. 17 Now, while Peter continued in himself being perplexed what the vision was that he saw, behold, the men having been sent by Cornelius, making inquiry for Simon's house, stood at the gate, 18 and calling, asked if Simon, the one being surnamed Peter, was being hosted in this place. 19 Now, as Peter was reflecting on the vision, the Spirit said to him, "Behold, three men are seeking you! 20 But arising, go down and travel with them—disputing nothing, because I myself have sent them!" 21 And going down, Peter said to the men, "Behold, I myself am he whom you are seeking. What is the reason for which you are present?"

22 οἱ δὲ εἶπαν·

Κορνήλιος ἑκατοντάρχης, ἀνὴρ δίκαιος καὶ φοβούμενος τὸν θεὸν μαρτυρούμενός τε ὑπὸ ὅλου τοῦ ἔθνους τῶν Ἰουδαίων, ἐχρηματίσθη ὑπὸ ἀγγέλου ἁγίου μεταπέμψασθαί σε εἰς τὸν οἶκον αὐτοῦ καὶ ἀκοῦσαι ῥήματα παρὰ σοῦ.

23 εἰσκαλεσάμενος οὖν αὐτοὺς ἐξένισεν.

τῇ δὲ ἐπαύριον ἀναστὰς ἐξῆλθεν σὺν αὐτοῖς, καί τινες τῶν ἀδελφῶν τῶν ἀπὸ Ἰόππης συνῆλθον αὐτῷ. **24** τῇ δὲ ἐπαύριον εἰσῆλθαν εἰς τὴν Καισάρειαν· ὁ δὲ Κορνήλιος ἦν προσδοκῶν αὐτοὺς συγκαλεσάμενος τοὺς συγγενεῖς αὐτοῦ καὶ τοὺς ἀναγκαίους φίλους.

26 ὁ δὲ Πέτρος ἤγειρεν αὐτὸν λέγων·

ἀνάστηθι· καὶ ἐγὼ αὐτὸς ἄνθρωπός εἰμι.

25 ὡς δὲ ἐγένετο τοῦ εἰσελθεῖν τὸν Πέτρον, συναντήσας αὐτῷ ὁ Κορνήλιος πεσὼν ἐπὶ τοὺς πόδας προσεκύνησεν.

22 And they said, "Cornelius, a centurion, a righteous man and fearing God, at the same time well-attested by the whole nation of the Judeans, was given revelation by a holy angel to summon you into his house and to hear words from you." 23 Therefore, having called them in, he hosted them. And on the next day, arising, he went out with them, and some of the brothers from Joppa accompanied him. 24 And on the next day, they entered into Caesarea. Moreover, Cornelius was waiting for them, having called together his relatives and his indispensable friends. 25 Additionally, when it happened that Peter entered in, after greeting him, Cornelius falling at his feet prostrated himself. 26 But Peter raised him up, saying, "Stand up! I myself am also a human!"

27 And conversing with him, he entered in and finds many having gathered together, 28 and at the same time he was saying to them, "You yourselves know how it is an unlawful thing for a Judean man to join himself to or to come to a foreigner of another nation; even to me God demonstrated to call no single person unholy or unclean. 29 Therefore, also without complaint I came having been summoned. I ask, therefore, for what matter did you summon me?" 30 And Cornelius was saying, "Four days ago until this hour, I was praying in my home during the ninth hour, and behold, a man stood before me in bright clothing, 31 and says, 'Cornelius, your prayer is heard, and your charitable gifts are remembered before God. 32 Send, therefore, into Joppa and call after Simon, who is also called Peter. This one is being hosted in the house of Simon, a tanner, along the seaside.' 33 Therefore, at once I sent to you, at the same time you yourself did well in coming. Now, therefore, we ourselves are all here present before God to hear all the things that have been commanded to you by the Lord."

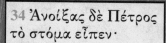

34 Ἀνοίξας δὲ Πέτρος τὸ στόμα εἶπεν·

ἐπ' ἀληθείας καταλαμβάνομαι ὅτι οὐκ ἔστιν προσωπολήμπτης ὁ θεός, 35 ἀλλ' ἐν παντὶ ἔθνει ὁ φοβούμενος αὐτὸν καὶ ἐργαζόμενος δικαιοσύνην δεκτὸς αὐτῷ ἐστιν.

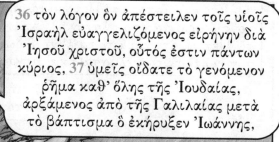

36 τὸν λόγον ὃν ἀπέστειλεν τοῖς υἱοῖς Ἰσραὴλ εὐαγγελιζόμενος εἰρήνην διὰ Ἰησοῦ χριστοῦ, οὗτός ἐστιν πάντων κύριος, 37 ὑμεῖς οἴδατε τὸ γενόμενον ῥῆμα καθ' ὅλης τῆς Ἰουδαίας, ἀρξάμενος ἀπὸ τῆς Γαλιλαίας μετὰ τὸ βάπτισμα ὃ ἐκήρυξεν Ἰωάννης,

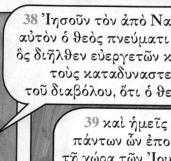

38 Ἰησοῦν τὸν ἀπὸ Ναζαρέθ, ὡς ἔχρισεν αὐτὸν ὁ θεὸς πνεύματι ἁγίῳ καὶ δυνάμει, ὃς διῆλθεν εὐεργετῶν καὶ ἰώμενος πάντας τοὺς καταδυναστευομένους ὑπὸ τοῦ διαβόλου, ὅτι ὁ θεὸς ἦν μετ' αὐτοῦ·

39 καὶ ἡμεῖς μάρτυρες πάντων ὧν ἐποίησεν ἔν τε τῇ χώρᾳ τῶν Ἰουδαίων καὶ ἐν Ἰερουσαλήμ· ὃν καὶ ἀνεῖλαν κρεμάσαντες ἐπὶ ξύλου.

40 τοῦτον ὁ θεὸς ἤγειρεν τῇ τρίτῃ ἡμέρᾳ καὶ ἔδωκεν αὐτὸν ἐμφανῆ γενέσθαι

41 οὐ παντὶ τῷ λαῷ, ἀλλὰ μάρτυσι τοῖς προκεχειροτονημένοις ὑπὸ τοῦ θεοῦ ἡμῖν, οἵτινες συνεφάγομεν καὶ συνεπίομεν αὐτῷ μετὰ τὸ ἀναστῆναι αὐτὸν ἐκ νεκρῶν·

42 καὶ παρήγγειλεν ἡμῖν κηρύξαι τῷ λαῷ καὶ διαμαρτύρασθαι ὅτι αὐτός ἐστιν ὁ ὡρισμένος ὑπὸ τοῦ θεοῦ κριτὴς ζώντων καὶ νεκρῶν.

43 τούτῳ πάντες οἱ προφῆται μαρτυροῦσιν ἄφεσιν ἁμαρτιῶν λαβεῖν διὰ τοῦ ὀνόματος αὐτοῦ πάντα τὸν πιστεύοντα εἰς αὐτόν.

34 And Peter, opening his mouth, said, "In truth I comprehend that God is no respecter of persons, 35 but in every nation the one fearing him and working justice is acceptable to him. 36 The Word which he sent to the children of Israel, proclaiming the good news of peace through Jesus Christ—this one is Lord of all— 37 you yourselves know the matter that happened across the whole of Judea beginning from Galilee after the baptism which John preached, 38—[concerning] Jesus the one from Nazareth—how God anointed him with the Holy Spirit and with power, who went about doing good deeds and healing all the ones being oppressed by the devil, because God was with him. 39 And we ourselves are witnesses of all that he did both in the country of the Judeans and in Jerusalem; whom also they killed, hanging [him] on a tree. 40 This One God raised up on the third day and gave him to be manifest 41 not to all the people but to witnesses who had been chosen before by God, to us, who ate with and drank with him after he rose from the dead. 42 And he gave command to us to preach to the people and to testify that he himself is the One who has been appointed by God to be judge of the living and the dead. 43 To this One, all the Prophets are testifying that through his name everyone believing in him receives deliverance from sins."

44 Ἔτι λαλοῦντος τοῦ Πέτρου τὰ ῥήματα ταῦτα ἐπέπεσεν τὸ πνεῦμα τὸ ἅγιον ἐπὶ πάντας τοὺς ἀκούοντας τὸν λόγον. 45 καὶ ἐξέστησαν οἱ ἐκ περιτομῆς πιστοὶ ὅσοι συνῆλθον τῷ Πέτρῳ, ὅτι καὶ ἐπὶ τὰ ἔθνη ἡ δωρεὰ τοῦ ἁγίου πνεύματος ἐκκέχυται· 46 ἤκουον γὰρ αὐτῶν λαλούντων γλώσσαις καὶ μεγαλυνόντων τὸν θεόν. τότε ἀπεκρίθη Πέτρος·

47 μήτι τὸ ὕδωρ δύναταί τις κωλῦσαί τοῦ μὴ βαπτισθῆναι τούτους, οἵτινες τὸ πνεῦμα τὸ ἅγιον ἔλαβον ὡς καὶ ἡμεῖς;

48 προσέταξεν δὲ αὐτοὺς ἐν τῷ ὀνόματι Ἰησοῦ χριστοῦ βαπτισθῆναι. τότε ἠρώτησαν αὐτὸν ἐπιμεῖναι ἡμέρας τινάς.

4 ἀρξάμενος δὲ Πέτρος ἐξετίθετο αὐτοῖς καθεξῆς λέγων·

Κεφ. ΙΑ΄

11:1 Ἤκουσαν δὲ οἱ ἀπόστολοι καὶ οἱ ἀδελφοὶ οἱ ὄντες κατὰ τὴν Ἰουδαίαν ὅτι καὶ τὰ ἔθνη ἐδέξαντο τὸν λόγον τοῦ θεοῦ. 2 Ὅτε δὲ ἀνέβη Πέτρος εἰς Ἰερουσαλήμ, διεκρίνοντο πρὸς αὐτὸν οἱ ἐκ περιτομῆς 3 λέγοντες ὅτι

5 ἐγὼ ἤμην ἐν πόλει Ἰόππῃ προσευχόμενος καὶ εἶδον ἐν ἐκστάσει ὅραμα καταβαῖνον σκεῦός τι ὡς ὀθόνην μεγάλην τέσσαρσιν ἀρχαῖς καθιεμένην ἐκ τοῦ οὐρανοῦ, καὶ ἦλθεν ἄχρι ἐμοῦ·

εἰσῆλθες πρὸς ἄνδρας ἀκροβυστίαν ἔχοντας καὶ συνέφαγες αὐτοῖς.

44 While Peter was still speaking these words, the Holy Spirit fell on all hearing the Word. 45 And the believers of the circumcision group, as many as came with Peter, were amazed, because also upon the Gentiles the gift of the Holy Spirit had been poured out. 46 For they were hearing them speaking in languages and magnifying God. Then Peter responded, 47 "Surely, someone is not able to forbid these people from being baptized with water who received the Holy Spirit as even we have? (Surely not!)" 48 And he commanded them to be baptized in the name of Jesus Christ. Then they asked him to stay some days. 11:1 Now, the apostles and the brothers who were throughout Judea heard that also the Gentiles received the Word of God. 2 And when Peter went up to Jerusalem, the ones from the circumcision group were disputing with him, 3 saying this: "You entered with men having uncircumcision and ate with them!" 4 But, starting in order, Peter was explaining to them saying, 5 "I myself was in the city of Joppa praying and in a trance I saw a vision, some vessel descending as a great sheet being let down from heaven by four corners, and it came as far as me;

6 εἰς ἣν ἀτενίσας κατενόουν καὶ εἶδον τὰ τετράποδα τῆς γῆς καὶ τὰ θηρία καὶ τὰ ἑρπετὰ καὶ τὰ πετεινὰ τοῦ οὐρανοῦ.

7 ἤκουσα δὲ καὶ φωνῆς λεγούσης μοι· **ἀναστὰς Πέτρε, θῦσον καὶ φάγε.** 8 εἶπον δέ· μηδαμῶς, κύριε· ὅτι κοινὸν ἢ ἀκάθαρτον οὐδέποτε εἰσῆλθεν εἰς τὸ στόμα μου. 9 ἀπεκρίθη δὲ φωνὴ ἐκ δευτέρου ἐκ τοῦ οὐρανοῦ· **ἃ ὁ θεὸς ἐκαθάρισεν, σὺ μὴ κοίνου.** 10 τοῦτο δὲ ἐγένετο ἐπὶ τρίς, καὶ ἀνεσπάσθη πάλιν ἅπαντα εἰς τὸν οὐρανόν.

11 καὶ ἰδοὺ ἐξαυτῆς τρεῖς ἄνδρες ἐπέστησαν ἐπὶ τὴν οἰκίαν ἐν ᾗ ἦμεν ἀπεσταλμένοι ἀπὸ Καισαρείας πρός με.

12 εἶπεν δὲ τὸ πνεῦμά μοι συνελθεῖν αὐτοῖς μηδὲν διακρίναντα. ἦλθον δὲ σὺν ἐμοὶ καὶ οἱ ἓξ ἀδελφοὶ οὗτοι, καὶ εἰσήλθομεν εἰς τὸν οἶκον τοῦ ἀνδρός.

13 ἀπήγγειλεν δὲ ἡμῖν πῶς εἶδεν τὸν ἄγγελον ἐν τῷ οἴκῳ αὐτοῦ σταθέντα καὶ εἰπόντα· **ἀπόστειλον εἰς Ἰόππην καὶ μετάπεμψαι Σίμωνα τὸν ἐπικαλούμενον Πέτρον,**

14 ὃς λαλήσει ῥήματα πρός σὲ ἐν οἷς σωθήσῃ σὺ καὶ πᾶς ὁ οἶκός σου.

6 into which gazing I was considering and saw the four-footed animals of the earth and wild animals and reptiles and birds of the sky. 7 Moreover, I also heard a voice saying to me, 'Arising, Peter, kill and eat!' 8 But I said, 'Certainly not, Lord, because a common or unclean thing never entered into my mouth!' 9 But the voice answered back to me the second time out of heaven, 'That which God made clean, you yourself must not make unclean!' 10 This occurred three times, and again all was snatched up into heaven. 11 And behold, immediately, three men stood at the house in which we were, having been sent from Caesarea to me. 12 And the Spirit said for me to go with them, disputing nothing. Moreover, they also went with me, these six brothers, and we entered into the man's house. 13 Moreover, he reported to us how he saw the angel standing in his house and saying, 'Send into Joppa and summon Simon, the one being called Peter, 14 who will speak to you words by which you yourself will be saved, and all your house.'

15 And when I began to speak, the Holy Spirit fell on them, just as also upon us at the beginning! 16 Moreover, I remembered the Word of the Lord, how he was saying, 'John indeed baptized with water, but you yourselves will be baptized in the Holy Spirit.' 17 If, therefore, God gave to them the same gift as also to us when believing in the Lord Jesus Christ, who was I able to hinder God?!" 18 And hearing these things, they remained at peace and glorified God, saying, "Then also to the Gentiles God has given repentance to life!"

19 Οἱ μὲν οὖν διασπαρέντες ἀπὸ τῆς θλίψεως τῆς γενομένης ἐπὶ Στεφάνῳ διῆλθον ἕως Φοινίκης καὶ Κύπρου καὶ Ἀντιοχείας μηδενὶ λαλοῦντες τὸν λόγον εἰ μὴ μόνον Ἰουδαίοις. 20 Ἦσαν δέ τινες ἐξ αὐτῶν ἄνδρες Κύπριοι καὶ Κυρηναῖοι, οἵτινες ἐλθόντες εἰς Ἀντιόχειαν ἐλάλουν καὶ πρὸς τοὺς Ἑλληνιστάς εὐαγγελιζόμενοι τὸν κύριον Ἰησοῦν. 21 καὶ ἦν χεὶρ κυρίου μετ' αὐτῶν, πολύς τε ἀριθμὸς ὁ πιστεύσας ἐπέστρεψεν ἐπὶ τὸν κύριον· 22 ἠκούσθη δὲ ὁ λόγος εἰς τὰ ὦτα τῆς ἐκκλησίας τῆς οὔσης ἐν Ἰερουσαλὴμ περὶ αὐτῶν καὶ ἐξαπέστειλαν Βαρνάβαν ἕως Ἀντιοχείας·

23 ὃς παραγενόμενος καὶ ἰδὼν τὴν χάριν τοῦ θεοῦ ἐχάρη καὶ παρεκάλει πάντας τῇ προθέσει τῆς καρδίας προσμένειν τῷ κυρίῳ· 24 ὅτι ἦν ἀνὴρ ἀγαθὸς καὶ πλήρης πνεύματος ἁγίου καὶ πίστεως. καὶ προσετέθη ὄχλος ἱκανὸς τῷ κυρίῳ. 25 ἐξῆλθεν δὲ εἰς Ταρσὸν ἀναζητῆσαι Σαῦλον, 26 καὶ εὑρὼν ἤγαγεν εἰς Ἀντιόχειαν. ἐγένετο δὲ αὐτοῖς καὶ ἐνιαυτὸν ὅλον συναχθῆναι ἐν τῇ ἐκκλησίᾳ καὶ διδάξαι ὄχλον ἱκανόν, χρηματίσαι τε πρώτως ἐν Ἀντιοχείᾳ τοὺς μαθητὰς Χριστιανούς. 27 Ἐν ταύταις δὲ ταῖς ἡμέραις κατῆλθον ἀπὸ Ἱεροσολύμων προφῆται εἰς Ἀντιόχειαν· 28 ἀναστὰς δὲ εἷς ἐξ αὐτῶν ὀνόματι Ἄγαβος ἐσήμανεν διὰ τοῦ πνεύματος

λιμὸν μεγάλην μέλλειν ἔσεσθαι ἐφ' ὅλην τὴν οἰκουμένην,

ἥτις ἐγένετο ἐπὶ Κλαυδίου. 29 τῶν δὲ μαθητῶν καθὼς εὐπορεῖτό τις, ὥρισαν ἕκαστος αὐτῶν εἰς διακονίαν πέμψαι τοῖς κατοικοῦσιν ἐν τῇ Ἰουδαίᾳ ἀδελφοῖς· 30 ὃ καὶ ἐποίησαν ἀποστείλαντες πρὸς τοὺς πρεσβυτέρους διὰ χειρὸς Βαρνάβα καὶ Σαύλου.

19 So then, the ones who were dispersed from the persecution that occurred with Stephen traveled throughout as far as Phoenicia and Cyprus and Antioch, speaking the Word to no one except only to Judeans. 20 But there were some of them, men of Cyprus and Cyrene, who, coming into Antioch, were speaking also to the Hellenists, proclaiming the good news of the Lord Jesus. 21 And the hand of the Lord was with them and at the same time a great number that believed turned to the Lord. 22 And the word concerning them was heard in the ears of the assembly which was in Jerusalem and they sent Barnabas out to go as far as Antioch, 23 who, arriving and seeing the grace of God, rejoiced and was encouraging them all in the resolve of the heart to keep remaining with the Lord; 24 because he was a good man and full of the Holy Spirit and of faith. And a sizeable crowd was added to the Lord. 25 Moreover, Barnabas went out to Tarsus to look for Saul, 26 and finding him, he brought him to Antioch. And it happened for them that also for a whole year they were welcomed in the assembly and taught a sizeable crowd; at the same time, the disciples were first named 'Christians' in Antioch. 27 Now in these days, prophets came down from Jerusalem into Antioch. 28 And one of them arising, Agabus by name, indicated through the Spirit that a great famine was about to come upon the whole inhabited [Roman] world, which happened with Claudius. 29 And regarding the disciples, just as someone was having plenty, each of them determined to send relief to the brothers dwelling in Judea; 30 which also they did, sending it to the elders through the hand of Barnabas and Saul.

Κεφ. ΙΒ΄

12:1 Κατ' ἐκεῖνον δὲ τὸν καιρὸν ἐπέβαλεν Ἡρώδης ὁ βασιλεὺς τὰς χεῖρας κακῶσαί τινας τῶν ἀπὸ τῆς ἐκκλησίας. 2 ἀνεῖλεν δὲ Ἰάκωβον τὸν ἀδελφὸν Ἰωάννου μαχαίρῃ.

3 ἰδὼν δὲ ὅτι ἀρεστόν ἐστιν τοῖς Ἰουδαίοις, προσέθετο συλλαβεῖν καὶ Πέτρον, ἦσαν δὲ ἡμέραι τῶν ἀζύμων,

4 ὃν καὶ πιάσας ἔθετο εἰς φυλακὴν παραδοὺς τέσσαρσιν τετραδίοις στρατιωτῶν φυλάσσειν αὐτόν, βουλόμενος μετὰ τὸ πάσχα ἀναγαγεῖν αὐτὸν τῷ λαῷ.

5 Ὁ μὲν οὖν Πέτρος ἐτηρεῖτο ἐν τῇ φυλακῇ· προσευχὴ δὲ ἦν ἐκτενῶς γινομένη ὑπὸ τῆς ἐκκλησίας πρὸς τὸν θεὸν περὶ αὐτοῦ.

6 ὅτε δὲ ἤμελλεν προσαγαγεῖν αὐτὸν ὁ Ἡρώδης, τῇ νυκτὶ ἐκείνῃ ἦν ὁ Πέτρος κοιμώμενος μεταξὺ δύο στρατιωτῶν δεδεμένος ἁλύσεσιν δυσίν, φύλακές τε πρὸ τῆς θύρας ἐτήρουν τὴν φυλακήν.

12:1 And about that time, Herod the king set his hands to harm some of the ones from the assembly. 2 And he killed James, the brother of John, with the sword. 3 And seeing that it was pleasing to the Judean officials, he added to lay hold of Peter also—and they were the days of the Unleavened Bread—4 whom also seizing he placed in prison, having delivered him to four squads of soldiers to be guarding him, intending after the Passover to bring him before the people. 5 So then, Peter, was being kept in the prison; and fervent prayer was being made by the assembly to God concerning him. 6 And when Herod was about to bring him forth, at that night Peter bound with two chains was sleeping between two soldiers, and at the same time guards before the door were keeping the watch.

7 And behold, an angel of the Lord stood by and a light shone in the building; moreover, striking the side of Peter, he raised him up, saying, "Arise in haste!" And the chains fell off of his hands. 8 Next, the angel said to him, "Gird yourself and bind up your sandals!" So, he did so. And he says to him, "Put your garment around and start following me!" 9 And going out, he was following him; and he did not know that what was happening through the angel was true, but was supposing that he was seeing a vision. 10 So, passing through the first guard and a second, they came to the iron gate leading to the city, which automatically opened for them, and going out, they went forward through one street and immediately the angel departed from him. 11 And Peter, coming to himself, said, "Now I know truly that the Lord sent forth His angel and delivered me out of the hand of Herod and every expectation of the people of the Judeans!"

12 συνιδών τε ἦλθεν ἐπὶ τὴν οἰκίαν τῆς Μαρίας τῆς μητρὸς Ἰωάννου τοῦ ἐπικαλουμένου Μάρκου, οὗ ἦσαν ἱκανοὶ συνηθροισμένοι καὶ προσευχόμενοι.

13 κρούσαντος δὲ αὐτοῦ τὴν θύραν τοῦ πυλῶνος προσῆλθεν παιδίσκη ὑπακοῦσαι ὀνόματι Ῥόδη· 14a καὶ ἐπιγνοῦσα τὴν φωνὴν τοῦ Πέτρου ἀπὸ τῆς χαρᾶς οὐκ ἤνοιξεν τὸν πυλῶνα

14b εἰσδραμοῦσα δὲ ἀπήγγειλεν

ἑστάναι τὸν Πέτρον πρὸ τοῦ πυλῶνος.

15 οἱ δὲ πρὸς αὐτὴν εἶπαν·

μαίνῃ.

ἡ δὲ διϊσχυρίζετο οὕτως ἔχειν. οἱ δὲ ἔλεγον·

ὁ ἄγγελός ἐστιν αὐτοῦ.

12 At the same time perceiving this, he came to the house of Mary, the mother of John, who is surnamed Mark, where there were a sufficient number gathered together and praying. 13 So, when Peter knocked at the door of the gate, a female servant, Rhoda by name, came to answer; 14 and knowing the voice of Peter, out of the joy she did not open the gate, but running in announced that Peter was standing before the gate. 15 But they said to her, "You are mad!" But she was confidently affirming that it was so. But they were saying, "It is his angel."

16 But Peter was continuing to keep knocking; so, opening up, they saw him and were astonished. 17 Moreover, motioning to them with the hand to be silent, he explained to them how the Lord brought him out of the prison; also, he said, "Report to James and to the brothers these things!" And going out, he traveled into another place. 18 Now, the day having arrived, there was not a little stir among the soldiers what then had become of Peter. 19 So, Herod having sought for him and not finding, after examining the guards, commanded [them] to be led away to punishment, and, going down from Judea to Caesarea, he was passing time [there].

20 ἦν δὲ θυμομαχῶν Τυρίοις καὶ Σιδωνίοις· ὁμοθυμαδὸν δὲ παρῆσαν πρὸς αὐτὸν καὶ πείσαντες Βλάστον τὸν ἐπὶ τοῦ κοιτῶνος τοῦ βασιλέως ἠτοῦντο εἰρήνην, διὰ τὸ τρέφεσθαι αὐτῶν τὴν χώραν ἀπὸ τῆς βασιλικῆς. 21 Τακτῇ δὲ ἡμέρᾳ ὁ Ἡρώδης ἐνδυσάμενος ἐσθῆτα βασιλικὴν καὶ καθίσας ἐπὶ τοῦ βήματος ἐδημηγόρει πρὸς αὐτούς.

22 ὁ δὲ δῆμος ἐπεφώνει·

θεοῦ φωνὴ καὶ οὐκ ἀνθρώπου.

23 παραχρῆμα δὲ ἐπάταξεν αὐτὸν ἄγγελος κυρίου ἀνθ' ὧν οὐκ ἔδωκεν τὴν δόξαν τῷ θεῷ, καὶ γενόμενος σκωληκόβρωτος ἐξέψυξεν.

24 Ὁ δὲ λόγος τοῦ θεοῦ ηὔξανεν καὶ ἐπληθύνετο. 25 Βαρνάβας δὲ καὶ Σαῦλος ὑπέστρεψαν εἰς Ἱερουσαλὴμ πληρώσαντες τὴν διακονίαν, συνπαραλαβόντες Ἰωάννην τὸν ἐπικληθέντα Μάρκον.

20 Moreover, Herod was highly displeased with the Tyrians and Sidonians. So, with one accord they came to him, and having won over Blastus, the one over the bed-chambers of the king, they were asking for peace, because their country was nourished from the king's [country]. 21 Then, on a set day, Herod, arraying himself in kingly apparel and sitting down upon the tribunal, was making a public address to them. 22 And the popular assembly was shouting, "The voice of a god, and not of a man!" 23 Then, immediately an angel of the Lord struck him because he did not give the glory to God, and becoming worm-eaten, he expired. 24 Moreover, the Word of God continued to grow and was multiplying. 25 Then, Barnabas and Saul returned back to Jerusalem, completing the ministry, taking along also John, the one who was surnamed Mark.

Κεφ. ΙΓ´

13:1 ἮΗσαν δὲ ἐν Ἀντιοχείᾳ κατὰ τὴν οὖσαν ἐκκλησίαν προφῆται καὶ διδάσκαλοι, ὅ τε Βαρνάβας καὶ Συμεὼν ὁ καλούμενος Νίγερ καὶ Λούκιος ὁ Κυρηναῖος, Μαναήν τε Ἡρῴδου τοῦ τετράρχου σύντροφος καὶ Σαῦλος. 2 λειτουργούντων δὲ αὐτῶν τῷ κυρίῳ καὶ νηστευόντων εἶπεν τὸ πνεῦμα τὸ ἅγιον·

ἀφορίσατε δή μοι τὸν Βαρνάβαν καὶ Σαῦλον εἰς τὸ ἔργον ὃ προσκέκλημαι αὐτούς.

3 τότε νηστεύσαντες καὶ προσευξάμενοι καὶ ἐπιθέντες τὰς χεῖρας αὐτοῖς ἀπέλυσαν.

13:1 Now, in the assembly that was in Antioch there were prophets and teachers: Barnabas and Simeon who was called Niger and Lucius of Cyrene, as well as Manaen the foster brother of Herod the tetrarch and Saul. 2 And, with them serving the Lord and fasting, the Holy Spirit said, "Separate indeed Barnabas and Saul for me for the work which I have called them." 3 Then, having fasted and prayed and laid their hands on them, they released [them].

4 Αὐτοὶ μὲν οὖν ἐκπεμφθέντες ὑπὸ τοῦ ἁγίου πνεύματος κατῆλθον εἰς Σελεύκειαν, ἐκεῖθέν τε ἀπέπλευσαν εἰς Κύπρον.

5 καὶ γενόμενοι ἐν Σαλαμῖνι κατήγγελλον τὸν λόγον τοῦ θεοῦ ἐν ταῖς συναγωγαῖς τῶν Ἰουδαίων· εἶχον δὲ καὶ Ἰωάννην ὑπηρέτην.

6 Διελθόντες δὲ ὅλην τὴν νῆσον ἄχρι Πάφου εὗρον ἄνδρα τινὰ μάγον ψευδο-προφήτην Ἰουδαῖον ᾧ ὄνομα Βαριησοῦς, 7 ὃς ἦν σὺν τῷ ἀνθυπάτῳ Σεργίῳ Παύλῳ, ἀνδρὶ συνετῷ.

7b οὗτος προσκαλεσάμενος Βαρνάβαν καὶ Σαῦλον ἐπεζήτησεν ἀκοῦσαι τὸν λόγον τοῦ θεοῦ. 8 ἀνθίστατο δὲ αὐτοῖς Ἐλύμας ὁ μάγος, οὕτως γὰρ μεθερμηνεύεται τὸ ὄνομα αὐτοῦ, ζητῶν διαστρέψαι τὸν ἀνθύπατον ἀπὸ τῆς πίστεως.

4 So then, being sent out by the Holy Spirit, they went down into Seleucia, and at the same time from there they sailed into Cyprus. 5 And being in Salamis, they were proclaiming God's Word in the synagogues of the Judeans. Moreover, they also were having John as an assistant. 6 Next, going through the whole island as far as Paphos, they found a certain man, a sorcerer, a Judean false prophet, whose name was Bar Jesus, 7 who was with the proconsul Sergius Paulus, a man of intelligence. This man, summoning Barnabas and Saul, sought to hear the Word of God. 8 But Elymas the sorcerer (for thus is his name interpreted) was opposing them, seeking to turn the proconsul away from the Faith.

9 Σαῦλος δὲ ὁ καὶ Παῦλος πλησθεὶς πνεύματος ἁγίου ἀτενίσας εἰς αὐτὸν 10 εἶπεν·

ὦ πλήρης παντὸς δόλου καὶ πάσης ῥαδιουργίας, υἱὲ διαβόλου, ἐχθρὲ πάσης δικαιοσύνης, οὐ παύσῃ διαστρέφων τὰς ὁδοὺς κυρίου τὰς εὐθείας;

11 καὶ νῦν ἰδοὺ χεὶρ κυρίου ἐπὶ σέ, καὶ ἔσῃ τυφλὸς μὴ βλέπων τὸν ἥλιον ἄχρι καιροῦ.

παραχρῆμα δὲ ἔπεσεν ἐπ' αὐτὸν ἀχλὺς καὶ σκότος, καὶ περιάγων ἐζήτει χειραγωγούς.

12 τότε ἰδὼν ὁ ἀνθύπατος τὸ γεγονὸς ἐπίστευσεν ἐκπλησσόμενος ἐπὶ τῇ διδαχῇ τοῦ κυρίου.

13a Ἀναχθέντες δὲ ἀπὸ τῆς Πάφου οἱ περὶ Παῦλον ἦλθον εἰς Πέργην τῆς Παμφυλίας.

13b Ἰωάννης δὲ ἀποχωρήσας ἀπ' αὐτῶν ὑπέστρεψεν εἰς Ἱεροσόλυμα.

9 But Saul, the one also [called] Paul, filled with the Holy Spirit, fastening his eyes on him, 10 said, "O full of all deceit and all cunning, You son of the devil, enemy of all justice, will you not stop perverting the straight paths of the Lord?! (Yes!) 11 And now, behold, the hand of the Lord is upon you, and you will be blind, not seeing the sun for a season!" So, immediately a mist and darkness fell upon him, and wandering around he was seeking a guide to lead him by hand. 12 Then, the proconsul seeing what had happened believed, being astonished at the teaching of the Lord. 13 Next, setting sail from Paphos, the ones around Paul came to Perga in Pamphylia. But John, departing from them, returned to Jerusalem.

14 αὐτοὶ δὲ διελθόντες ἀπὸ τῆς Πέργης παρεγένοντο εἰς Ἀντιόχειαν τὴν Πισιδίαν, καὶ ἐλθόντες εἰς τὴν συναγωγὴν τῇ ἡμέρᾳ τῶν σαββάτων ἐκάθισαν. 15 Μετὰ δὲ τὴν ἀνάγνωσιν τοῦ νόμου καὶ τῶν προφητῶν ἀπέστειλαν οἱ ἀρχισυνάγωγοι πρὸς αὐτοὺς λέγοντες·

ἄνδρες ἀδελφοί, εἴ τίς ἐστιν ἐν ὑμῖν λόγος παρακλήσεως πρὸς τὸν λαόν, λέγετε.

16 Ἀναστὰς δὲ Παῦλος καὶ κατασείσας τῇ χειρὶ εἶπεν·

ἄνδρες Ἰσραηλεῖται καὶ οἱ φοβούμενοι τὸν θεόν, ἀκούσατε. 17 ὁ θεὸς τοῦ λαοῦ τούτου Ἰσραὴλ ἐξελέξατο τοὺς πατέρας ἡμῶν καὶ τὸν λαὸν ὕψωσεν ἐν τῇ παροικίᾳ ἐν γῇ Αἰγύπτου καὶ μετὰ βραχίονος ὑψηλοῦ ἐξήγαγεν αὐτοὺς ἐξ αὐτῆς·

18 καὶ ὡς τεσσερακονταετῆ χρόνον ἐτροποφόρησεν αὐτοὺς ἐν τῇ ἐρήμῳ, 19 καὶ καθελὼν ἔθνη ἑπτὰ ἐν γῇ Χαναὰν κατεκληρονόμησεν τὴν γῆν αὐτῶν 20 ὡς ἔτεσι τετρακοσίοις καὶ πεντήκοντα·

καὶ μετὰ ταῦτα ἔδωκεν κριτὰς ἕως Σαμουὴλ τοῦ προφήτου· 21 κἀκεῖθεν ᾐτήσαντο βασιλέα, καὶ ἔδωκεν αὐτοῖς ὁ θεὸς τὸν Σαοὺλ υἱὸν Κείς, ἄνδρα ἐκ φυλῆς Βενιαμείν, ἔτη τεσσεράκοντα·

22 καὶ μεταστήσας αὐτὸν ἤγειρεν τὸν Δαυεὶδ αὐτοῖς εἰς βασιλέα, ᾧ καὶ εἶπεν μαρτυρήσας· *εὗρον Δαυεὶδ τὸν τοῦ Ἰεσσαί, ἄνδρα κατὰ τὴν καρδίαν μου, ὃς ποιήσει πάντα τὰ θελήματά μου.*

14 But they themselves, passing on from Perga, came into Antioch of Pisidia, and coming into the synagogue on the Sabbath day, they sat down. 15 Moreover, after the reading of the Law and the Prophets, the rulers of the synagogue sent to them, saying, "Brothers, if you have any word of exhortation for the people, speak." 16 So, Paul standing and motioning with his hand said, "Israelite men and you fearing God, listen! 17 The God of this people, Israel, chose our fathers and lifted up the people in the foreign country in the land of Egypt and with an uplifted arm he led them out from it. 18 And for about forty years he put up with them in the wilderness, 19 and after destroying seven nations in the land of Canaan, he gave them their land for an inheritance 20 for about four hundred fifty years. And after these things, he gave them judges until Samuel the prophet. 21 And afterward they asked for a king, and God gave to them Saul, the son of Kish, a man of the tribe of Benjamin, for forty years. 22 And after removing him, he raised up David for them as king, to whom also he said testifying, 'I found David, the son of Jesse, a man according to my heart, who will do all my desires.'

23 From this man's offspring according to promise, God brought salvation to Israel, the savior Jesus, 24 in the face of his entrance John having proclaimed beforehand the baptism of repentance to Israel. 25 Moreover, as John was fulfilling his course, he was saying, 'What do you suppose me to be? I myself am not he! But behold, one comes after me, the sandals of whose feet I am not worthy to untie!' 26 Fellow brothers, sons of the stock of Abraham and those among you who fear God, to you the Word of this salvation has been sent out! 27 For, the ones residing in Jerusalem and their rulers, not recognizing this One and the voices of the Prophets which are being read every Sabbath, condemning [him] fulfilled [them]. 28 And having found no reason for death, they asked Pilate that he be killed.

29 ὡς δὲ ἐτέλεσαν πάντα τὰ περὶ αὐτοῦ γεγραμμένα, καθελόντες ἀπὸ τοῦ ξύλου ἔθηκαν εἰς μνημεῖον.

31 ὃς ὤφθη ἐπὶ ἡμέρας πλείους τοῖς συναναβᾶσιν αὐτῷ ἀπὸ τῆς Γαλιλαίας εἰς Ἰερουσαλήμ, οἵτινές εἰσιν μάρτυρες αὐτοῦ πρὸς τὸν λαόν.

30 ὁ δὲ θεὸς ἤγειρεν αὐτὸν ἐκ νεκρῶν,

32 καὶ ἡμεῖς ὑμᾶς εὐαγγελιζόμεθα τὴν πρὸς τοὺς πατέρας ἐπαγγελίαν γενομένην, 33 ὅτι ταύτην ὁ θεὸς ἐκπεπλήρωκεν τοῖς τέκνοις αὐτῶν ἡμῖν ἀναστήσας Ἰησοῦν, ὡς καὶ ἐν τῷ ψαλμῷ γέγραπται τῷ δευτέρῳ·

υἱός μου εἶ σύ, ἐγὼ σήμερον γεγέννηκά σε.

34 ὅτι δὲ ἀνέστησεν αὐτὸν ἐκ νεκρῶν μηκέτι μέλλοντα ὑποστρέφειν εἰς διαφθοράν, οὕτως εἴρηκεν ὅτι

δώσω ὑμῖν τὰ ὅσια Δαυεὶδ τὰ πιστά.

35 διότι καὶ ἐν ἑτέρῳ λέγει·

οὐ δώσεις τὸν ὅσιόν σου ἰδεῖν διαφθοράν.

36 Δαυεὶδ μὲν γὰρ ἰδίᾳ γενεᾷ ὑπηρετήσας τῇ τοῦ θεοῦ βουλῇ ἐκοιμήθη καὶ προσετέθη πρὸς τοὺς πατέρας αὐτοῦ καὶ εἶδεν διαφθοράν· 37 ὃν δὲ ὁ θεὸς ἤγειρεν, οὐκ εἶδεν διαφθοράν.

29 Moreover, when they fulfilled all things written about him, taking him down from the tree, they laid him into a tomb. 30 But God raised him from the dead, 31 who appeared for many days to the ones coming up with him from Galilee into Jerusalem, who are his witnesses to the people. 32 And we ourselves are proclaiming to you the good news of the promise made to the fathers, 33 that God has fulfilled this for their children—for us! — by raising up Jesus, as also in the second psalm it has been written, 'You yourself are my Son! Today I myself have begotten you!' 34 "Now, that he raised him up from the dead so that no longer would he be about to return to corruption, thus has he spoken this: 'I will give you the holy, assured things of David.' 35 Because also in another psalm he says, 'You will not allow your Holy One to see decay.' 36 For indeed David, having served the counsel of God in his own generation, fell asleep and was laid away with his fathers and saw decay. 37 But he, whom God raised up, saw no decay!

38 Γνωστὸν οὖν ἔστω ὑμῖν, ἄνδρες ἀδελφοί, ὅτι διὰ τούτου ὑμῖν ἄφεσις ἁμαρτιῶν καταγγέλλεται· καὶ ἀπὸ πάντων ὧν οὐκ ἠδυνήθητε ἐν νόμῳ Μωϋσέως δικαιωθῆναι, 39 ἐν τούτῳ πᾶς ὁ πιστεύων δικαιοῦται. 40 βλέπετε οὖν μὴ ἐπέλθῃ τὸ εἰρημένον ἐν τοῖς προφήταις·

41 ἴδετε, οἱ καταφρονηταί, καὶ θαυμάσατε καὶ ἀφανίσθητε, ὅτι ἔργον ἐργάζομαι ἐγὼ ἐν ταῖς ἡμέραις ὑμῶν, ἔργον ὃ οὐ μὴ πιστεύσητε ἐάν τις ἐκδιηγῆται ὑμῖν.

42 Ἐξιόντων δὲ αὐτῶν παρεκάλουν εἰς τὸ μεταξὺ σάββατον λαληθῆναι αὐτοῖς τὰ ῥήματα ταῦτα. 43 λυθείσης δὲ τῆς συναγωγῆς ἠκολούθησαν πολλοὶ τῶν Ἰουδαίων καὶ τῶν σεβομένων προσηλύτων τῷ Παύλῳ καὶ τῷ Βαρνάβᾳ, οἵτινες προσλαλοῦντες αὐτοῖς ἔπειθον αὐτοὺς προσμένειν τῇ χάριτι τοῦ θεοῦ.

44 τῷ δὲ ἐρχομένῳ σαββάτῳ σχεδὸν πᾶσα ἡ πόλις συνήχθη ἀκοῦσαι τὸν λόγον τοῦ κυρίου.

38 Therefore, let it be known to you, fellow brothers, that through this one the deliverance from sins is being proclaimed to you; and from all which you were not able to be justified in the Law of Moses, 39 in this One, everyone who believes is justified! 40 Beware, therefore, that what has been spoken in the Prophets does not come about: 41 'Look, you scoffers, and be amazed and disappear! Because I myself am working a work in your days, a work which you will never ever believe if someone would delineate it to you.' 42 So, while they were departing, the Gentiles were asking in order that these words would be spoken to them next Sabbath. 43 Moreover, after the synagogue was released, many of the Judeans and of the devout proselytes followed Paul and Barnabas, who, speaking to them, were urging them to continue in the grace of God. 44 So, at the coming of the Sabbath, nearly the whole city was gathered together to hear the Word of the Lord.

45 ἰδόντες δὲ οἱ Ἰουδαῖοι τοὺς ὄχλους ἐπλήσθησαν ζήλου καὶ ἀντέλεγον τοῖς ὑπὸ Παύλου λαλουμένοις βλασφημοῦντες. **46** παρρησιασάμενοί τε ὁ Παῦλος καὶ ὁ Βαρνάβας εἶπαν·

ὑμῖν ἦν ἀναγκαῖον πρῶτον λαληθῆναι τὸν λόγον τοῦ θεοῦ· ἐπειδὴ δὲ ἀπωθεῖσθε αὐτὸν καὶ οὐκ ἀξίους κρίνετε ἑαυτοὺς τῆς αἰωνίου ζωῆς, ἰδοὺ στρεφόμεθα εἰς τὰ ἔθνη. **47** οὕτως γὰρ ἐντέταλται ἡμῖν ὁ κύριος·

τέθεικά σε εἰς φῶς ἐθνῶν τοῦ εἶναί σε εἰς σωτηρίαν ἕως ἐσχάτου τῆς γῆς.

48 Ἀκούοντα δὲ τὰ ἔθνη ἔχαιρον καὶ ἐδόξαζον τὸν λόγον τοῦ κυρίου καὶ ἐπίστευσαν ὅσοι ἦσαν τεταγμένοι εἰς ζωὴν αἰώνιον.

49 διεφέρετο δὲ ὁ λόγος τοῦ κυρίου δι᾽ ὅλης τῆς χώρας. **50** οἱ δὲ Ἰουδαῖοι παρώτρυναν τὰς σεβομένας γυναῖκας τὰς εὐσχήμονας καὶ τοὺς πρώτους τῆς πόλεως καὶ ἐπήγειραν διωγμὸν ἐπὶ τὸν Παῦλον καὶ Βαρνάβαν καὶ ἐξέβαλον αὐτοὺς ἀπὸ τῶν ὁρίων αὐτῶν.

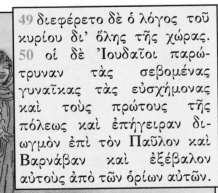

51 οἱ δὲ ἐκτιναξάμενοι τὸν κονιορτὸν τῶν ποδῶν ἐπ᾽ αὐτοὺς ἦλθον εἰς Ἰκόνιον. **52** οἵ τε μαθηταὶ ἐπληροῦντο χαρᾶς καὶ πνεύματος ἁγίου.

45 But, the Judeans, seeing the multitudes, were filled with jealousy and were contradicting the things being spoken by Paul, slandering [him]. 46 At the same time, speaking boldly, Paul and Barnabas said, "To you it was necessary first that the Word of God would be spoken. Moreover, since you are thrusting it from yourselves and are judging yourselves not worthy of everlasting life, behold, we are turning to the Gentiles. 47 For thus the Lord has commanded us: 'I have set you as a light for the Gentiles, so that you would be for the salvation as far as the uttermost parts of the earth!'" 48 And, hearing, the Gentiles were rejoicing and were glorifying the Word of the Lord and they believed, as many as appointed themselves to everlasting life. 49 So, the Word of the Lord was being carried throughout the whole region. 50 But the Judeans stirred up the devout, prominent women and the chief men of the city and roused up a persecution against Paul and Barnabas and threw them out of their borders. 51 So, they, shaking off the dust of their feet against them, went into Iconium. 52 At the same time, the disciples continued to be filled with joy and with the Holy Spirit.

Κεφ. ΙΔ΄

14:1 Ἐγένετο δὲ ἐν Ἰκονίῳ κατὰ τὸ αὐτὸ εἰσελθεῖν αὐτοὺς εἰς τὴν συναγωγὴν τῶν Ἰουδαίων καὶ λαλῆσαι οὕτως ὥστε πιστεῦσαι Ἰουδαίων τε καὶ Ἑλλήνων πολὺ πλῆθος.

2 οἱ δὲ ἀπειθήσαντες Ἰουδαῖοι ἐπήγειραν καὶ ἐκάκωσαν τὰς ψυχὰς τῶν ἐθνῶν κατὰ τῶν ἀδελφῶν.

3 Ἱκανὸν μὲν οὖν χρόνον διέτριψαν παρρησιαζόμενοι ἐπὶ τῷ κυρίῳ τῷ μαρτυροῦντι τῷ λόγῳ τῆς χάριτος αὐτοῦ, διδόντι σημεῖα καὶ τέρατα γίνεσθαι διὰ τῶν χειρῶν αὐτῶν.

14:1 So, it happened in Iconium in the same way that they entered into the synagogue of the Judeans and spoke in such a way that a great multitude both of Judeans and of Greeks believed. 2 But the disbelieving Judeans roused up and embittered the souls of the Gentiles against the brothers. 3 So then, they stayed there a sufficient time, speaking boldly in the Lord who was testifying to the Word of his grace, granting signs and wonders to be occurring by their hands.

4 ἐσχίσθη δὲ τὸ πλῆθος τῆς πόλεως, καὶ οἱ μὲν ἦσαν σὺν τοῖς Ἰουδαίοις, οἱ δὲ σὺν τοῖς ἀποστόλοις.

5 ὡς δὲ ἐγένετο ὁρμὴ τῶν ἐθνῶν τε καὶ Ἰουδαίων σὺν τοῖς ἄρχουσιν αὐτῶν ὑβρίσαι καὶ λιθοβολῆσαι αὐτούς, 6 συνιδόντες κατέφυγον εἰς τὰς πόλεις τῆς Λυκαονίας, Λύστραν καὶ Δέρβην καὶ τὴν περίχωρον, 7 κἀκεῖ εὐαγγελιζόμενοι ἦσαν.

8 Καί τις ἀνὴρ ἐν Λύστροις ἀδύνατος τοῖς ποσὶν ἐκάθητο, χωλὸς ἐκ κοιλίας μητρὸς αὐτοῦ, ὃς οὐδέποτε περιεπάτησεν.

4 But the multitude of the city was divided, and, on the one hand, some were with the Judeans and, on the other hand, some with the apostles. 5 So, when a violent attempt from both the Gentiles and the Judeans with their rulers occurred to mistreat and to stone them, 6 learning about it, they fled for safety into the cities of Lycaonia, Lystra, and Derbe and the surrounding region. 7 And there they were preaching the good news. 8 And a certain man in Lystra, disabled in feet, was sitting, a cripple from his mother's womb, who never had walked.

9 This man heard Paul speaking, who, staring at him and seeing that he was having faith to be made whole, 10 said with a loud voice, "Stand up straight on your feet!" And he sprung up and was walking around. 11 At the same time, the multitude, seeing what Paul did, lifted up their voice saying in the language of Lycaonia, "The gods, becoming like people, have come down to us!" 12 Additionally, they were calling Barnabas "Jupiter" and Paul "Mercury" since he himself was the one leading the speech. 13 At the same time, the priest of Jupiter (who was foremost of the city), bringing oxen and garlands to the gates, was wanting to conduct sacrifices along with the crowds. 14 But, hearing [this], the apostles Barnabas and Paul, tearing their clothes, rushed out in the crowd crying out,

15 καὶ λέγοντες·

ἄνδρες, τί ταῦτα ποιεῖτε; καὶ ἡμεῖς ὁμοιοπαθεῖς ἐσμεν ὑμῖν ἄνθρωποι, εὐαγγελιζόμενοι ὑμᾶς ἀπὸ τούτων τῶν ματαίων ἐπιστρέφειν ἐπὶ θεὸν ζῶντα, ὃς ἐποίησεν τὸν οὐρανὸν καὶ τὴν γῆν καὶ τὴν θάλασσαν καὶ πάντα τὰ ἐν αὐτοῖς,

16 ὃς ἐν ταῖς παρῳχημέναις γενεαῖς εἴασεν πάντα τὰ ἔθνη πορεύεσθαι ταῖς ὁδοῖς αὐτῶν· **17** καίτοι οὐκ ἀμάρτυρον αὐτὸν ἀφῆκεν ἀγαθουργῶν, οὐρανόθεν ὑμῖν ὑετοὺς διδοὺς καὶ καιροὺς καρποφόρους, ἐμπιπλῶν τροφῆς καὶ εὐφροσύνης τὰς καρδίας ὑμῶν.

18 καὶ ταῦτα λέγοντες μόλις κατέπαυσαν τοὺς ὄχλους τοῦ μὴ θύειν αὐτοῖς.

19 Ἐπῆλθαν δὲ ἀπὸ Ἀντιοχείας καὶ Ἰκονίου Ἰουδαῖοι, καὶ πείσαντες τοὺς ὄχλους καὶ λιθάσαντες τὸν Παῦλον ἔσυρον ἔξω τῆς πόλεως νομίζοντες αὐτὸν τεθνηκέναι.

20 κυκλωσάντων δὲ τῶν μαθητῶν αὐτὸν ἀναστὰς εἰσῆλθεν εἰς τὴν πόλιν καὶ τῇ ἐπαύριον ἐξῆλθεν σὺν τῷ Βαρνάβᾳ εἰς Δέρβην.

15 and saying, "Men, why are you doing these things? We ourselves are also persons of like nature to you, proclaiming to you the good news to turn away from these vain things to the living God, who made the heaven and the earth and the sea and all things in them, 16 who in bygone generations allowed all the nations to walk in their own ways; 17 although he did not leave himself without witness in doing good, in giving you rains from the heaven and fruitful seasons, in filling our hearts with food and gladness." 18 And saying these things, they hardly stopped the crowds from conducting sacrifices to them. 19 Next, some Judeans from Antioch and Iconium came there, both having persuaded the crowds and having stoned Paul, they were dragging him out of the city supposing that he had died. 20 But, after the disciples stood around him, arising he entered into the city and on the next day he went out with Barnabas into Derbe.

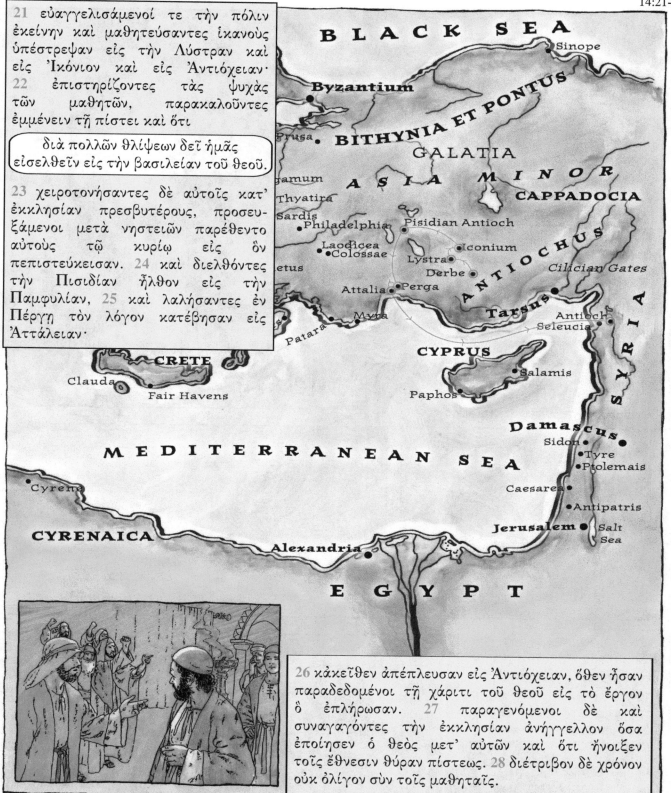

21 εὐαγγελισάμενοί τε τὴν πόλιν ἐκείνην καὶ μαθητεύσαντες ἱκανοὺς ὑπέστρεψαν εἰς τὴν Λύστραν καὶ εἰς Ἰκόνιον καὶ εἰς Ἀντιόχειαν· 22 ἐπιστηρίζοντες τὰς ψυχὰς τῶν μαθητῶν, παρακαλοῦντες ἐμμένειν τῇ πίστει καὶ ὅτι

διὰ πολλῶν θλίψεων δεῖ ἡμᾶς εἰσελθεῖν εἰς τὴν βασιλείαν τοῦ θεοῦ.

23 χειροτονήσαντες δὲ αὐτοῖς κατ’ ἐκκλησίαν πρεσβυτέρους, προσευ-ξάμενοι μετὰ νηστειῶν παρέθεντο αὐτοὺς τῷ κυρίῳ εἰς ὃν πεπιστεύκεισαν. 24 καὶ διελθόντες τὴν Πισιδίαν ἦλθον εἰς τὴν Παμφυλίαν, 25 καὶ λαλήσαντες ἐν Πέργῃ τὸν λόγον κατέβησαν εἰς Ἀττάλειαν·

26 κἀκεῖθεν ἀπέπλευσαν εἰς Ἀντιόχειαν, ὅθεν ἦσαν παραδεδομένοι τῇ χάριτι τοῦ θεοῦ εἰς τὸ ἔργον ὃ ἐπλήρωσαν. 27 παραγενόμενοι δὲ καὶ συναγαγόντες τὴν ἐκκλησίαν ἀνήγγελλον ὅσα ἐποίησεν ὁ θεὸς μετ’ αὐτῶν καὶ ὅτι ἤνοιξεν τοῖς ἔθνεσιν θύραν πίστεως. 28 διέτριβον δὲ χρόνον οὐκ ὀλίγον σὺν τοῖς μαθηταῖς.

21 At the same time, proclaiming the good news to that city and having discipled a sufficient number, they returned into Lystra and into Iconium and into Antioch, 22 strengthening the souls of the disciples, encouraging them to continue in the Faith, and [saying] this: "Through many afflictions it is necessary that we enter into the kingdom of God!" 23 So, appointing elders for them in every assembly, praying with fasting, they commended them to the Lord, in whom they had believed. 24 And passing through Pisidia, they went into Pamphylia. 25 And having spoken the Word in Perga, they went down into Attalia. 26 And from there they sailed to Antioch, from where they had been committed to the grace of God for the work which they fulfilled. 27 So, arriving and gathering the assembly together, they were reporting how many things God did with them and that he had opened a door of faith to the Gentiles. 28 Moreover, they were staying not a small time there with the disciples.

Κεφ.
ΙΕ΄

15:1 Καί τινες κατελθόντες ἀπὸ τῆς Ἰουδαίας ἐδίδασκον τοὺς ἀδελφοὺς ὅτι

ἐὰν μὴ περιτμηθῆτε τῷ ἔθει τῷ Μωϋσέως, οὐ δύνασθε σωθῆναι.

2 γενομένης δὲ στάσεως καὶ ζητήσεως οὐκ ὀλίγης τῷ Παύλῳ καὶ τῷ Βαρνάβᾳ πρὸς αὐτοὺς ἔταξαν ἀναβαίνειν Παῦλον καὶ Βαρνάβαν καί τινας ἄλλους ἐξ αὐτῶν πρὸς τοὺς ἀποστόλους καὶ πρεσβυτέρους εἰς Ἱερουσαλὴμ περὶ τοῦ ζητήματος τούτου.

3 Οἱ μὲν οὖν προπεμφθέντες ὑπὸ τῆς ἐκκλησίας διήρχοντο τήν τε Φοινίκην καὶ Σαμάρειαν ἐκδιηγούμενοι τὴν ἐπιστροφὴν τῶν ἐθνῶν καὶ ἐποίουν χαρὰν μεγάλην πᾶσι τοῖς ἀδελφοῖς.

4 παραγενόμενοι δὲ εἰς Ἱεροσόλυμα παρεδέχθησαν ὑπὸ τῆς ἐκκλησίας καὶ τῶν ἀποστόλων καὶ τῶν πρεσβυτέρων, ἀνήγγειλάν τε ὅσα ὁ θεὸς ἐποίησεν μετ' αὐτῶν.

15:1 And some persons, coming down from Judea, were teaching the brothers this: "Unless you are circumcised after the custom of Moses, you are not able to be saved!" 2 So, after no small discord and dispute for Paul and Barnabas occurred with them, they arranged that Paul and Barnabas and some others from them would go up into Jerusalem to the apostles and elders concerning this dispute. 3 So then, they, being sent forth by the assembly, were passing through both Phoenicia and Samaria, recounting in full the conversion of the Gentiles and were creating a great joy for all the brothers. 4 So, arriving into Jerusalem, they were received by the assembly and the apostles and the elders, and at the same time they reported how many things God did with them.

5 Ἐξανέστησαν δέ τινες τῶν ἀπὸ τῆς αἱρέσεως τῶν Φαρισαίων πεπιστευκότες, λέγοντες ὅτι

δεῖ περιτέμνειν αὐτοὺς παραγγέλλειν τε τηρεῖν τὸν νόμον Μωϋσέως.

6 Συνήχθησαν δὲ οἱ ἀπόστολοι καὶ οἱ πρεσβύτεροι ἰδεῖν περὶ τοῦ λόγου τούτου. 7 πολλῆς δὲ ζητήσεως γενομένης, ἀναστὰς Πέτρος εἶπεν πρὸς αὐτούς·

ἄνδρες ἀδελφοί, ὑμεῖς ἐπίστασθε ὅτι ἀφ' ἡμερῶν ἀρχαίων ἐν ὑμῖν ἐξελέξατο ὁ θεὸς διὰ τοῦ στόματός μου ἀκοῦσαι τὰ ἔθνη τὸν λόγον τοῦ εὐαγγελίου καὶ πιστεῦσαι.

8 καὶ ὁ καρδιογνώστης θεὸς ἐμαρτύρησεν αὐτοῖς δοὺς τὸ πνεῦμα τὸ ἅγιον καθὼς καὶ ἡμῖν· 9 καὶ οὐθὲν διέκρινεν μεταξὺ ἡμῶν τε καὶ αὐτῶν τῇ πίστει καθαρίσας τὰς καρδίας αὐτῶν.

10 νῦν οὖν τί πειράζετε τὸν θεὸν ἐπιθεῖναι ζυγὸν ἐπὶ τὸν τράχηλον τῶν μαθητῶν, ὃν οὔτε οἱ πατέρες ἡμῶν οὔτε ἡμεῖς ἰσχύσαμεν βαστάσαι;

11 ἀλλὰ διὰ τῆς χάριτος τοῦ κυρίου Ἰησοῦ πιστεύομεν σωθῆναι καθ' ὃν τρόπον κἀκεῖνοι.

5 But some of the ones from the sect of the Pharisees who had believed rose up, saying this: "It is necessary to be circumcising them as well as to be commanding them to continue keeping the Law of Moses!" 6 So, the apostles and the elders were gathered together to see about this matter. 7 Moreover, with a large dispute occurring, rising up Peter said to them, "Fellow brothers, you yourselves know that many days ago God made a choice among you that by my mouth the Gentiles would hear the Word of the good news and believe. 8 And God, the Knower of hearts, testified, giving to them the Holy Spirit just like also to us. 9 And he made no distinction between both us and them, by faith cleansing their hearts. 10 Now, therefore, why are you tempting God to put a yoke on the neck of the disciples which neither our fathers nor we ourselves were able to bear?! 11 But through the grace of the Lord Jesus we believe that we are saved in like manner as also those ones are!"

12 ἐσίγησεν δὲ πᾶν τὸ πλῆθος καὶ ἤκουον Βαρνάβα καὶ Παύλου ἐξηγουμένων ὅσα ἐποίησεν ὁ θεὸς σημεῖα καὶ τέρατα ἐν τοῖς ἔθνεσιν δι' αὐτῶν.

13 Μετὰ δὲ τὸ σιγῆσαι αὐτοὺς ἀπεκρίθη Ἰάκωβος λέγων·

ἄνδρες ἀδελφοί, ἀκούσατέ μου.

14 Συμεὼν ἐξηγήσατο καθὼς πρῶτον ὁ θεὸς ἐπεσκέψατο λαβεῖν ἐξ ἐθνῶν λαὸν τῷ ὀνόματι αὐτοῦ· 15 καὶ τούτῳ συμφωνοῦσιν οἱ λόγοι τῶν προφητῶν καθὼς γέγραπται·

16 μετὰ ταῦτα ἀναστρέψω καὶ ἀνοικοδομήσω τὴν σκηνὴν Δαυεὶδ τὴν πεπτωκυῖαν καὶ τὰ κατεσκαμμένα αὐτῆς ἀνοικοδομήσω καὶ ἀνορθώσω αὐτήν· 17 ὅπως ἂν ἐκζητήσωσιν οἱ κατάλοιποι τῶν ἀνθρώπων τὸν κύριον καὶ πάντα τὰ ἔθνη, ἐφ' οὓς ἐπικέκληται τὸ ὄνομά μου ἐπ' αὐτούς, λέγει κύριος ὁ ποιῶν ταῦτα 18 γνωστὰ ἀπ' αἰῶνος.

19 διὸ ἐγὼ κρίνω μὴ παρενοχλεῖν τοῖς ἀπὸ τῶν ἐθνῶν ἐπιστρέφουσιν ἐπὶ τὸν θεόν,

20 ἀλλὰ ἐπιστεῖλαι αὐτοῖς τοῦ ἀπέχεσθαι τῶν ἀλισγημάτων τῶν εἰδώλων καὶ τῆς πορνείας καὶ τοῦ πνικτοῦ καὶ τοῦ αἵματος. 21 Μωϋσῆς γὰρ ἐκ γενεῶν ἀρχαίων κατὰ πόλιν τοὺς κηρύσσοντας αὐτὸν ἔχει ἐν ταῖς συναγωγαῖς κατὰ πᾶν σάββατον ἀναγινωσκόμενος.

12 Then, all the multitude went silent and they were listening to Barnabas and Paul reporting how many signs and wonders God had done among the Gentiles through them. 13 Moreover, after they were silent, James responded, saying, "Fellow brothers, listen to me. 14 Simeon reported just how God first sought out to take from the Gentiles a people for his name. 15 And to this the words of the Prophets are agreeing, just as it has been written, 16 'After these things, I will return and I will again build the tabernacle of David which has fallen and its demolished pieces I will again build and I will set it up 17 in order that the remaining ones of people would seek after the Lord, and all the Gentiles upon whom my name is called upon them, says the Lord who accomplishes these things 18 known from eternity.' 19 Therefore, I myself propose not to trouble the ones turning to God from among the Gentiles, 20 but to write to them to abstain from the pollution of idols and from sexual immorality and from what is strangled and from blood. 21 For Moses from generations of old has from city to city the ones preaching him, being read in the synagogues every Sabbath."

22 Τότε ἔδοξε τοῖς ἀποστόλοις καὶ τοῖς πρεσβυτέροις σὺν ὅλῃ τῇ ἐκκλησίᾳ ἐκλεξαμένους ἄνδρας ἐξ αὐτῶν πέμψαι εἰς Ἀντιόχειαν σὺν τῷ Παύλῳ καὶ Βαρνάβᾳ, Ἰούδαν τὸν καλούμενον Βαρσαββᾶν καὶ Σίλαν, ἄνδρας ἡγουμένους ἐν τοῖς ἀδελφοῖς, 23 γράψαντες διὰ χειρὸς αὐτῶν·

Οἱ ἀπόστολοι καὶ οἱ πρεσβύτεροι ἀδελφοὶ τοῖς κατὰ τὴν Ἀντιόχειαν καὶ Συρίαν καὶ Κιλικίαν ἀδελφοῖς τοῖς ἐξ ἐθνῶν χαίρειν. 24 Ἐπειδὴ ἠκούσαμεν ὅτι τινὲς ἐξ ἡμῶν ἐξελθόντες ἐτάραξαν ὑμᾶς λόγοις ἀνασκευάζοντες τὰς ψυχὰς ὑμῶν, οἷς οὐ διεστειλάμεθα, 25 ἔδοξεν ἡμῖν γενομένοις ὁμοθυμαδὸν ἐκλεξαμένους ἄνδρας πέμψαι πρὸς ὑμᾶς σὺν τοῖς ἀγαπητοῖς ἡμῶν Βαρνάβᾳ καὶ Παύλῳ, 26 ἀνθρώποις παραδεδωκόσι τὰς ψυχὰς αὐτῶν ὑπὲρ τοῦ ὀνόματος τοῦ κυρίου ἡμῶν Ἰησοῦ χριστοῦ. 27 ἀπεστάλκαμεν οὖν Ἰούδαν καὶ Σίλαν, καὶ αὐτοὺς διὰ λόγου ἀπαγγέλλοντας τὰ αὐτά. 28 ἔδοξεν γὰρ τῷ πνεύματι τῷ ἁγίῳ καὶ ἡμῖν μηδὲν πλέον ἐπιτίθεσθαι ὑμῖν βάρος πλὴν τούτων τῶν ἐπάναγκες 29 ἀπέχεσθαι εἰδωλοθύτων καὶ αἵματος καὶ πνικτῶν καὶ πορνείας· ἐξ ὧν διατηροῦντες ἑαυτοὺς εὖ πράξετε. ἔρρωσθε.

30 Οἱ μὲν οὖν ἀπολυθέντες κατῆλθον εἰς Ἀντιόχειαν, καὶ συναγαγόντες τὸ πλῆθος ἐπέδωκαν τὴν ἐπιστολήν.

31 ἀναγνόντες δὲ ἐχάρησαν ἐπὶ τῇ παρακλήσει. 32 Ἰούδας τε καὶ Σίλας, καὶ αὐτοὶ προφῆται ὄντες, διὰ λόγου πολλοῦ παρεκάλεσαν τοὺς ἀδελφοὺς καὶ ἐπεστήριξαν.

22 Then, it seemed good to the apostles and to the elders with the whole assembly, choosing men from them to send into Antioch with Paul and Barnabas: Judas the one being called Barsabbas and Silas—chief men among the brothers— 23 writing these things by their hand: "The apostles and the elders, brothers, to the brothers across Antioch and Syria and Cilicia who are from the Gentiles: Greetings! 24 Because we heard that some coming out from us have troubled you with words, unsettling your souls, to whom we gave no orders, 25 it seemed good to us coming to one accord, to send chosen men to you with our beloved Barnabas and Paul, 26 persons having offered their souls for the name of our Lord, Jesus Christ. 27 Therefore, we have sent Judas and Silas, also themselves reporting by word the same things. 28 For it seemed good to the Holy Spirit and to us to keep laying no greater burden on you except these necessary things: 29 to abstain from things sacrificed to idols and from blood and from things strangled and from sexual immorality; from which things keeping yourselves, you would do well! Farewell." 30 So then, being sent off, they went down into Antioch, and having gathered the multitude together, they delivered the letter. 31 And, having read it, they rejoiced at the encouragement. 32 Both Judas and Silas, also being prophets themselves, with a great word encouraged the brothers and strengthened [them].

33 ποιήσαντες δὲ χρόνον ἀπελύθησαν μετ᾽ εἰρήνης ἀπὸ τῶν ἀδελφῶν πρὸς τοὺς ἀποστείλαντας αὐτούς.

35* Παῦλος δὲ καὶ Βαρνάβας διέτριβον ἐν Ἀντιοχείᾳ διδάσκοντες καὶ εὐαγγελιζόμενοι μετὰ καὶ ἑτέρων πολλῶν τὸν λόγον τοῦ κυρίου.

36 Μετὰ δέ τινας ἡμέρας εἶπεν πρὸς Βαρνάβαν Παῦλος·

ἐπιστρέψαντες δὴ ἐπισκεψώμεθα τοὺς ἀδελφοὺς κατὰ πόλιν πᾶσαν ἐν αἷς κατηγγείλαμεν τὸν λόγον τοῦ κυρίου, πῶς ἔχουσιν.

37 Βαρνάβας δὲ ἐβούλετο συν-παραλαβεῖν καὶ τὸν Ἰωάννην τὸν καλούμενον Μάρκον·

38 Παῦλος δὲ ἠξίου τὸν ἀπο-στάντα ἀπ᾽ αὐτῶν ἀπὸ Παμφυλίας καὶ μὴ συνελθ-όντα αὐτοῖς εἰς τὸ ἔργον μὴ συνπαραλαμβάνειν τοῦτον. 39 Ἐγένετο δὲ παροξυσμός, ὥστε ἀποχωρισθῆναι αὐτοὺς ἀπ᾽ ἀλλήλων,

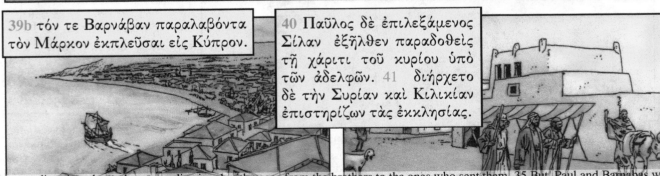

39b τόν τε Βαρνάβαν παραλαβόντα τὸν Μάρκον ἐκπλεῦσαι εἰς Κύπρον.

40 Παῦλος δὲ ἐπιλεξάμενος Σίλαν ἐξῆλθεν παραδοθεὶς τῇ χάριτι τοῦ κυρίου ὑπὸ τῶν ἀδελφῶν. 41 διήρχετο δὲ τὴν Συρίαν καὶ Κιλικίαν ἐπιστηρίζων τὰς ἐκκλησίας.

33 So, spending time there, they were dismissed with peace from the brothers to the ones who sent them. 35 But, Paul and Barnabas were staying in Antioch, teaching and proclaiming, with many others also, the good news of the Word of the Lord. 36 Then, after some days Paul said to Barnabas, "Returning now, let's check up on our brothers in every city in which we proclaimed the Word of the Lord, to see how they are doing." 37 So, Barnabas was intending to take along also John, the one being called Mark. 38 But Paul was evaluating the one who deserted them at Pamphylia and did not go with them for the work, [deciding] not to bring this one along. 39 So, a sharp disagreement occurred with the result that they separated from each other, at the same time Barnabas taking Mark with him to sail away into Cyprus. 40 But Paul, choosing Silas, went out commended to the grace of God by the brothers. 41 Moreover, he was going throughout Syria and Cilicia strengthening the assemblies.

72

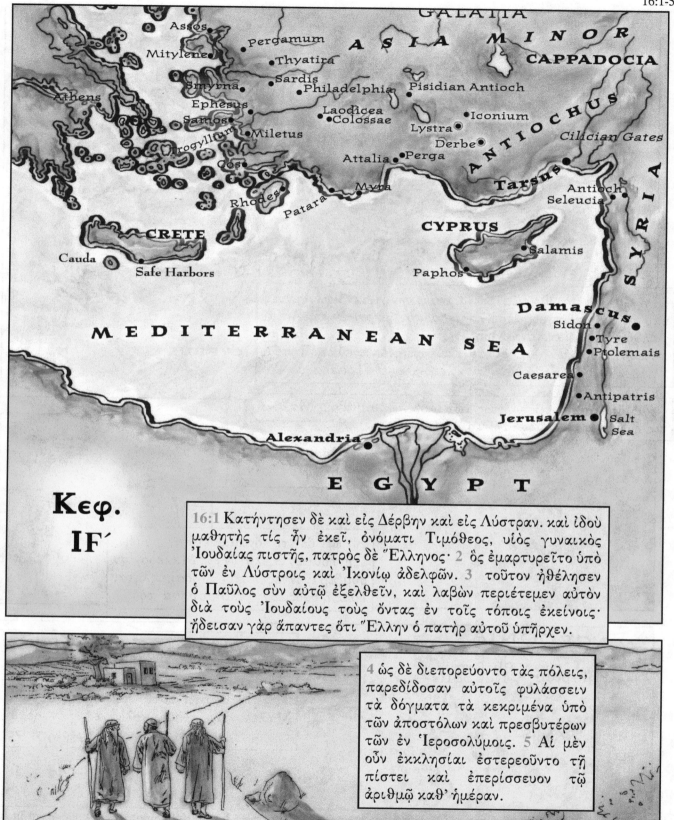

**Κεφ.
ΙϚ΄**

16:1 Κατήντησεν δὲ καὶ εἰς Δέρβην καὶ εἰς Λύστραν. καὶ ἰδοὺ μαθητής τίς ἦν ἐκεῖ, ὀνόματι Τιμόθεος, υἱὸς γυναικὸς Ἰουδαίας πιστῆς, πατρὸς δὲ Ἕλληνος· **2** ὃς ἐμαρτυρεῖτο ὑπὸ τῶν ἐν Λύστροις καὶ Ἰκονίῳ ἀδελφῶν. **3** τοῦτον ἠθέλησεν ὁ Παῦλος σὺν αὐτῷ ἐξελθεῖν, καὶ λαβὼν περιέτεμεν αὐτὸν διὰ τοὺς Ἰουδαίους τοὺς ὄντας ἐν τοῖς τόποις ἐκείνοις· ᾔδεισαν γὰρ ἅπαντες ὅτι Ἕλλην ὁ πατὴρ αὐτοῦ ὑπῆρχεν.

4 ὡς δὲ διεπορεύοντο τὰς πόλεις, παρεδίδοσαν αὐτοῖς φυλάσσειν τὰ δόγματα τὰ κεκριμένα ὑπὸ τῶν ἀποστόλων καὶ πρεσβυτέρων τῶν ἐν Ἱεροσολύμοις. **5** Αἱ μὲν οὖν ἐκκλησίαι ἐστερεοῦντο τῇ πίστει καὶ ἐπερίσσευον τῷ ἀριθμῷ καθ᾽ ἡμέραν.

16:1 Next, he came both into Derbe and into Lystra. And, behold, a certain disciple was there, Timothy by name—a son of a faithful Judean woman and of a Greek father—2 who was being affirmed by the brothers in Lystra and Iconium. 3 Paul wanted this fellow to go out with him, and, receiving him, he circumcised him on account of the Judeans who were in those regions; for all of them knew that his father was in fact a Greek. 4 So, as they were traveling through the cities, they were delivering to them the decrees to continue keeping that had been decided by the apostles and elders who were in Jerusalem. 5 So then, the assemblies were being strengthened in the Faith and were increasing in number each day.

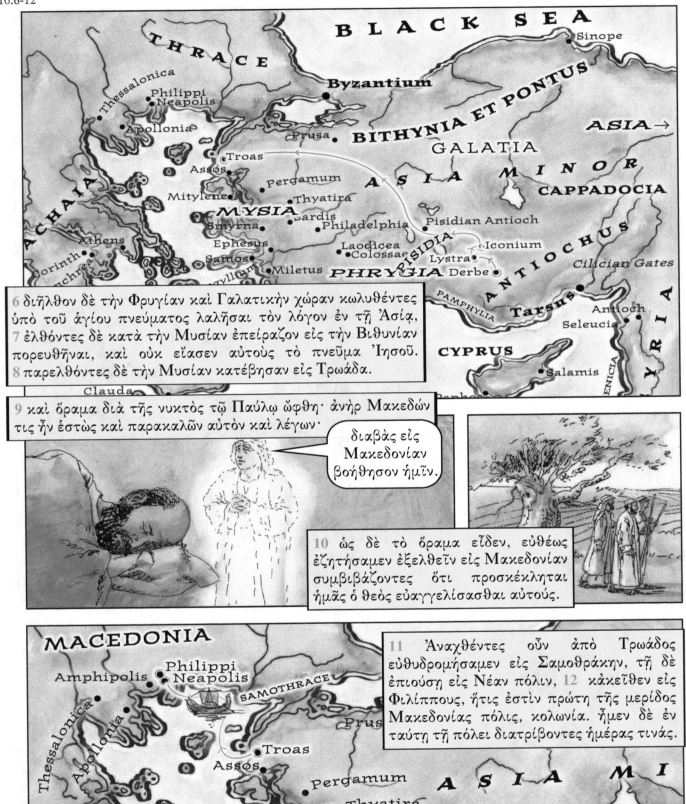

6 διῆλθον δὲ τὴν Φρυγίαν καὶ Γαλατικὴν χώραν κωλυθέντες ὑπὸ τοῦ ἁγίου πνεύματος λαλῆσαι τὸν λόγον ἐν τῇ Ἀσίᾳ, 7 ἐλθόντες δὲ κατὰ τὴν Μυσίαν ἐπείραζον εἰς τὴν Βιθυνίαν πορευθῆναι, καὶ οὐκ εἴασεν αὐτοὺς τὸ πνεῦμα Ἰησοῦ. 8 παρελθόντες δὲ τὴν Μυσίαν κατέβησαν εἰς Τρωάδα.

9 καὶ ὅραμα διὰ τῆς νυκτὸς τῷ Παύλῳ ὤφθη· ἀνὴρ Μακεδών τις ἦν ἑστὼς καὶ παρακαλῶν αὐτὸν καὶ λέγων·

διαβὰς εἰς Μακεδονίαν βοήθησον ἡμῖν.

10 ὡς δὲ τὸ ὅραμα εἶδεν, εὐθέως ἐζητήσαμεν ἐξελθεῖν εἰς Μακεδονίαν συμβιβάζοντες ὅτι προσκέκληται ἡμᾶς ὁ θεὸς εὐαγγελίσασθαι αὐτούς.

11 Ἀναχθέντες οὖν ἀπὸ Τρωάδος εὐθυδρομήσαμεν εἰς Σαμοθράκην, τῇ δὲ ἐπιούσῃ εἰς Νέαν πόλιν, 12 κἀκεῖθεν εἰς Φιλίππους, ἥτις ἐστὶν πρώτη τῆς μερίδος Μακεδονίας πόλις, κολωνία. ἦμεν δὲ ἐν ταύτῃ τῇ πόλει διατρίβοντες ἡμέρας τινάς.

6 Next, they went through the Phrygian and Galatian region having been prevented by the Holy Spirit to speak the Word in Asia. 7 Moreover, going opposite Mysia, they were attempting to travel into Bithynia, and the Spirit of Jesus did not allow them. 8 Next, passing by Mysia, they went down into Troas. 9 And a vision in the night appeared to Paul: A certain Macedonian man was standing and calling on him and saying, "Crossing over into Macedonia, help us!" 10 So, when he saw the vision, immediately we sought to go out into Macedonia, concluding that God had called us to proclaim the good news to them. 11 Therefore, setting sail from Troas, we made a straight course into Samothrace, and on the day following into Neapolis, 12 and from there into Philippi, which is the leading city of the district of Macedonia, a Roman colony. So, in this city we were staying some days.

13 τῇ τε ἡμέρᾳ τῶν σαββάτων ἐξήλθομεν ἔξω τῆς πύλης παρὰ ποταμὸν οὗ ἐνομίζομεν προσευχὴν εἶναι, καὶ καθίσαντες ἐλαλοῦμεν ταῖς συνελθούσαις γυναιξίν.

14 Καί τις γυνὴ ὀνόματι Λυδία, πορφυρόπωλις πόλεως Θυατείρων σεβομένη τὸν θεόν, ἤκουεν ἧς ὁ κύριος διήνοιξεν τὴν καρδίαν προσέχειν τοῖς λαλουμένοις ὑπὸ τοῦ Παύλου. 15 ὡς δὲ ἐβαπτίσθη καὶ ὁ οἶκος αὐτῆς, παρεκάλεσεν λέγουσα·

εἰ κεκρίκατέ με πιστὴν τῷ κυρίῳ εἶναι, εἰσελθόντες εἰς τὸν οἶκόν μου μένετε·

καὶ παρεβιάσατο ἡμᾶς.

13 At the same time, on the Sabbath day we went outside of the city along a riverside where we were presuming a prayer [place] to exist, and sitting down, we were speaking to the women assembled. 14 And a certain woman, Lydia by name, a seller of purple of the city of Thyatira, one worshipping God, was listening, whose heart the Lord opened to be paying attention to the things being spoken by Paul. 15 Moreover, when she was baptized and her household, she invited us, saying, "If you have judged me to be faithful to the Lord, coming into my house, stay." And she successfully persuaded us.

16 Ἐγένετο δὲ πορευομένων ἡμῶν εἰς τὴν προσευχήν, παιδίσκην τινὰ ἔχουσαν πνεῦμα πύθωνα ὑπαντῆσαι ἡμῖν, ἥτις ἐργασίαν πολλὴν παρεῖχεν τοῖς κυρίοις αὐτῆς μαντευομένη.

17 αὕτη κατακολουθοῦσα τῷ Παύλῳ καὶ ἡμῖν ἔκραζεν λέγουσα·

οὗτοι οἱ ἄνθρωποι δοῦλοι τοῦ θεοῦ τοῦ ὑψίστου εἰσίν, οἵτινες καταγγέλλουσιν ὑμῖν ὁδὸν σωτηρίας.

παραγγέλλω σοι ἐν ὀνόματι Ἰησοῦ χριστοῦ ἐξελθεῖν ἀπ' αὐτῆς.

18a τοῦτο δὲ ἐποίει ἐπὶ πολλὰς ἡμέρας. διαπονηθεὶς δὲ Παῦλος καὶ ἐπιστρέψας τῷ πνεύματι εἶπεν·

18b καὶ ἐξῆλθεν αὐτῇ τῇ ὥρᾳ. 19 ἰδόντες δὲ οἱ κύριοι αὐτῆς ὅτι ἐξῆλθεν ἡ ἐλπὶς τῆς ἐργασίας αὐτῶν, ἐπιλαβόμενοι τὸν Παῦλον καὶ τὸν Σίλαν εἵλκυσαν εἰς τὴν ἀγορὰν ἐπὶ τοὺς ἄρχοντας,

16 Next, it happened that as we were traveling to the prayer [place], a certain servant girl having a spirit of divination met us, who was supplying her masters much business telling fortunes. 17 This woman following Paul and us was crying out, saying, "These persons are servants of the Most High God, who are declaring to us the way of salvation!" 18 Moreover, she was doing this for many days. But Paul, becoming greatly annoyed and turning, said to the spirit, "I command you in the name of Jesus Christ to come out of her!" And it came out at that very hour. 19 But, her masters, seeing that the hope of their business had departed, seizing Paul and Silas, dragged them into the marketplace to the rulers.

20 And bringing them to the magistrates, they said, "These persons are agitating our city, being in fact Judeans! 21 And they are declaring customs which are not lawful for us to be receiving nor to be observing, being Romans!" 22 And the crowd rose up together against them, and the magistrates, tearing their clothes from them, were commanding them to be beaten with rods. 23 At the same time, laying many stripes on them, they threw them into prison charging the jailer to be guarding them securely, 24 who, receiving such a command, threw them into the inner prison and secured their feet into the wood [stocks].

25 Κατὰ δὲ τὸ μεσονύκτιον Παῦλος καὶ Σίλας προσ-ευχόμενοι ὕμνουν τὸν θεόν· ἐπηκροῶντο δὲ αὐτῶν οἱ δέσμιοι. **26a** ἄφνω δὲ σεισμὸς ἐγένετο μέγας ὥστε σαλευθῆναι τὰ θεμέλια τοῦ δεσμωτηρίου·

26b ἠνεῴχθησαν δὲ παραχρῆμα αἱ θύραι πᾶσαι, καὶ πάντων τὰ δεσμὰ ἀνέθη.

27 ἔξυπνος δὲ γενόμενος ὁ δεσμοφύλαξ καὶ ἰδὼν ἀνεῳγμένας τὰς θύρας τῆς φυλακῆς, σπασάμενος μάχαιραν ἤμελλεν ἑαυτὸν ἀναιρεῖν νομίζων ἐκπεφευγέναι τοὺς δεσμίους.

25 But about midnight Paul and Silas, praying, were singing hymns to God; moreover, the prisoners were listening to them. 26 Then, suddenly a great earthquake occurred, so that the foundations of the prison were shaken; and immediately all the doors were opened, and the bonds of all were unfastened! 27 So, the jailer, being roused out of sleep and seeing the prison doors opened, drawing his sword, was about to kill himself, supposing that the prisoners had escaped.

28 Ἐφώνησεν δὲ φωνῇ μεγάλῃ Παῦλος λέγων·

μηδὲν πράξῃς σεαυτῷ κακόν· ἅπαντες γὰρ ἐσμὲν ἐνθάδε.

29 αἰτήσας δὲ φῶτα εἰσεπήδησεν καὶ ἔντρομος γενόμενος προσέπεσεν τῷ Παύλῳ καὶ τῷ Σίλᾳ, 30 καὶ προαγαγὼν αὐτοὺς ἔξω ἔφη·

κύριοι, τί με δεῖ ποιεῖν ἵνα σωθῶ;

31 οἱ δὲ εἶπαν·

πίστευσον ἐπὶ τὸν κύριον Ἰησοῦν, καὶ σωθήσῃ σὺ καὶ ὁ οἶκός σου.

32 καὶ ἐλάλησαν αὐτῷ τὸν λόγον τοῦ κυρίου σὺν πᾶσιν τοῖς ἐν τῇ οἰκίᾳ αὐτοῦ. 33 καὶ παραλαβὼν αὐτοὺς ἐν ἐκείνῃ τῇ ὥρᾳ τῆς νυκτὸς ἔλουσεν ἀπὸ τῶν πληγῶν, καὶ ἐβαπτίσθη αὐτὸς καὶ οἱ αὐτοῦ πάντες παραχρῆμα. 34 ἀναγαγών τε αὐτοὺς εἰς τὸν οἶκον παρέθηκεν τράπεζαν καὶ ἠγαλλιάσατο πανοικεὶ πεπιστευκὼς τῷ θεῷ.

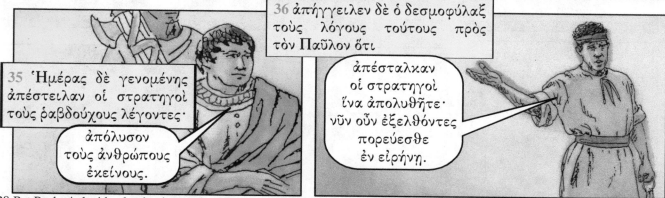

36 ἀπήγγειλεν δὲ ὁ δεσμοφύλαξ τοὺς λόγους τούτους πρὸς τὸν Παῦλον ὅτι

35 Ἡμέρας δὲ γενομένης ἀπέστειλαν οἱ στρατηγοὶ τοὺς ῥαβδούχους λέγοντες·

ἀπόλυσον τοὺς ἀνθρώπους ἐκείνους.

ἀπέσταλκαν οἱ στρατηγοὶ ἵνα ἀπολυθῆτε· νῦν οὖν ἐξελθόντες πορεύεσθε ἐν εἰρήνῃ.

28 But Paul cried with a loud voice, saying, "Do not do any harm to yourself, for all of us are here!" 29 So, calling for lights, he sprang in and, becoming awestruck, he fell down before Paul and Silas, 30 and bringing them outside, he said, "Sirs, what is necessary for me to be doing in order that I would be saved?" 31 And they said, "Believe in the Lord Jesus, and you will be saved, you and your household!" 32 And they spoke the Word of the Lord to him with the ones in his house. 33 And taking them at the same hour of the night, he washed their stripes, and he was baptized and all his household immediately. 34 At the same time, leading them up into his house, he laid out a table [of food] and rejoiced greatly, with all his household, having believed in God. 35 But with the day having come, the magistrates sent lictors, saying, "Release those men!" 36 Moreover, the jailer reported these words to Paul, [saying] this: "The magistrates have been sent in order that you would be released; now, therefore, departing, go in peace."

37 Ὁ δὲ Παῦλος ἔφη πρὸς αὐτούς·

δείραντες ἡμᾶς δημοσίᾳ ἀκατακρίτους, ἀνθρώπους Ῥωμαίους ὑπάρχοντας, ἔβαλαν εἰς φυλακήν, καὶ νῦν λάθρα ἡμᾶς ἐκβάλλουσιν; οὐ γάρ, ἀλλὰ ἐλθόντες αὐτοὶ ἡμᾶς ἐξαγαγέτωσαν.

38 ἀπήγγειλαν δὲ τοῖς στρατηγοῖς οἱ ῥαβδοῦχοι τὰ ῥήματα ταῦτα· ἐφοβήθησαν δὲ ἀκούσαντες ὅτι Ῥωμαῖοι εἰσίν, 39 καὶ ἐλθόντες παρεκάλεσαν αὐτούς, καὶ ἐξαγαγόντες ἠρώτων ἀπελθεῖν ἀπὸ τῆς πόλεως.

40 Ἐξελθόντες δὲ ἐκ τῆς φυλακῆς εἰσῆλθον πρὸς τὴν Λυδίαν· καὶ ἰδόντες παρεκάλεσαν τοὺς ἀδελφοὺς καὶ ἐξῆλθαν.

37 But Paul was saying to them, "Beating us in public without a trial, persons being in fact Romans, they cast us into prison, and secretly they are releasing us?! Indeed, no! Rather, coming, let they themselves bring us out!" 38 So, the lictors reported these words to the magistrates; moreover, they were terrified hearing that they were Romans, 39 and coming, they summoned them, and leading [them] out, they were asking them to depart from the city. 40 So, coming out from the prison, they went to Lydia. And seeing the brothers, they encouraged [them] and departed.

17:1 Next, passing through Amphipolis and Apollonia, they came into Thessalonica, where there was a synagogue of the Judeans. 2 Moreover, according to his custom, Paul went in to them, and for three Sabbath days reasoned with them from the Scriptures, 3 explaining and demonstrating that it was necessary for the Christ to suffer and rise again from the dead, and [saying] this: "This One is Christ Jesus, whom I myself am announcing to you!" 4 And some of them were persuaded and were added to Paul and Silas, both a great multitude of the devout Greeks and not a few of the chief women. 5 But the Judeans, showing zeal and taking along some wicked men from the marketplace and gathering a crowd, were throwing the city into an uproar,

5b καὶ ἐπιστάντες τῇ οἰκίᾳ Ἰάσονος ἐζήτουν αὐτοὺς προαγαγεῖν εἰς τὸν δῆμον· 6 μὴ εὑρόντες δὲ αὐτοὺς ἔσυρον Ἰάσονα καί τινας ἀδελφοὺς ἐπὶ τοὺς πολιτάρχας βοῶντες ὅτι

οἱ τὴν οἰκουμένην ἀναστατώσαντες οὗτοι καὶ ἐνθάδε πάρεισιν, 7 οὓς ὑποδέδεκται Ἰάσων· καὶ οὗτοι πάντες ἀπέναντι τῶν δογμάτων Καίσαρος πράσσουσιν βασιλέα ἕτερον λέγοντες εἶναι Ἰησοῦν.

8 ἐτάραξαν δὲ τὸν ὄχλον καὶ τοὺς πολιτάρχας ἀκούοντας ταῦτα· 9 καὶ λαβόντες τὸ ἱκανὸν παρὰ τοῦ Ἰάσονος καὶ τῶν λοιπῶν ἀπέλυσαν αὐτούς.

10 Οἱ δὲ ἀδελφοὶ εὐθέως διὰ νυκτὸς ἐξέπεμψαν τόν τε Παῦλον καὶ τὸν Σίλαν εἰς Βέροιαν, οἵτινες παραγενόμενοι εἰς τὴν συναγωγὴν τῶν Ἰουδαίων ἀπῄεσαν.

5b and setting out to the house of Jason, they were seeking to lead them out to the people. 6 And, not finding them, they were dragging Jason and certain brothers before the rulers of the city, crying out this: "These persons, upsetting the inhabited [Roman] world, are also present here, 7 whom Jason has hosted! And all these are acting contrary to the decrees of Caesar, saying that there is another king, Jesus!" 8 So, they troubled the multitude and the rulers of the city hearing these things. 9 And receiving sufficient [bond] from Jason and the rest, they released them. 10 Now, the brothers immediately by night sent both Paul and Silas away into Berea, who arriving went into the synagogue of the Judeans.

11 οὗτοι δὲ ἦσαν εὐγενέστεροι τῶν ἐν Θεσσαλονίκῃ, οἵτινες ἐδέξαντο τὸν λόγον μετὰ πάσης προθυμίας καθ' ἡμέραν ἀνακρίνοντες τὰς γραφὰς εἰ ἔχοι ταῦτα οὕτως. 12 Πολλοὶ μὲν οὖν ἐξ αὐτῶν ἐπίστευσαν, καὶ τῶν Ἑλληνίδων γυναικῶν τῶν εὐσχημόνων καὶ ἀνδρῶν οὐκ ὀλίγοι.

13 Ὡς δὲ ἔγνωσαν οἱ ἀπὸ τῆς Θεσσαλονίκης Ἰουδαῖοι ὅτι καὶ ἐν τῇ Βεροίᾳ κατηγγέλη ὑπὸ τοῦ Παύλου ὁ λόγος τοῦ θεοῦ, ἦλθον κἀκεῖ σαλεύοντες καὶ ταράσσοντες τοὺς ὄχλους.

14 εὐθέως δὲ τότε τὸν Παῦλον ἐξαπέστειλαν οἱ ἀδελφοὶ πορεύεσθαι ἕως ἐπὶ τὴν θάλασσαν· ὑπέμεινάν τε ὅ τε Σίλας καὶ ὁ Τιμόθεος ἐκεῖ. 15 οἱ δὲ καθιστάνοντες τὸν Παῦλον ἤγαγον ἕως Ἀθηνῶν, καὶ λαβόντες ἐντολὴν πρὸς τὸν Σίλαν καὶ τὸν Τιμόθεον ἵνα ὡς τάχιστα ἔλθωσιν πρὸς αὐτὸν ἐξῄεσαν.

11 Now these were more noble than those in Thessalonica, who indeed received the Word with all willingness, examining the Scriptures each day if these things might actually be so. 12 So then, many of them believed—and not a few of the prominent Greek women and men. 13 But when the Judeans from Thessalonica knew that also in Berea the Word of God was proclaimed by Paul, they came there also, agitating and troubling the crowds. 14 So, then immediately the brothers sent out Paul to travel as far as to the sea, and at the same time both Silas and Timothy stayed there. 15 But the ones put in charge of Paul brought him as far as Athens, and receiving a command for Silas and Timothy that they should come to him as quickly as possible, they left.

16 So, in Athens, as Paul was waiting for them, his spirit was being provoked within him beholding the city being full of idols. 17 So then, he was reasoning in the synagogue with the Judeans and the devout persons and in the marketplace every day with the ones happening to be there. 18 Now, some also of the Epicurean and Stoic philosophers were conversing with him. And some were saying, "What could this babbler want to say?" But others [said], "He seems to be a herald of foreign deities"; because he was proclaiming the good news of Jesus and the resurrection.

19 Ἐπιλαβόμενοί τε αὐτοῦ ἐπὶ τὸν Ἄρειον πάγον ἤγαγον λέγοντες·

δυνάμεθα γνῶναι τίς ἡ καινὴ αὕτη ἡ ὑπὸ σοῦ λαλουμένη διδαχή; 20 ξενίζοντα γάρ τινα εἰσφέρεις εἰς τὰς ἀκοὰς ἡμῶν· βουλόμεθα οὖν γνῶναι τίνα θέλει ταῦτα εἶναι.

21 Ἀθηναῖοι δὲ πάντες καὶ οἱ ἐπιδημοῦντες ξένοι εἰς οὐδὲν ἕτερον ηὐκαίρουν ἢ λέγειν τι ἢ ἀκούειν τι καινότερον.

22 Σταθεὶς δὲ Παῦλος ἐν μέσῳ τοῦ Ἀρείου πάγου ἔφη·

ἄνδρες Ἀθηναῖοι, κατὰ πάντα ὡς δεισιδαιμονεστέρους ὑμᾶς θεωρῶ· 23 διερχόμενος γὰρ καὶ ἀναθεωρῶν τὰ σεβάσματα ὑμῶν εὗρον καὶ βωμὸν ἐν ᾧ ἐπεγέγραπτο· ἀγνώστῳ θεῷ. ὃ οὖν ἀγνοοῦντες εὐσεβεῖτε, τοῦτο ἐγὼ καταγγέλλω ὑμῖν.

TO A GOD WHO IS NOT KNOWN

24 ὁ θεὸς ὁ ποιήσας τὸν κόσμον καὶ πάντα τὰ ἐν αὐτῷ, οὗτος οὐρανοῦ καὶ γῆς ὑπάρχων κύριος οὐκ ἐν χειροποιήτοις ναοῖς κατοικεῖ, 25 οὐδὲ ὑπὸ χειρῶν ἀνθρωπίνων θεραπεύεται προσδεόμενός τινος, αὐτὸς διδοὺς πᾶσι ζωὴν καὶ πνοὴν καὶ τὰ πάντα·

26 ἐποίησέν τε ἐξ ἑνὸς πᾶν ἔθνος ἀνθρώπων κατοικεῖν ἐπὶ παντὸς προσώπου τῆς γῆς, ὁρίσας προστεταγμένους καιροὺς καὶ τὰς ὁροθεσίας τῆς κατοικίας αὐτῶν 27 ζητεῖν τὸν θεόν, εἰ ἄρα γε ψηλαφήσειαν αὐτὸν καὶ εὕροιεν, καί γε οὐ μακρὰν ἀπὸ ἑνὸς ἑκάστου ἡμῶν ὑπάρχοντα.

19 At the same time, taking hold of him, they brought him to the Areopagus, saying, "Are we able to know what this new teaching is that is being spoken by you? 20 For you are bringing certain strange things to our ears. Therefore, we are wanting to know what these things mean." 21 Now all the Athenians and the foreigners living there enjoyed spending their time in nothing other than to say something or to hear something rather novel. 22 So, Paul, standing in the middle of the Areopagus, was saying, "Athenian Men, in every way I perceive you as being rather reverent of the gods. 23 For, passing along and observing the objects of your worship, I found also an altar on which it had been inscribed: 'TO AN UNKNOWN GOD.' Therefore, that which, being uninformed about, you worship, I am announcing to you! 24 The God who made the world and all things in it, this One, being in fact Lord of heaven and earth, does not dwell in hand made temples, 25 nor by human hands is he served, [as though] needing anything, he himself giving to all life and breath and all things. 26 At the same time, he made from one person every nation of humans to dwell upon all the face of the earth, determining appointed seasons and the boundaries of their habitation 27 to be seeking God, if then indeed they might reach out for him and find him, also indeed being in fact not far from each one of us.

28 ἐν αὐτῷ γὰρ ζῶμεν καὶ κεινούμεθα καὶ ἐσμέν, ὡς καί τινες τῶν καθ' ὑμᾶς ποιητῶν εἰρήκασιν· τοῦ γὰρ καὶ γένος ἐσμέν. 29 γένος οὖν ὑπάρχοντες τοῦ θεοῦ οὐκ ὀφείλομεν νομίζειν χρυσῷ ἢ ἀργύρῳ ἢ λίθῳ, χαράγματι τέχνης καὶ ἐνθυμήσεως ἀνθρώπου, τὸ θεῖον εἶναι ὅμοιον.

30 τοὺς μὲν οὖν χρόνους τῆς ἀγνοίας ὑπεριδὼν ὁ θεὸς τὰ νῦν παραγγέλλει τοῖς ἀνθρώποις πάντας πανταχοῦ μετανοεῖν·

31 καθότι ἔστησεν ἡμέραν ἐν ᾗ μέλλει κρίνειν τὴν οἰκουμένην ἐν δικαιοσύνῃ ἐν ἀνδρὶ ᾧ ὥρισεν πίστιν παρασχὼν πᾶσιν, ἀναστήσας αὐτὸν ἐκ νεκρῶν.

32 Ἀκούσαντες δὲ ἀνάστασιν νεκρῶν οἱ μὲν ἐχλεύαζον, οἱ δὲ εἶπαν· ἀκουσόμεθά σου περὶ τούτου καὶ πάλιν.

33 οὕτως ὁ Παῦλος ἐξῆλθεν ἐκ μέσου αὐτῶν. 34 Τινὲς δὲ ἄνδρες κολληθέντες αὐτῷ ἐπίστευσαν, ἐν οἷς καὶ Διονύσιος ὁ Ἀρεοπαγίτης καὶ γυνὴ ὀνόματι Δάμαρις καὶ ἕτεροι σὺν αὐτοῖς.

28 'For in him we live and move and exist,' as also some of your own poets have said, 'For we are also his offspring.' 29 Therefore, being in fact offspring of God, we ought not to think the Divine Nature to be like gold or silver or stone—the representation from the art and idea of a person! 30 So then, overlooking the times of ignorance, presently now he issues a command to persons that everywhere all should repent, 31 because he appointed a day on which he determines to judge the inhabited world in justice by a man whom he has determined, offering proof/faith to all people [by] raising him from the dead." 32 Now, having heard about the resurrection of the dead, some were mocking; but others said, "We will hear you concerning this also again." 33 Thus Paul went out from the middle of them. 34 But certain men, being joined to him, believed, among whom also was Dionysius the Areopagite and a woman, Damaris by name, and others with them.

Κεφ. ΙΗ´

18:1 Μετὰ ταῦτα χωρισθεὶς ἐκ τῶν Ἀθηνῶν ἦλθεν εἰς Κόρινθον,

2 καὶ εὑρών τινα Ἰουδαῖον ὀνόματι Ἀκύλαν, Ποντικὸν τῷ γένει, προσφάτως ἐληλυθότα ἀπὸ τῆς Ἰταλίας, καὶ Πρίσκιλλαν γυναῖκα αὐτοῦ, διὰ τὸ διατεταχέναι Κλαύδιον χωρίζεσθαι πάντας τοὺς Ἰουδαίους ἀπὸ τῆς Ῥώμης, προσῆλθεν αὐτοῖς·

3 καὶ διὰ τὸ ὁμότεχνον εἶναι ἔμενεν παρ᾽ αὐτοῖς καὶ ἠργάζετο· ἦσαν γὰρ σκηνοποιοὶ τῇ τέχνῃ·

4 διελέγετο δὲ ἐν τῇ συναγωγῇ κατὰ πᾶν σάββατον, ἔπειθέν τε Ἰουδαίους καὶ Ἕλληνας.

5 Ὡς δὲ κατῆλθον ἀπὸ τῆς Μακεδονίας ὅ τε Σίλας καὶ ὁ Τιμόθεος, συνείχετο τῷ λόγῳ ὁ Παῦλος διαμαρτυρόμενος τοῖς Ἰουδαίοις εἶναι τὸν χριστὸν Ἰησοῦν.

18:1 After these things, being separated from Athens, he came to Corinth. 2 And finding a certain Judean, Aquila by name, a man of Pontus by race, having come recently from Italy, and his wife Priscilla, because Claudius had commanded all the Judeans to be separated from Rome, he came to them, 3 and, because he practiced the same trade, he remained with them and was working; for by trade they were tent makers. 4 Moreover, he was reasoning in the synagogue every Sabbath, and at the same time he was persuading Judeans and Greeks. 5 But, when both Silas and Timothy came down from Macedonia, Paul was completely occupied with the Word, testifying to the Judeans that the Christ was Jesus.

6 Ἀντιτασσομένων δὲ αὐτῶν καὶ βλασφημούντων, ἐκτιναξάμενος τὰ ἱμάτια εἶπεν πρὸς αὐτούς·

τὸ αἷμα ὑμῶν ἐπὶ τὴν κεφαλὴν ὑμῶν, καθαρὸς ἐγώ· ἀπὸ τοῦ νῦν εἰς τὰ ἔθνη πορεύσομαι.

7 Καὶ μεταβὰς ἐκεῖθεν ἦλθεν εἰς οἰκίαν τινὸς ὀνόματι Ἰούστου σεβομένου τὸν θεόν, οὗ ἡ οἰκία ἦν συνομοροῦσα τῇ συναγωγῇ.

8 Κρίσπος δὲ ὁ ἀρχισυνάγωγος ἐπίστευσεν τῷ κυρίῳ σὺν ὅλῳ τῷ οἴκῳ αὐτοῦ, καὶ πολλοὶ τῶν Κορινθίων ἀκούοντες ἐπίστευον καὶ ἐβαπτίζοντο.

9 Εἶπεν δὲ ὁ κύριος ἐν νυκτὶ δι' ὁράματος τῷ Παύλῳ·

μὴ φοβοῦ ἀλλὰ λάλει καὶ μὴ σιωπήσῃς, 10 διότι ἐγώ εἰμι μετὰ σοῦ, καὶ οὐδεὶς ἐπιθήσεταί σοι τοῦ κακῶσαί σε· διότι λαός ἐστί μοι πολὺς ἐν τῇ πόλει ταύτῃ·

11 ἐκάθισεν δὲ ἐνιαυτὸν καὶ μῆνας ἓξ διδάσκων ἐν αὐτοῖς τὸν λόγον τοῦ θεοῦ.

6 But, while they were opposing him and slandering, shaking out his garments, he said to them, "Your blood is on your heads! I am clean! From now on, I will go to the Gentiles!" 7 And passing from there, he went into the house of a certain man, Justus by name, one worshipping God, whose house was adjoined to the synagogue. 8 So, Crispus, the ruler of the synagogue, believed in the Lord with his whole house, and many of the Corinthians, hearing, were believing and were being baptized. 9 Moreover, the Lord said to Paul in the night by a vision, "Do not be afraid, but continue speaking and do not be silent; 10 for I myself am with you, and no one will attack you in order to harm you, for numerous people of mine are in this city." 11 So, he sat there a year and six months, teaching the Word of God among them.

12 But, with Gallio being proconsul of Achaia, the Judeans with one accord rose up against Paul and brought him to the judgment seat, 13 saying this: "This person persuades people to be worshiping God contrary to the Law!" 14 But, with Paul being about to open his mouth, Gallio said to the Judeans, "If, on the one hand, it were some wrong or wicked crime, O Judeans, for each matter I would be putting up with you; 15 but, on the other hand, if they are questions about speech and names and your particular Law, you will see [to it] yourselves; I myself am not wanting to be a judge of these matters!" 16 And he expelled them from the judgment seat. 17 Moreover, seizing Sosthenes, the ruler of the synagogue, all were beating him before the judgment seat; and nothing of these things was concerning to Gallio.

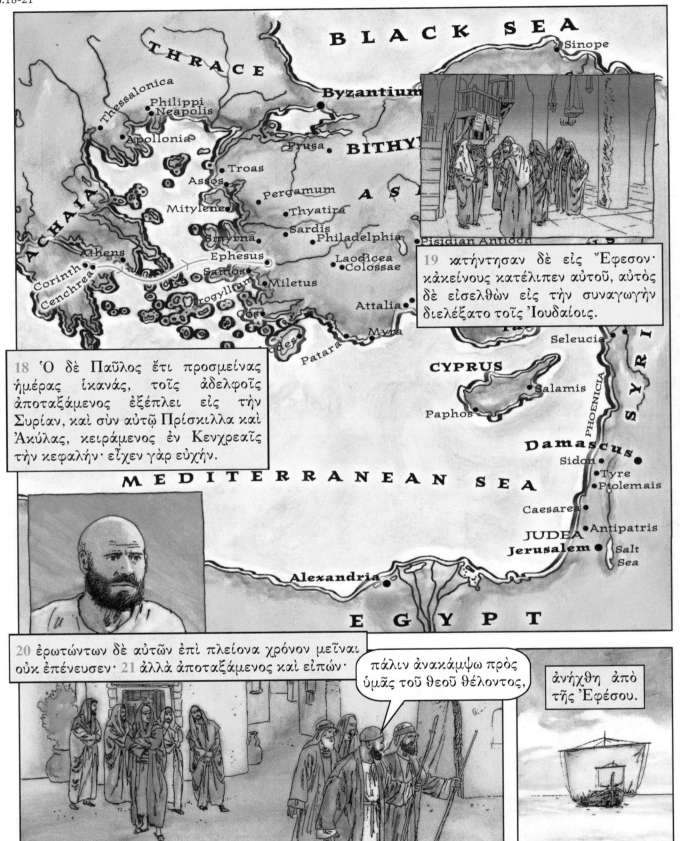

19 κατήντησαν δὲ εἰς Ἔφεσον· κἀκείνους κατέλιπεν αὐτοῦ, αὐτὸς δὲ εἰσελθὼν εἰς τὴν συναγωγὴν διελέξατο τοῖς Ἰουδαίοις.

18 Ὁ δὲ Παῦλος ἔτι προσμείνας ἡμέρας ἱκανάς, τοῖς ἀδελφοῖς ἀποταξάμενος ἐξέπλει εἰς τὴν Συρίαν, καὶ σὺν αὐτῷ Πρίσκιλλα καὶ Ἀκύλας, κειράμενος ἐν Κεγχρεαῖς τὴν κεφαλήν· εἶχεν γὰρ εὐχήν.

20 ἐρωτώντων δὲ αὐτῶν ἐπὶ πλείονα χρόνον μεῖναι οὐκ ἐπένευσεν· **21** ἀλλὰ ἀποταξάμενος καὶ εἰπών·

πάλιν ἀνακάμψω πρὸς ὑμᾶς τοῦ θεοῦ θέλοντος,

ἀνήχθη ἀπὸ τῆς Ἐφέσου.

18 Next, Paul, still staying for considerable days, saying farewell to the brothers, was sailing into Syria (and with him were Priscilla and Aquila), shaving his head in Cenchrea, for he was holding a vow. 19 So, he came down into Ephesus; and he left them there, but he himself, entering into the synagogue, reasoned with the Judeans. 20 Moreover, with them asking him to stay for a longer time, he declined; 21 but bidding farewell and saying, "Again I will return to you, God willing," he set sail from Ephesus.

22 καὶ κατελθὼν εἰς Καισάρειαν, ἀναβὰς καὶ ἀσπασάμενος τὴν ἐκκλησίαν κατέβη εἰς Ἀντιόχειαν·

23 καὶ ποιήσας χρόνον τινὰ ἐξῆλθεν διερχόμενος καθεξῆς τὴν Γαλατικὴν χώραν καὶ Φρυγίαν, στηρίζων πάντας τοὺς μαθητάς.

24 Ἰουδαῖος δέ τις Ἀπολλὼς ὀνόματι, Ἀλεξανδρεὺς τῷ γένει, ἀνὴρ λόγιος, κατήντησεν εἰς Ἔφεσον δυνατὸς ὢν ἐν ταῖς γραφαῖς.

25 οὗτος ἦν κατηχημένος τὴν ὁδὸν τοῦ κυρίου, καὶ ζέων τῷ πνεύματι ἐλάλει καὶ ἐδίδασκεν ἀκριβῶς τὰ περὶ τοῦ Ἰησοῦ ἐπιστάμενος μόνον τὸ βάπτισμα Ἰωάννου· 26a οὗτός τε ἤρξατο παρρησιάζεσθαι ἐν τῇ συναγωγῇ.

26b ἀκούσαντες δὲ αὐτοῦ Πρίσκιλλα καὶ Ἀκύλας προσελάβοντο αὐτὸν καὶ ἀκριβέστερον αὐτῷ ἐξέθεντο τὴν ὁδὸν τοῦ θεοῦ.

27 βουλομένου δὲ αὐτοῦ διελθεῖν εἰς τὴν Ἀχαΐαν, προτρεψάμενοι οἱ ἀδελφοὶ ἔγραψαν τοῖς μαθηταῖς ἀποδέξασθαι αὐτόν· ὃς παραγενόμενος συνεβάλετο πολὺ τοῖς πεπιστευκόσιν διὰ τῆς χάριτος·

22 And putting in at Caesarea, going up and greeting the assembly, he went down to Antioch. 23 And spending some time [there], he departed, successively going throughout the region of Galatia and Phrygia establishing all the disciples. 24 Now a certain Judean, Apollos by name, an Alexandrian by race, a learned man, came down into Ephesus, being competent in the Scriptures. 25 This man had been instructed in the Way of the Lord, and being zealous in spirit, he was speaking and was teaching accurately the things concerning Jesus, [although] knowing only the baptism of John. 26 At the same time, this person began to be speaking boldly in the synagogue. But, hearing him, Priscilla and Aquila took him in and more accurately set out for him the Way of God. 27 So, with his wanting to pass over into Achaia, encouraging [him], the brothers wrote to the disciples to receive him, who arriving contributed greatly to the ones having believed through grace;

91

28 εὐτόνως γὰρ τοῖς Ἰουδαίοις δια-κατηλέγχετο δημοσίᾳ ἐπιδεικνὺς διὰ τῶν γραφῶν εἶναι τὸν χριστὸν Ἰησοῦν.

Κεφ. ΙΘ΄

19:1 Ἐγένετο δὲ ἐν τῷ τὸν Ἀπολλὼ εἶναι ἐν Κορίνθῳ, Παῦλον διελθόντα τὰ ἀνωτερικὰ μέρη ἐλθεῖν εἰς Ἔφεσον καὶ εὑρεῖν τινας μαθητάς,

2 εἶπέν τε πρὸς αὐτούς·

εἰ πνεῦμα ἅγιον ἐλάβετε πιστεύσαντες;

οἱ δὲ πρὸς αὐτόν·

ἀλλ' οὐδ' εἰ πνεῦμα ἅγιόν ἐστιν ἠκούσαμεν.

3 εἶπέν τε·

εἰς τί οὖν ἐβαπτίσθητε;

οἱ δὲ εἶπαν·

εἰς τὸ Ἰωάννου βάπτισμα.

4 Εἶπεν δὲ Παῦλος·

Ἰωάννης ἐβάπτισεν βάπτισμα μετανοίας τῷ λαῷ λέγων εἰς τὸν ἐρχόμενον μετ' αὐτὸν ἵνα πιστεύσωσιν, τουτέστιν εἰς τὸν Ἰησοῦν.

5 ἀκούσαντες δὲ ἐβαπτίσθησαν εἰς τὸ ὄνομα τοῦ κυρίου Ἰησοῦ· 6 καὶ ἐπιθέντος αὐτοῖς τοῦ Παύλου χεῖρας ἦλθε τὸ πνεῦμα τὸ ἅγιον ἐπ'

αὐτούς, ἐλάλουν τε γλώσσαις καὶ ἐπροφήτευον. 7 ἦσαν δὲ οἱ πάντες ἄνδρες ὡσεὶ δώδεκα.

28 for he powerfully was thoroughly refuting the Judeans, publicly showing through the Scriptures that the Christ was Jesus. 19:1 Now, it happened that while Apollos was at Corinth, Paul, passing through the upper regions, came into Ephesus and found certain disciples. 2 At the same time, he said to them, "Did you receive the Holy Spirit having believed?" And they said to him, "No, rather neither did we hear whether there is a Holy Spirit!" 3 Additionally, he said, "Into what, therefore, were you baptized?" And they said, "Into John's baptism." 4 So, Paul said, "John indeed baptized with a baptism of repentance, speaking to the people in order that, in the One coming after him, they should believe, that is, in Jesus." 5 Moreover, hearing this, they were baptized into the name of the Lord Jesus, 6 and, with Paul laying his hands on them, the Holy Spirit came upon them, and at the same time they were speaking with other languages and were prophesying. 7 Additionally, all the men were about twelve [in number].

8 Εἰσελθὼν δὲ εἰς τὴν συναγωγὴν ἐπαρρησιάζετο ἐπὶ μῆνας τρεῖς διαλεγόμενος καὶ πείθων τὰ περὶ τῆς βασιλείας τοῦ θεοῦ.

9 ὡς δέ τινες ἐσκληρύνοντο καὶ ἠπείθουν κακολογοῦντες τὴν ὁδὸν ἐνώπιον τοῦ πλήθους,

9b ἀποστὰς ἀπ᾽ αὐτῶν ἀφώρισεν τοὺς μαθητὰς καθ᾽ ἡμέραν διαλεγόμενος ἐν τῇ σχολῇ Τυράννου.

10 τοῦτο δὲ ἐγένετο ἐπὶ ἔτη δύο, ὥστε πάντας τοὺς κατοικοῦντας τὴν Ἀσίαν ἀκοῦσαι τὸν λόγον τοῦ κυρίου, Ἰουδαίους τε καὶ Ἕλληνας.

11 δυνάμεις τε οὐ τὰς τυχούσας ὁ θεὸς ἐποίει διὰ τῶν χειρῶν Παύλου, 12 ὥστε καὶ ἐπὶ τοὺς ἀσθενοῦντας ἀποφέρεσθαι ἀπὸ τοῦ χρωτὸς αὐτοῦ σουδάρια ἢ σιμικίνθια καὶ ἀπαλλάσσεσθαι ἀπ᾽ αὐτῶν τὰς νόσους τά τε πνεύματα τὰ πονηρὰ ἐκπορεύεσθαι.

13 Ἐπεχείρησαν δέ τινες καὶ τῶν περιερχομένων Ἰουδαίων ἐξορκιστῶν ὀνομάζειν ἐπὶ τοὺς ἔχοντας τὰ πνεύματα τὰ πονηρὰ τὸ ὄνομα τοῦ κυρίου Ἰησοῦ λέγοντες·

ὁρκίζω ὑμᾶς τὸν Ἰησοῦν ὃν Παῦλος κηρύσσει.

14 ἦσαν δέ τινος Σκευᾶ Ἰουδαίου ἀρχιερέως ἑπτὰ υἱοὶ τοῦτο ποιοῦντες.

8 Next, entering into the synagogue, he was speaking boldly for three months, reasoning and persuading about the things concerning the kingdom of God. 9 But when some were being hardened and were disbelieving, speaking evil of the Way before the multitude, giving up on them, he separated the disciples, each day reasoning in the lecture hall of Tyrannus. 10 Now, this occurred for two years with the result that all those residing in Asia heard the Word of the Lord, both Judeans and Greeks. 11 At the same time, God was working not coincidental miracles through the hands of Paul, 12 with the result that, even to the sick, handkerchiefs or aprons were being carried away from his body and the diseases were departing from them; at the same time the evil spirits were going out. 13 But some also of the itinerant Judeans, exorcists, attempted to invoke over those having evil spirits the name of the Lord Jesus, saying, "We adjure you by the Jesus whom Paul is preaching." 14 Now, doing this were the seven sons of one Sceva, a Judean chief priest.

15 ἀποκριθὲν δὲ τὸ πνεῦμα τὸ πονηρὸν εἶπεν αὐτοῖς·

τὸν Ἰησοῦν γινώσκω καὶ τὸν Παῦλον ἐπίσταμαι· ὑμεῖς δὲ τίνες ἐστέ;

16 καὶ ἐφαλόμενος ὁ ἄνθρωπος ἐπ' αὐτούς, ἐν ᾧ ἦν τὸ πνεῦμα τὸ πονηρόν, κατακυριεύσας ἀμφοτέρων ἴσχυσεν κατ' αὐτῶν, ὥστε γυμνοὺς καὶ τετραυματισμένους ἐκφυγεῖν ἐκ τοῦ οἴκου ἐκείνου.

17 τοῦτο δὲ ἐγένετο γνωστὸν πᾶσιν Ἰουδαίοις τε καὶ Ἕλλησιν τοῖς κατοικοῦσιν τὴν Ἔφεσον καὶ ἐπέπεσεν φόβος ἐπὶ πάντας αὐτούς, καὶ ἐμεγαλύνετο τὸ ὄνομα τοῦ κυρίου Ἰησοῦ, 18 πολλοί τε τῶν πεπιστευκότων ἤρχοντο ἐξομολογούμενοι καὶ ἀναγγέλλοντες τὰς πράξεις αὐτῶν.

19 ἱκανοὶ δὲ τῶν τὰ περίεργα πραξάντων συνενέγκαντες τὰς βίβλους κατέκαιον ἐνώπιον πάντων· καὶ συνεψήφισαν τὰς τιμὰς αὐτῶν καὶ εὗρον ἀργυρίου μυριάδας πέντε.

20 οὕτως κατὰ κράτος τοῦ κυρίου ὁ λόγος ηὔξανεν καὶ ἴσχυεν.

15 But, answering back, the evil spirit said to them, "Jesus I know, and Paul I know, but you, who are you guys?!" 16 And the man, in whom was the evil spirit, jumping upon them, overpowering each, prevailed against them with the result that they fled out of that house naked and having been wounded. 17 So, this became known to all—both Judeans and Greeks—who resided in Ephesus and fear fell upon them all, and the name of the Lord Jesus was being exalted. 18 At the same time, many of the ones who had believed were coming, confessing and reporting their deeds. 19 Moreover, considerable numbers of the ones who practiced the magical arts, bringing their books together, were burning [them] in the sight of all. And they counted their value and found [it to be] fifty thousand pieces of silver! 20 Thus, with strength the Word of the Lord was growing and having power.

21 Ὡς δὲ ἐπληρώθη ταῦτα, ἔθετο ὁ Παῦλος ἐν τῷ πνεύματι διελθὼν τὴν Μακεδονίαν καὶ Ἀχαΐαν πορεύεσθαι εἰς Ἱεροσόλυμα εἰπὼν ὅτι

μετὰ τὸ γενέσθαι με ἐκεῖ, δεῖ με καὶ Ῥώμην ἰδεῖν.

22 ἀποστείλας δὲ εἰς τὴν Μακεδονίαν δύο τῶν διακονούντων αὐτῷ, Τιμόθεον καὶ Ἔραστον, αὐτὸς ἐπέσχεν χρόνον εἰς τὴν Ἀσίαν.

23 Ἐγένετο δὲ κατὰ τὸν καιρὸν ἐκεῖνον τάραχος οὐκ ὀλίγος περὶ τῆς ὁδοῦ. 24 Δημήτριος γάρ τις ὀνόματι, ἀργυροκόπος ποιῶν ναοὺς ἀργυροῦς Ἀρτέμιδος, παρείχετο τοῖς τεχνίταις οὐκ ὀλίγην ἐργασίαν, 25 οὓς συναθροίσας καὶ τοὺς περὶ τὰ τοιαῦτα ἐργάτας εἶπεν·

ἄνδρες, ἐπίστασθε ὅτι ἐκ ταύτης τῆς ἐργασίας ἡ εὐπορία ἡμῖν ἐστιν, 26 καὶ θεωρεῖτε καὶ ἀκούετε ὅτι οὐ μόνον Ἐφέσου ἀλλὰ σχεδὸν πάσης τῆς Ἀσίας ὁ Παῦλος οὗτος πείσας μετέστησεν ἱκανὸν ὄχλον λέγων ὅτι οὐκ εἰσὶν θεοὶ οἱ διὰ χειρῶν γινόμενοι.

21 Now when these things were completed, Paul determined in the Spirit, passing through Macedonia and Achaia, to go into Jerusalem, saying this: "After I have been there, it is necessary that I see also Rome." 22 So, sending into Macedonia two of the ones ministering to him, Timothy and Erastus, he himself stayed back for a time in Asia. 23 Moreover, it happened about that time there was no small disturbance concerning the Way. 24 For a certain person, Demetrius by name, a silversmith making silver shrines of Artemis, was supplying no little business for the craftsmen, 25 to whom, gathering also with the workmen of such things, he said, "Men, you know that from this business we have our wealth, 26 and you are beholding and hearing that not at Ephesus alone, but nearly throughout all Asia, this Paul, with persuading, turned away a considerable crowd, saying that they are not gods which are being made through hands!

27 οὐ μόνον δὲ τοῦτο κινδυνεύει ἡμῖν τὸ μέρος εἰς ἀπελεγμὸν ἐλθεῖν ἀλλὰ καὶ τὸ τῆς μεγάλης θεᾶς Ἀρτέμιδος ἱερὸν εἰς οὐθὲν λογισθῆναι, μέλλειν τε καὶ καθαιρεῖσθαι τῆς μεγαλειότητος αὐτῆς ἣν ὅλη ἡ Ἀσία καὶ ἡ οἰκουμένη σέβεται.

28 Ἀκούσαντες δὲ καὶ γενόμενοι πλήρεις θυμοῦ ἔκραζον λέγοντες·

μεγάλη ἡ Ἄρτεμις Ἐφεσίων.

29 καὶ ἐπλήσθη ἡ πόλις τῆς συγχύσεως· ὥρμησάν τε ὁμοθυμαδὸν εἰς τὸ θέατρον συναρπάσαντες Γάϊον καὶ Ἀρίσταρχον Μακεδόνας, συνεκδήμους Παύλου. 30 Παύλου δὲ βουλομένου εἰσελθεῖν εἰς τὸν δῆμον οὐκ εἴων αὐτὸν οἱ μαθηταί· 31 τινὲς δὲ καὶ τῶν Ἀσιαρχῶν ὄντες αὐτῷ φίλοι, πέμψαντες πρὸς αὐτὸν παρεκάλουν μὴ δοῦναι ἑαυτὸν εἰς τὸ θέατρον. 32 ἄλλοι μὲν οὖν ἄλλο τι ἔκραζον· ἦν γὰρ ἡ ἐκκλησία συνκεχυμένη, καὶ οἱ πλείους οὐκ ᾔδεισαν τίνος ἕνεκα συνεληλύθεισαν.

27 But, not only is this risking the share of ours to come into disrepute, but also [risking] the temple of the great goddess Artemis to be accounted for nothing, and at the same time to destine also to destroy her majesty, whom the whole of Asia and inhabited [Roman] world worships!" 28 So, hearing and becoming full of wrath, they were crying out, saying, "Great is Artemis of the Ephesians!" 29 And the city was filled with confusion. At the same time, they rushed together into the theater, seizing Gaius and Aristarchus, men of Macedonia, travel companions of Paul. 30 Moreover, with Paul wanting to enter to the people, the disciples were not allowing him. 31 Additionally, certain persons also of the Asiarchs, being friends of his, sending to him, were imploring not to bring himself into the theater. 32 So then, different ones were shouting something different; for the assembly was in confusion and the majority did not know for what reason they had come together.

μεγάλη ἡ Ἄρτεμις Ἐφεσίων.

33 ἐκ δὲ τοῦ ὄχλου συνεβίβασαν Ἀλέξανδρον προβαλόντων αὐτὸν τῶν Ἰουδαίων· ὁ δὲ Ἀλέξανδρος κατασείσας τὴν χεῖρα ἤθελεν ἀπολογεῖσθαι τῷ δήμῳ. 34 ἐπιγνόντες δὲ ὅτι Ἰουδαῖός ἐστιν, φωνὴ ἐγένετο μία ἐκ πάντων ὡς ἐπὶ ὥρας δύο κραζόντων·

35 καταστείλας δὲ ὁ γραμματεὺς τὸν ὄχλον φησίν·

ἄνδρες Ἐφέσιοι, τίς γάρ ἐστιν ἀνθρώπων ὃς οὐ γινώσκει τὴν Ἐφεσίων πόλιν νεωκόρον οὖσαν τῆς μεγάλης Ἀρτέμιδος καὶ τοῦ διοπετοῦς; 36 ἀναντιρρήτων οὖν ὄντων τούτων δέον ἐστὶν ὑμᾶς κατεσταλμένους ὑπάρχειν καὶ μηδὲν προπετὲς πράσσειν. 37 ἠγάγετε γὰρ τοὺς ἄνδρας τούτους οὔτε ἱεροσύλους οὔτε βλασφημοῦντας τὴν θεὸν ἡμῶν. 38 εἰ μὲν οὖν Δημήτριος καὶ οἱ σὺν αὐτῷ τεχνῖται ἔχουσι πρός τινα λόγον, ἀγοραῖοι ἄγονται καὶ ἀνθύπατοί εἰσιν· ἐγκαλείτωσαν ἀλλήλοις. 39 εἰ δέ τι περαιτέρω ἐπιζητεῖτε, ἐν τῇ ἐννόμῳ ἐκκλησίᾳ ἐπιλυθήσεται.

33 Then, from the crowd they united around Alexander, the Judeans having put him forward. So, Alexander, motioning down by hand, was wanting to make a defense to the people. 34 But learning that he was a Judean, one voice came from all for about two hours crying out, "Great is Artemis of the Ephesians!" 35 So, restraining the crowd, the town clerk says, "Ephesian men, who among people, indeed, is there who does not know that the city of the Ephesians is temple keeper of the great goddess Artemis and of the image fallen from Zeus? 36 Therefore, with these things being indisputable, it is a necessity that you should in fact be calmed down and do nothing reckless! 37 For you have brought these men here, neither robbers of temples nor blaspheming your goddess. 38 So then, if Demetrius and the craftsmen with him have a matter against anyone, the courts are being directed and there are proconsuls. Let them press charges against one another. 39 But if you are seeking anything further, it will be settled in the lawful assembly.

40* καὶ γὰρ κινδυνεύομεν ἐγκαλεῖσθαι στάσεως περὶ τῆς σήμερον μηδενὸς αἰτίου ὑπάρχοντος περὶ οὗ οὐ δυνησόμεθα ἀποδοῦναι λόγον περὶ τῆς συστροφῆς ταύτης.

καὶ ταῦτα εἰπὼν ἀπέλυσεν τὴν ἐκκλησίαν.

Κεφ. Κ´

20:1 Μετὰ δὲ τὸ παύσασθαι τὸν θόρυβον μεταπεμψάμενος ὁ Παῦλος τοὺς μαθητὰς καὶ παρακαλέσας ἀσπασά-μενος ἐξῆλθεν πορεύεσθαι εἰς Μακεδονίαν.

2 Διελθὼν δὲ τὰ μέρη ἐκεῖνα καὶ παρακαλέσας αὐτοὺς λόγῳ πολλῷ ἦλθεν εἰς τὴν Ἑλλάδα· 3 ποιήσας τε μῆνας τρεῖς, γενομένης ἐπιβουλῆς αὐτῷ ὑπὸ τῶν Ἰουδαίων μέλλοντι ἀνάγεσθαι εἰς τὴν Συρίαν, ἐγένετο γνώμης τοῦ ὑποστρέφειν διὰ Μακεδονίας.

40 For we are also risking being accused of a riot concerning today's events with there being in fact no reason for which we would be able to give an account of this mass gathering." And saying these things, he dismissed the assembly. 20:1 Now, after the uproar ceased, sending for the disciples and encouraging [them], having said farewell, Paul departed to travel into Macedonia. 2 So, going through those regions and encouraging them with a substantial message, he came into Greece. 3 At the same time, spending three months [there], after a plot was made against him by Judeans with him about to set sail for Syria, the opinion was that he should return through Macedonia.

4 συνείπετο δὲ αὐτῷ ἄχρι τῆς Ἀσίας Σώπατρος Πύρρου Βεροιαῖος, Θεσσαλονικέων δὲ Ἀρίσταρχος καὶ Σεκοῦνδος καὶ Γάϊος Δερβαῖος καὶ Τιμόθεος· Ἀσιανοὶ δὲ Τυχικὸς καὶ Τρόφιμος,

5 οὗτοι δὲ προσελθόντες ἔμενον ἡμᾶς ἐν Τρῳάδι· 6 ἡμεῖς δὲ ἐξεπλεύσαμεν μετὰ τὰς ἡμέρας τῶν ἀζύμων ἀπὸ Φιλίππων καὶ ἤλθομεν πρὸς αὐτοὺς εἰς τὴν Τρῳάδα ἄχρι ἡμερῶν πέντε οὗ διετρίψαμεν ἡμέρας ἑπτά.

7 Ἐν δὲ τῇ μιᾷ τῶν σαββάτων συνηγμένων ἡμῶν κλάσαι ἄρτον ὁ Παῦλος διελέγετο αὐτοῖς μέλλων ἐξιέναι τῇ ἐπαύριον παρέτεινέν τε τὸν λόγον μέχρι μεσονυκτίου· 8 ἦσαν δὲ λαμπάδες ἱκαναὶ ἐν τῷ ὑπερῴῳ οὗ ἦμεν συνηγμένοι. 9a καθεζόμενος δέ τις νεανίας ὀνόματι Εὔτυχος ἐπὶ τῆς θυρίδος, καταφερόμενος ὕπνῳ βαθεῖ, διαλεγομένου τοῦ Παύλου ἐπὶ πλεῖον,

4 Now, Sopater of Berea accompanied him as far as Asia; moreover, from the Thessalonians were Aristarchus and Secundus and Gaius of Derbe and Timothy; additionally, from Asia were Tychicus and Trophimus. 5 But these, going ahead, were awaiting us at Troas. 6 But we ourselves sailed away from Philippi after the days of Unleavened Bread and came to them at Troas five days later, where we stayed seven days. 7 Moreover, on the first day of the week, with us having gathered together to break bread, Paul was conversing with them, intending to depart on the next day; at the same time, he was prolonging his message until midnight. 8 Now, a sufficient number of lamps were in the upper room where we had gathered together. 9 But, a certain young man, Eutychus by name, sitting in the window, being weighed down with deep sleep with Paul conversing still longer,

99

9b κατενεχθεὶς ἀπὸ τοῦ ὕπνου ἔπεσεν ἀπὸ τοῦ τριστέγου κάτω καὶ ἤρθη νεκρός.

10 καταβὰς δὲ ὁ Παῦλος ἐπέπεσεν αὐτῷ καὶ συν-περιλαβὼν εἶπεν·

μὴ θορυβεῖσθε· ἡ γὰρ ψυχὴ αὐτοῦ ἐν αὐτῷ ἐστιν.

11 ἀναβὰς δὲ καὶ κλάσας τὸν ἄρτον καὶ γευσάμενος, ἐφ᾽ ἱκανόν τε ὁμιλήσας ἄχρι αὐγῆς, οὕτως ἐξῆλθεν. 12 ἤγαγον δὲ τὸν παῖδα ζῶντα καὶ παρεκλήθησαν οὐ μετρίως.

13 Ἡμεῖς δὲ προσελθόντες ἐπὶ τὸ πλοῖον ἀνήχθημεν ἐπὶ τὴν Ἄσσον, ἐκεῖθεν μέλλοντες ἀναλαμβάνειν τὸν Παῦλον· οὕτως γὰρ διατεταγμένος ἦν, μέλλων αὐτὸς πεζεύειν.

9b sinking down from sleep, he fell down from the third floor and was lifted up as dead. 10 But, going down, Paul fell upon him and embracing said, "Do not be troubled! For his life is in him!" 11 So, going up and breaking bread and eating, at the same time talking sufficiently until daybreak, he departed. 12 Moreover, they brought the boy in alive and were greatly comforted not moderately! 13 But we ourselves, going ahead to the ship, set sail for Assos, from there intending to take Paul aboard; for he had so arranged, intending himself to go on foot.

14 ὡς δὲ συνέβαλλεν ἡμῖν εἰς τὴν Ἄσσον, ἀναλαβόντες αὐτὸν ἤλθομεν εἰς Μιτυλήνην· κἀκεῖθεν ἀποπλεύσαντες τῇ ἐπιούσῃ κατηντήσαμεν ἄντικρυς Χίου, τῇ δὲ ἑτέρᾳ παρεβάλομεν εἰς Σάμον, τῇ δὲ ἐχομένῃ ἤλθομεν εἰς Μίλητον.

16 κεκρίκει γὰρ ὁ Παῦλος παραπλεῦσαι τὴν Ἔφεσον, ὅπως μὴ γένηται αὐτῷ χρονοτριβῆσαι ἐν τῇ Ἀσίᾳ· ἔσπευδεν γὰρ εἰ δυνατὸν εἴη αὐτῷ τὴν ἡμέραν τῆς Πεντηκοστῆς γενέσθαι εἰς Ἱεροσόλυμα. 17 Ἀπὸ δὲ τῆς Μιλήτου πέμψας εἰς Ἔφεσον μετεκαλέσατο τοὺς πρεσβυτέρους τῆς ἐκκλησίας.

18 ὡς δὲ παρεγένοντο πρὸς αὐτὸν εἶπεν αὐτοῖς·

ὑμεῖς ἐπίστασθε ἀπὸ πρώτης ἡμέρας ἀφ᾽ ἧς ἐπέβην εἰς τὴν Ἀσίαν πῶς μεθ᾽ ὑμῶν τὸν πάντα χρόνον ἐγενόμην 19 δουλεύων τῷ κυρίῳ μετὰ πάσης ταπεινοφροσύνης καὶ δακρύων καὶ πειρασμῶν τῶν συμβάντων μοι ἐν ταῖς ἐπιβουλαῖς τῶν Ἰουδαίων·

20 ὡς οὐδὲν ὑπεστειλάμην τῶν συμφερόντων τοῦ μὴ ἀναγγεῖλαι ὑμῖν καὶ διδάξαι ὑμᾶς δημοσίᾳ καὶ κατ᾽ οἴκους, 21 διαμαρτυρόμενος Ἰουδαίοις τε καὶ Ἕλλησιν τὴν εἰς θεὸν μετάνοιαν καὶ πίστιν εἰς τὸν κύριον ἡμῶν Ἰησοῦν.

14 Next, as he was meeting us at Assos, taking him aboard, we came into Mitylene. 15 Sailing from there on the following day, we arrived opposite Chios and on the next day we cast into Samos and on the day following we came into Miletus. 16 For Paul had determined to sail past Ephesus, in order that he would not have to spend time in Asia; for he was hastening, if it were possible for him, to be in Jerusalem during the day of Pentecost. 17 Next, from Miletus, sending into Ephesus, he called to himself the elders of the assembly. 18 So, when they had come to him, he said to them, "You yourselves know, from the first day upon which I set foot into Asia, how I was with you all the time, 19 serving the Lord with all humility and with many tears and with trials that met me by the plots of the Judeans; 20 how I did not in any single respect hold back from declaring to you anything that was profitable and teaching you publicly and from house-to-house, 21 testifying both to Judeans and to Greeks repentance toward God and faith toward our Lord, Jesus.

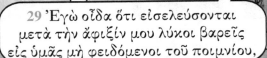

22 Καὶ νῦν ἰδοὺ δεδεμένος ἐγὼ τῷ πνεύματι πορεύομαι εἰς Ἰερουσαλὴμ τὰ ἐν αὐτῇ συναντήσοντά μοι μὴ εἰδώς, 23 πλὴν ὅτι τὸ πνεῦμα τὸ ἅγιον κατὰ πόλιν διαμαρτύρεταί μοι λέγον ὅτι δεσμὰ καὶ θλίψεις με μένουσιν.

24 ἀλλ' οὐδενὸς λόγου ποιοῦμαι τὴν ψυχὴν τιμίαν ἐμαυτῷ, ὡς τελειῶσαι τὸν δρόμον μου καὶ τὴν διακονίαν ἣν ἔλαβον παρὰ τοῦ κυρίου Ἰησοῦ, διαμαρτύρασθαι τὸ εὐαγγέλιον τῆς χάριτος τοῦ θεοῦ.

25 καὶ νῦν ἰδοὺ ἐγὼ οἶδα ὅτι οὐκέτι ὄψεσθε τὸ πρόσωπόν μου ὑμεῖς πάντες, ἐν οἷς διῆλθον κηρύσσων τὴν βασιλείαν. 26 διότι μαρτύρομαι ὑμῖν ἐν τῇ σήμερον ἡμέρᾳ ὅτι καθαρός εἰμι ἀπὸ τοῦ αἵματος πάντων· 27 οὐ γὰρ ὑπεστειλάμην τοῦ μὴ ἀναγγεῖλαι πᾶσαν τὴν βουλὴν τοῦ θεοῦ ὑμῖν.

28 προσέχετε ἑαυτοῖς καὶ παντὶ τῷ ποιμνίῳ, ἐν ᾧ ὑμᾶς τὸ πνεῦμα τὸ ἅγιον ἔθετο ἐπισκόπους, ποιμαίνειν τὴν ἐκκλησίαν τοῦ κυρίου, ἣν περιεποιήσατο διὰ τοῦ αἵματος τοῦ ἰδίου.

29 Ἐγὼ οἶδα ὅτι εἰσελεύσονται μετὰ τὴν ἄφιξίν μου λύκοι βαρεῖς εἰς ὑμᾶς μὴ φειδόμενοι τοῦ ποιμνίου,

30 καὶ ἐξ ὑμῶν αὐτῶν ἀναστήσονται ἄνδρες λαλοῦντες διεστραμμένα τοῦ ἀποσπᾶν τοὺς μαθητὰς ὀπίσω ἑαυτῶν.

31 διὸ γρηγορεῖτε μνημονεύοντες ὅτι τριετίαν νύκτα καὶ ἡμέραν οὐκ ἐπαυσάμην μετὰ δακρύων νουθετῶν ἕνα ἕκαστον.

22 And now, behold, having been bound in the Spirit, I myself am traveling to Jerusalem, not knowing in it the things that will happen to me, 23 except that the Holy Spirit testifies to me city by city, saying that bonds and afflictions are waiting for me. 24 But in no single matter do I hold my life as valuable to myself as to finish my race and the ministry which I received from the Lord Jesus, to fully testify to the good news of the grace of God. 25 And now, behold, I myself know that no longer will all of you see my face, among whom I went about preaching the kingdom. 26 Therefore, I testify to you in the present day that I am clean from the blood of all people! 27 For I did not hold back from declaring to you all the counsel of God. 28 Pay attention to yourselves and to all the flock, in which the Holy Spirit has made you overseers to shepherd the assembly of the Lord which he purchased with his own blood. 29 I myself know that with my departure will come vicious wolves in among you, not sparing the flock, 30 and from you yourselves will arise men speaking different things in order to draw away the disciples after them. 31 Therefore, be watching, remembering that for three years night and day I did not cease with tears to admonish each one.

32 καὶ τὰ νῦν παρατίθεμαι ὑμᾶς τῷ θεῷ καὶ τῷ λόγῳ τῆς χάριτος αὐτοῦ, τῷ δυναμένῳ οἰκοδομῆσαι καὶ δοῦναι τὴν κληρονομίαν ἐν τοῖς ἡγιασμένοις πᾶσιν.

33 ἀργυρίου ἢ χρυσίου ἢ ἱματισμοῦ οὐδενὸς ἐπεθύμησα· 34 αὐτοὶ γινώσκετε ὅτι ταῖς χρείαις μου καὶ τοῖς οὖσιν μετ' ἐμοῦ ὑπηρέτησαν αἱ χεῖρες αὗται. 35 πάντα ὑπέδειξα ὑμῖν ὅτι οὕτως κοπιῶντας δεῖ ἀντιλαμβάνεσθαι τῶν ἀσθενούντων, μνημονεύειν τε τῶν λόγων τοῦ κυρίου Ἰησοῦ, ὅτι αὐτὸς εἶπεν· **μακάριόν ἐστιν μᾶλλον διδόναι ἢ λαμβάνειν.**

36 καὶ ταῦτα εἰπὼν θεὶς τὰ γόνατα αὐτοῦ σὺν πᾶσιν αὐτοῖς προσηύξατο. 37 ἱκανὸς δὲ κλαυθμὸς ἐγένετο πάντων, καὶ ἐπιπεσόντες ἐπὶ τὸν τράχηλον τοῦ Παύλου κατεφίλουν αὐτόν, 38a ὀδυνώμενοι μάλιστα ἐπὶ τῷ λόγῳ ᾧ εἰρήκει ὅτι οὐκέτι μέλλουσιν τὸ πρόσωπον αὐτοῦ θεωρεῖν.

38b προέπεμπον δὲ αὐτὸν εἰς τὸ πλοῖον.

32 And with respect to the present affairs, I am entrusting you to God and to the Word of his grace that is capable to build up and to give the inheritance among all the ones who have been sanctified. 33 The silver or gold or clothing of no single person did I covet. 34 You yourselves know that these hands served my necessities and the ones being with me. 35 In all things, I demonstrated to you that so laboring it is necessary to keep helping the ones being weak as well as to keep remembering the words of the Lord Jesus, that he himself said, 'It is more blessed to be giving than to be receiving.'" 36 And saying these things, setting down on his knees, he prayed with them all. 37 Moreover, a considerable weeping from all occurred, and falling on Paul's neck, they were kissing him, 38 feeling pained most of all at the word which he had spoken, that no longer would they behold his face. Then, they were sending him forth into the ship.

21:1 Ὡς δὲ ἐγένετο ἀναχθῆναι ἡμᾶς ἀποσπασθέντας ἀπ᾿ αὐτῶν, εὐθυδρομήσαντες ἤλθομεν εἰς τὴν Κῶ, τῇ δὲ ἑξῆς εἰς τὴν Ῥόδον, κἀκεῖθεν εἰς Πάταρα. 2 καὶ εὑρόντες πλοῖον διαπερῶν εἰς Φοινίκην ἐπιβάντες ἀνήχθημεν. 3 ἀναφάναντες δὲ τὴν Κύπρον καὶ καταλιπόντες αὐτὴν εὐώνυμον ἐπλέομεν εἰς Συρίαν καὶ κατήλθομεν εἰς Τύρον· ἐκεῖσε γὰρ τὸ πλοῖον ἦν ἀποφορτιζόμενον τὸν γόμον.

4 Ἀνευρόντες δὲ τοὺς μαθητὰς ἐπεμείναμεν αὐτοῦ ἡμέρας ἑπτά, οἵτινες τῷ Παύλῳ ἔλεγον διὰ τοῦ πνεύματος μὴ ἐπιβαίνειν εἰς Ἱεροσόλυμα. 5 ὅτε δὲ ἐγένετο ἐξαρτίσαι ἡμᾶς τὰς ἡμέρας, ἐξελθόντες ἐπορευόμεθα προπεμπόντων ἡμᾶς πάντων σὺν γυναιξὶν καὶ τέκνοις ἕως ἔξω τῆς πόλεως, καὶ θέντες τὰ γόνατα ἐπὶ τὸν αἰγιαλὸν προσευξάμενοι

6 ἀπησπασάμεθα ἀλλήλους καὶ ἐνέβημεν εἰς τὸ πλοῖον, ἐκεῖνοι δὲ ὑπέστρεψαν εἰς τὰ ἴδια.

21:1 Next, when it happened that we set sail departing from them, sailing a straight course, we came into Cos, and on the next day into Rhodes, and from there into Patara. 2 And finding a ship crossing over into Phoenicia, embarking, we set sail. 3 Next, sighting Cyprus and leaving it on the left hand, we were sailing into Syria and put in at Tyre; for there the ship was unloading her cargo. 4 Moreover, discovering disciples, we stayed there for seven days, who were saying to Paul through the Spirit that he should not embark for Jerusalem. 5 But, when it happened that we completed those days, going out we were traveling with all [of them] with wives and children sending us forth until outside of the city, and setting our knees down on the beach, [we] prayed. 6 We said goodbye to one another and we stepped into the ship, but those ones returned to their own affairs.

8 Τῇ δὲ ἐπαύριον ἐξελθόντες ἤλθομεν εἰς Καισάρειαν, καὶ εἰσελθόντες εἰς τὸν οἶκον Φιλίππου τοῦ εὐαγγελιστοῦ ὄντος ἐκ τῶν ἑπτὰ ἐμείναμεν παρ' αὐτῷ.

7 ἡμεῖς δὲ τὸν πλοῦν διανύσαντες ἀπὸ Τύρου κατηντήσαμεν εἰς Πτολεμαΐδα, καὶ ἀσπασάμενοι τοὺς ἀδελφοὺς ἐμείναμεν ἡμέραν μίαν παρ' αὐτοῖς.

9 τούτῳ δὲ ἦσαν θυγατέρες τέσσαρες παρθένοι προφητεύουσαι. 10 Ἐπιμενόντων δὲ ἡμέρας πλείους κατῆλθέν τις ἀπὸ τῆς Ἰουδαίας προφήτης ὀνόματι Ἄγαβος, 11 καὶ ἐλθὼν πρὸς ἡμᾶς καὶ ἄρας τὴν ζώνην τοῦ Παύλου, δήσας ἑαυτοῦ τοὺς πόδας καὶ τὰς χεῖρας εἶπεν·

τάδε λέγει τὸ πνεῦμα τὸ ἅγιον· τὸν ἄνδρα οὗ ἐστιν ἡ ζώνη αὕτη, οὕτως δήσουσιν ἐν Ἰερουσαλὴμ οἱ Ἰουδαῖοι καὶ παραδώσουσιν εἰς χεῖρας ἐθνῶν.

12 ὡς δὲ ἠκούσαμεν ταῦτα, παρεκαλοῦμεν ἡμεῖς τε καὶ οἱ ἐντόπιοι τοῦ μὴ ἀναβαίνειν αὐτὸν εἰς Ἰερουσαλήμ.

13 τότε ἀπεκρίθη ὁ Παῦλος·

τί ποιεῖτε κλαίοντες καὶ συνθρύπτοντές μου τὴν καρδίαν;

ἐγὼ γὰρ οὐ μόνον δεθῆναι ἀλλὰ καὶ ἀποθανεῖν εἰς Ἰερουσαλὴμ ἑτοίμως ἔχω ὑπὲρ τοῦ ὀνόματος τοῦ κυρίου Ἰησοῦ.

14 μὴ πειθομένου δὲ αὐτοῦ ἡσυχάσαμεν εἰπόντες·

τοῦ κυρίου τὸ θέλημα γινέσθω.

7 But we ourselves, continuing the voyage from Tyre, arrived at Ptolemais, and greeting the brothers, we stayed one day with them. 8 Then, on the next day departing, we came into Caesarea, and entering into the house of Philip the evangelist, being one of the seven, we stayed with him. 9 Moreover, to this man were four virgin daughters who were prophesying. 10 So, with us staying many days, a certain prophet came down from Judea, Agabus by name, 11 and coming to us and taking Paul's belt, binding his own feet and hands, he said, "These things the Holy Spirit says: 'The man who owns this belt, so the Judeans at Jerusalem will bind and will deliver him into the hands of the Gentiles.'" 12 Moreover, when we heard these things, both we ourselves and the people of that place were encouraging that he not go up to Jerusalem. 13 Then Paul answered back, "What are you doing weeping and breaking my heart? For I myself am ready not only to be bound, but also to die at Jerusalem for the name of the Lord Jesus!" 14 But, with him not being persuaded, we ceased, saying, "Let the Lord's will be done!"

15 Μετὰ δὲ τὰς ἡμέρας ταύτας ἐπισκευασάμενοι ἀνεβαίνομεν εἰς Ἰεροσόλυμα. **16** συνῆλθον δὲ καὶ τῶν μαθητῶν ἀπὸ Καισαρείας σὺν ἡμῖν, ἄγοντες παρ' ᾧ ξενισθῶμεν, Μνάσωνί τινι Κυπρίῳ, ἀρχαίῳ μαθητῇ.

17 Γενομένων δὲ ἡμῶν εἰς Ἰεροσόλυμα ἀσμένως ἀπεδέξαντο ἡμᾶς οἱ ἀδελφοί. **18** τῇ δὲ ἐπιούσῃ εἰσῄει ὁ Παῦλος σὺν ἡμῖν πρὸς Ἰάκωβον, πάντες τε παρεγένοντο οἱ πρεσβύτεροι.

19 καὶ ἀσπασάμενος αὐτοὺς ἐξηγεῖτο καθ' ἓν ἕκαστον ὧν ἐποίησεν ὁ θεὸς ἐν τοῖς ἔθνεσιν διὰ τῆς διακονίας αὐτοῦ.

15 So, after these days, making preparations, we were going up into Jerusalem. 16 Moreover, some also of the disciples from Caesarea went with us, bringing along one by whom we would be hosted, a certain Mnason of Cyprus, an early disciple. 17 Then, with us coming into Jerusalem, gladly the brothers received us. 18 So, on the following day, Paul was going with us to James, and at the same time all the elders were present. 19 And, greeting them, he was reporting each thing one at a time which God did among the Gentiles through his ministry.

20 οἱ δὲ ἀκούσαντες ἐδόξαζον τὸν θεόν, εἶπάν τε αὐτῷ·

θεωρεῖς ἀδελφέ, πόσαι μυριάδες εἰσὶν ἐν τοῖς Ἰουδαίοις τῶν πεπιστευκότων καὶ πάντες ζηλωταὶ τοῦ νόμου ὑπάρχουσιν.

21 κατηχήθησαν δὲ περὶ σοῦ ὅτι ἀποστασίαν διδάσκεις ἀπὸ Μωϋσέως τοὺς κατὰ τὰ ἔθνη πάντας Ἰουδαίους λέγων μὴ περιτέμνειν αὐτοὺς τὰ τέκνα μηδὲ τοῖς ἔθεσιν περιπατεῖν. **22** τί οὖν ἐστιν; πάντως ἀκούσονται ὅτι ἐλήλυθας. **23a** τοῦτο οὖν ποίησον ὅ σοι λέγομεν·

23b εἰσὶν ἡμῖν ἄνδρες τέσσαρες εὐχὴν ἔχοντες ἐφ' ἑαυτῶν· **24** τούτους παραλαβὼν ἁγνίσθητι σὺν αὐτοῖς καὶ δαπάνησον ἐπ' αὐτοῖς ἵνα ξυρήσονται τὴν κεφαλήν, καὶ γνώσονται πάντες ὅτι ὧν κατήχηνται περὶ σοῦ οὐδέν ἐστιν, ἀλλὰ στοιχεῖς καὶ αὐτὸς φυλάσσων τὸν νόμον.

25 περὶ δὲ τῶν πεπιστευκότων ἐθνῶν ἡμεῖς ἐπεστείλαμεν κρίναντες φυλάσσεσθαι αὐτοὺς τό τε εἰδωλόθυτον καὶ αἷμα καὶ πνικτὸν καὶ πορνείαν.

26 Τότε ὁ Παῦλος παραλαβὼν τοὺς ἄνδρας τῇ ἐχομένῃ ἡμέρᾳ σὺν αὐτοῖς ἁγνισθεὶς εἰσῄει εἰς τὸ ἱερὸν διαγγέλλων τὴν ἐκπλήρωσιν τῶν ἡμερῶν τοῦ ἁγνισμοῦ, ἕως οὗ προσηνέχθη ὑπὲρ ἑνὸς ἑκάστου αὐτῶν ἡ προσφορά.

20 Moreover, they, hearing it, were glorifying God, and at the same time they said to him, "You are beholding, brother, how many thousands there are among the Judeans of the ones who have believed and all are in fact zealous for the Law! 21 Moreover, they were taught about you, that you are teaching apostasy from Moses to all the Judeans who are among the Gentiles, telling them not to be circumcising their children and not to be walking in the customs. 22 What, therefore, is this?! Certainly, they will hear that you have come. 23 Therefore, do this, what we tell you. There are four men of ours having taken a vow upon themselves; 24 taking these, be purified with them and pay their expenses for them in order that they will shave their head, and [then] all will know that there is nothing behind the things they were taught about you, but that you are living in line with and yourself keeping the Law. 25 But concerning the Gentiles who have believed, we ourselves sent out message, deciding that they should observe no such thing, except that they should guard themselves from food offered to idols and from blood and from strangled things and from sexual immorality." 26 Then Paul, taking the men on the following day, being purified with them, was going into the temple, declaring the fulfillment of the days of purification, until the offering was offered for each one of them.

27 ὡς δὲ ἔμελλον αἱ ἑπτὰ ἡμέραι συντελεῖσθαι, οἱ ἀπὸ τῆς Ἀσίας Ἰουδαῖοι θεασάμενοι αὐτὸν ἐν τῷ ἱερῷ συνέχεον πάντα τὸν ὄχλον καὶ ἐπέβαλον ἐπ' αὐτὸν τὰς χεῖρας 28 κράζοντες·

ἄνδρες Ἰσραηλεῖται, βοηθεῖτε. οὗτός ἐστιν ὁ ἄνθρωπος ὁ κατὰ τοῦ λαοῦ καὶ τοῦ νόμου καὶ τοῦ τόπου τούτου πάντας πανταχῇ διδάσκων, ἔτι τε καὶ Ἕλληνας εἰσήγαγεν εἰς τὸ ἱερὸν καὶ κεκοίνωκεν τὸν ἅγιον τόπον τοῦτον.

29 ἦσαν γὰρ προεωρακότες Τρόφιμον τὸν Ἐφέσιον ἐν τῇ πόλει σὺν αὐτῷ, ὃν ἐνόμιζον ὅτι εἰς τὸ ἱερὸν εἰσήγαγεν ὁ Παῦλος.

30 ἐκεινήθη τε ἡ πόλις ὅλη καὶ ἐγένετο συνδρομὴ τοῦ λαοῦ, καὶ ἐπιλαβόμενοι τοῦ Παύλου εἷλκον αὐτὸν ἔξω τοῦ ἱεροῦ· καὶ εὐθέως ἐκλείσθησαν αἱ θύραι. 31 ζητούντων τε αὐτὸν ἀποκτεῖναι ἀνέβη φάσις τῷ χιλιάρχῳ τῆς σπείρης ὅτι ὅλη συνχύννεται Ἰερουσαλήμ·

32 ὃς ἐξαυτῆς παραλαβὼν στρατιώτας καὶ ἑκατοντάρχας κατέδραμεν ἐπ' αὐτούς. οἱ δὲ ἰδόντες τὸν χιλίαρχον καὶ τοὺς στρατιώτας ἐπαύσαντο τύπτοντες τὸν Παῦλον.

27 So, when the seven days were about to be completed, the Judeans from Asia, seeing him in the temple, stirred up all the crowd and laid hands on him, 28 crying out, "Israelite Men, help! This is the person teaching all persons everywhere against the people and the Law and this place, yet at the same time also he brought Greeks into the temple and has defiled this holy place!" 29 For they had beheld earlier Trophimus, the Ephesian, with him in the city, whom they were supposing Paul had brought into the temple. 30 At the same time, the whole city was shaken and a rushing together of the people occurred, and seizing Paul, they dragged him outside of the temple. And immediately the doors were shut. 31 At the same time, with them seeking to kill him, a report went up to the commanding officer of the [Roman] regiment that the whole of Jerusalem was being stirred up, 32 who immediately, taking soldiers and centurions, ran down to them. But, seeing the commanding officer and the soldiers, they stopped beating Paul.

33 τότε ἐγγίσας ὁ χιλίαρχος ἐπελάβετο αὐτοῦ καὶ ἐκέλευσεν δεθῆναι ἁλύσεσι δυσὶ καὶ ἐπυνθάνετο τίς εἴη καὶ τί ἐστιν πεποιηκώς. 34 ἄλλοι δὲ ἄλλο τι ἐπεφώνουν ἐν τῷ ὄχλῳ. μὴ δυναμένου δὲ αὐτοῦ γνῶναι τὸ ἀσφαλὲς διὰ τὸν θόρυβον ἐκέλευσεν ἄγεσθαι αὐτὸν εἰς τὴν παρεμβολήν.

35 ὅτε δὲ ἐγένετο ἐπὶ τοὺς ἀναβαθμούς, συνέβη βαστάζεσθαι αὐτὸν ὑπὸ τῶν στρατιωτῶν διὰ τὴν βίαν τοῦ ὄχλου· 36 ἠκολούθει γὰρ τὸ πλῆθος τοῦ λαοῦ κράζοντες·

αἶρε αὐτόν.

37 μέλλων τε εἰσάγεσθαι εἰς τὴν παρεμβολὴν ὁ Παῦλος λέγει τῷ χιλιάρχῳ·

εἰ ἔξεστίν μοι εἰπεῖν τι πρὸς σέ;

ὁ δὲ ἔφη·

ἑλληνιστὶ γινώσκεις; 38 οὐκ ἄρα σὺ εἶ ὁ Αἰγύπτιος ὁ πρὸ τούτων τῶν ἡμερῶν ἀναστατώσας καὶ ἐξαγαγὼν εἰς τὴν ἔρημον τοὺς τετρακισχιλίους ἄνδρας τῶν σικαρίων;

39 Εἶπεν δὲ ὁ Παῦλος·

ἐγὼ ἄνθρωπος μέν εἰμι Ἰουδαῖος Ταρσεὺς τῆς Κιλικίας οὐκ ἀσήμου πόλεως πολίτης, δέομαι δέ σου· ἐπίτρεψόν μοι λαλῆσαι πρὸς τὸν λαόν.

40 ἐπιτρέψαντος δὲ αὐτοῦ ὁ Παῦλος ἑστὼς ἐπὶ τῶν ἀναβαθμῶν κατέσεισε τῇ χειρὶ τῷ λαῷ, πολλῆς δὲ σιγῆς γενομένης προσεφώνησεν τῇ Ἑβραΐδι διαλέκτῳ λέγων·

33 Then, approaching, the commanding officer arrested him and commanded him to be bound with two chains and he was inquiring who he was and what he had done. 34 But, different ones were shouting something different in the crowd. So, with him not being able to know the certainty because of the uproar, he commanded him to be brought into the barracks. 35 But, when he came to the stairs, it turned out that he was being carried by the soldiers due to the violence of the crowd; 36 for the multitude of the people was following, crying out, "Away with him!" 37 At the same time, about to be brought into the barracks, Paul says to the commanding officer, "It is allowable for me to speak something to you?" And he was saying, "Do you understand the Greek language? Are you not yourself, then, the Egyptian who revolted early these days and led out the four thousand men of the Assassins into the desert? (Yes.)" 39 But Paul said, "I myself am, on the one hand, a Judean person from Tarsus of Cilicia, a citizen of no insignificant city. But on the other hand, I beg you, allow me to speak to the people." 40 So, with him granting permission, Paul, standing on the stairs, motioned the people down with his hand; then, with a great silence occurring, he spoke to them in the Hebrew language, saying,

Κεφ. ΚΒ´

22:1 Ἄνδρες ἀδελφοὶ καὶ πατέρες, ἀκούσατέ μου τῆς πρὸς ὑμᾶς νυνὶ ἀπολογίας.

2 ἀκούσαντες δὲ ὅτι τῇ Ἑβραΐδι διαλέκτῳ προσεφώνει αὐτοῖς, μᾶλλον παρέσχον ἡσυχίαν.

Καὶ φησίν·

3 ἐγὼ εἰμι ἀνὴρ Ἰουδαῖος γεγεννημένος ἐν Ταρσῷ τῆς Κιλικίας, ἀνατεθραμμένος δὲ ἐν τῇ πόλει ταύτῃ,

παρὰ τοὺς πόδας Γαμαλιὴλ πεπαιδευμένος κατὰ ἀκρίβειαν τοῦ πατρῴου νόμου, ζηλωτὴς ὑπάρχων τοῦ θεοῦ καθὼς πάντες ὑμεῖς ἐστε σήμερον, **4** ὃς ταύτην τὴν ὁδὸν ἐδίωξα ἄχρι θανάτου δεσμεύων καὶ παραδιδοὺς εἰς φυλακὰς ἄνδρας τε καὶ γυναῖκας, **5** ὡς καὶ ὁ ἀρχιερεὺς μαρτυρεῖ μοι καὶ πᾶν τὸ πρεσβυτέριον,

παρ' ὧν καὶ ἐπιστολὰς δεξάμενος πρὸς τοὺς ἀδελφοὺς εἰς Δαμασκὸν ἐπορευόμην, ἄξων καὶ τοὺς ἐκεῖσε ὄντας δεδεμένους εἰς Ἱερουσαλὴμ ἵνα τιμωρηθῶσιν.

6 ἐγένετο δέ μοι πορευομένῳ καὶ ἐγγίζοντι τῇ Δαμασκῷ περὶ μεσημβρίαν ἐξαίφνης ἐκ τοῦ οὐρανοῦ περιαστράψαι φῶς ἱκανὸν περὶ ἐμέ· **7** ἔπεσά τε εἰς τὸ ἔδαφος καὶ ἤκουσα φωνῆς λεγούσης μοι· **Σαοὺλ Σαούλ, τί με διώκεις;**

8 ἐγὼ δὲ ἀπεκρίθην· τίς εἶ κύριε; εἶπέν τε πρὸς ἐμέ· **ἐγώ εἰμι Ἰησοῦς ὁ Ναζωραῖος ὃν σὺ διώκεις.** **9** οἱ δὲ σὺν ἐμοὶ ὄντες τὸ μὲν φῶς ἐθεάσαντο, τὴν δὲ φωνὴν οὐκ ἤκουσαν τοῦ λαλοῦντός μοι. **10** εἶπον δέ· τί ποιήσω κύριε; ὁ δὲ κύριος εἶπεν πρός με· **ἀναστὰς πορεύου εἰς Δαμασκόν, κἀκεῖ σοι λαληθήσεται περὶ πάντων ὧν τέτακταί σοι ποιῆσαι.** **11** ὡς δὲ οὐκ ἐνέβλεπον ἀπὸ τῆς δόξης τοῦ φωτὸς ἐκείνου, χειραγωγούμενος ὑπὸ τῶν συνόντων μοι ἦλθον εἰς Δαμασκόν.

22:1 "Fellow brothers and fathers, listen to my defense now to you!" 2 So, hearing that he was speaking to them in the Hebrew language, they showed even more silence. And he says, 3 "I myself am indeed a Judean, having been born in Tarsus of Cilicia, but having been brought up in this city at the feet of Gamaliel, having been instructed according to the strict tradition of the inherited Law, being in fact zealous for God, even as you all are today. 4 [I] who persecuted this Way to the point of death, binding and delivering into prisons both men and women, 5 as also the high priest testifies for me, and all the council of the elders, from whom also letters receiving for the brothers, I was traveling into Damascus in order to bring even the ones being there bound up [back] into Jerusalem in order that they would be punished. 6 So, it happened to me traveling and nearing to Damascus, that about noon suddenly from heaven a considerable light shone around me. 7 At the same time, I fell to the ground and heard a voice saying to me, 'Saul, Saul, why are you persecuting me?' 8 So, I myself answered back, 'Who are you, Lord?' At the same time, he said to me, 'I myself am Jesus, the Nazarene, whom you yourself are persecuting.' 9 "But the ones being with me, on the one hand, saw the light, but on the other hand, they did not pay attention to the voice of the one speaking to me. 10 But, I said, 'What shall I do, Lord?' Then, the Lord said to me, 'Arising, go into Damascus and there it will be spoken to you about all that has been appointed for you to do!' 11 So, when I was not seeing clearly from the glory of that light, being led by hand by the ones accompanying me, I came into Damascus.

12 Ἀνανίας δέ τις, ἀνὴρ εὐλαβὴς κατὰ τὸν νόμον, μαρτυρούμενος ὑπὸ πάντων τῶν κατοικούντων Ἰουδαίων, 13 ἐλθὼν πρὸς ἐμὲ καὶ ἐπιστὰς εἶπέν μοι· Σαοὺλ ἀδελφέ, ἀνάβλεψον. κἀγὼ αὐτῇ τῇ ὥρᾳ ἀνέβλεψα εἰς αὐτόν.

14 ὁ δὲ εἶπεν· ὁ θεὸς τῶν πατέρων ἡμῶν προεχειρίσατό σε γνῶναι τὸ θέλημα αὐτοῦ καὶ ἰδεῖν τὸν δίκαιον καὶ ἀκοῦσαι φωνὴν ἐκ τοῦ στόματος αὐτοῦ· 15 ὅτι ἔσῃ μάρτυς αὐτῷ πρὸς πάντας ἀνθρώπους ὧν ἑώρακας καὶ ἤκουσας. 16 καὶ νῦν τί μέλλεις; ἀναστὰς βάπτισαι καὶ ἀπόλουσαι τὰς ἁμαρτίας σου ἐπικαλεσάμενος τὸ ὄνομα αὐτοῦ.

17 Ἐγένετο δέ μοι ὑποστρέψαντι εἰς Ἰερουσαλὴμ καὶ προσευχομένου μου ἐν τῷ ἱερῷ γενέσθαι με ἐν ἐκστάσει 18 καὶ ἰδεῖν αὐτὸν λέγοντά μοι· *σπεῦσον καὶ ἔξελθε ἐν τάχει ἐξ Ἰερουσαλήμ, διότι οὐ παραδέξονταί σου μαρτυρίαν περὶ ἐμοῦ.*

19 κἀγὼ εἶπον· κύριε, αὐτοὶ ἐπίστανται ὅτι ἐγὼ ἤμην φυλακίζων καὶ δέρων κατὰ τὰς συναγωγὰς τοὺς πιστεύοντας ἐπὶ σέ·

20 καὶ ὅτε ἐξεχύννετο τὸ αἷμα Στεφάνου τοῦ μάρτυρός σου, καὶ αὐτὸς ἤμην ἐφεστὼς καὶ συνευδοκῶν καὶ φυλάσσων τὰ ἱμάτια τῶν ἀναιρούντων αὐτόν. 21 καὶ εἶπεν πρός με· *πορεύου, ὅτι ἐγὼ εἰς ἔθνη μακρὰν ἐξαποστελῶ σε.*

12 Moreover, a certain Ananias, a devout man according to the Law, well-attested by all the Judeans living in Damascus, 13 coming to me and standing by, said to me, 'Brother Saul, receive your sight!' And I myself at that very hour looked up at him! 14 So, he said, 'The God of our fathers appointed you to know his will and to see the Righteous One and to hear a sound from his mouth; 5 because you will be a witness for him to all people of what you have seen and heard. 16 And now, what are you intending to do?! Arising, be baptized and wash away your sins, calling upon his name!' 17 So, it happened to me having returned into Jerusalem, and with me praying in the temple, that I fell into a trance 18 and saw him saying to me, 'Hurry and get out of Jerusalem quickly, because they will not receive your testimony concerning me!' 19 And I said, 'Lord, they themselves know that I myself was imprisoning and flogging in each synagogue the ones believing in you. 20 And when the blood of Stephen, your witness, was being shed, I myself also was standing by and consenting to his death and guarding the garments of the ones killing him.' 21 "And he said to me, 'Go, because I myself will send you out far from here to the Gentiles.'"

22 So, they listened to him until this statement and they lifted up their voice saying, "Rid the earth of such a fellow as this! For it is not proper that he lives!" 23 At the same time, as they were shouting out and hurling their garments and throwing dust into the air, 24 the commanding officer ordered him to be brought into the barracks, saying that with flogging he should be examined carefully in order that he would know for what crime they were thus shouting against him. 25 But, as they tied him up with thongs, Paul said to the centurion standing there, "Is it lawful for you to be flogging a person who is Roman and not found guilty?"

26 ἀκούσας δὲ ὁ ἑκατόνταρχος προσελθὼν τῷ χιλιάρχῳ ἀπήγγειλεν λέγων·

τί μέλλεις ποιεῖν; ὁ γὰρ ἄνθρωπος οὗτος Ῥωμαῖός ἐστιν.

27 προσελθὼν δὲ ὁ χιλίαρχος εἶπεν αὐτῷ·

λέγε μοι, σὺ Ῥωμαῖος εἶ;

ὁ δὲ ἔφη· ναί.

28 ἀπεκρίθη δὲ ὁ χιλίαρχος·

ἐγὼ πολλοῦ κεφαλαίου τὴν πολιτείαν ταύτην ἐκτησάμην.

ὁ δὲ Παῦλος ἔφη· ἐγὼ δὲ καὶ γεγέννημαι.

29 εὐθέως οὖν ἀπέστησαν ἀπ᾽ αὐτοῦ οἱ μέλλοντες αὐτὸν ἀνετάζειν. καὶ ὁ χιλίαρχος δὲ ἐφοβήθη ἐπιγνοὺς ὅτι Ῥωμαῖός ἐστιν καὶ ὅτι αὐτὸν ἦν δεδεκώς. 30 Τῇ δὲ ἐπαύριον βουλόμενος γνῶναι τὸ ἀσφαλές, τὸ τί κατηγορεῖται ὑπὸ τῶν Ἰουδαίων, ἔλυσεν αὐτὸν καὶ ἐκέλευσεν συνελθεῖν τοὺς ἀρχιερεῖς καὶ πᾶν τὸ συνέδριον, καὶ καταγαγὼν τὸν Παῦλον ἔστησεν εἰς αὐτούς.

26 So, hearing [this], the centurion, going to the commanding officer, reported saying, "What are you intending to do? For this person is a Roman!" 27 Then, approaching, the commanding officer said to him, "Tell me, are you yourself a Roman?" And he was saying, "Yes." 28 So, the commanding officer answered back, "I myself bought this citizenship with a great price." But, Paul was saying, "But I myself even have been born a Roman!" 29 Therefore, immediately the ones intending to examine him stood away from him. Moreover, also the commanding officer was afraid realizing that he was a Roman and because he had bound him. 30 But on the next day, wanting to know the certainty about why he was being accused by the Judeans, he freed him from the bonds and commanded the chief priests and all the council to come together and, leading down Paul, he set [him] before them.

Κεφ. ΚΓ΄

23:1 Ἀτενίσας δὲ τῷ συνεδρίῳ ὁ Παῦλος εἶπεν·

ἄνδρες ἀδελφοί, ἐγὼ πάσῃ συνειδήσει ἀγαθῇ πεπολίτευμαι τῷ θεῷ ἄχρι ταύτης τῆς ἡμέρας.

2 ὁ δὲ ἀρχιερεὺς Ἀνανίας ἐπέταξεν τοῖς παρεστῶσιν αὐτῷ τύπτειν αὐτοῦ τὸ στόμα.

3 τότε ὁ Παῦλος πρὸς αὐτὸν εἶπεν·

τύπτειν σε μέλλει ὁ θεός, τοῖχε κεκονιαμένε· καὶ σὺ κάθῃ κρίνων με κατὰ τὸν νόμον, καὶ παρανομῶν κελεύεις με τύπτεσθαι;

4 οἱ δὲ παρεστῶτες εἶπαν·

τὸν ἀρχιερέα τοῦ θεοῦ λοιδορεῖς;

5 ἔφη τε ὁ Παῦλος·

οὐκ ᾔδειν, ἀδελφοί, ὅτι ἐστὶν ἀρχιερεύς· γέγραπται γὰρ ὅτι ἄρχοντα τοῦ λαοῦ σου οὐκ ἐρεῖς κακῶς.

23:1 So, looking steadfastly at the council, Paul said, "Fellow brothers, I myself in all good conscience have lived as a citizen for God up until this day." 2 But, the high priest, Ananias, gave command to the ones standing nearby him to strike his mouth. 3 Then, to him Paul said, "God intends to strike you, you whitewashed wall! Are you both sitting [there] judging me according to the Law and, acting contrary to the Law, are you commanding me to be struck?" 4 But the ones standing there said, "Are you maligning the high priest of God?" 5 At the same time, Paul was saying, "I did not know, brothers, that he is high priest. For it is written this: 'You shall not speak evil of a ruler of your people.'"

6 Γνοὺς δὲ ὁ Παῦλος ὅτι τὸ ἓν μέρος ἐστὶν Σαδδουκαίων τὸ δὲ ἕτερον Φαρισαίων ἔκραζεν ἐν τῷ συνεδρίῳ·

ἄνδρες ἀδελφοί, ἐγὼ Φαρισαῖός εἰμι, υἱὸς Φαρισαίων· περὶ ἐλπίδος καὶ ἀναστάσεως νεκρῶν ἐγὼ κρίνομαι.

7 Τοῦτο δὲ αὐτοῦ εἰπόντος ἐγένετο στάσις τῶν Φαρισαίων καὶ Σαδδουκαίων, καὶ ἐσχίσθη τὸ πλῆθος. 8 Σαδδουκαῖοι μὲν γὰρ λέγουσιν μὴ εἶναι ἀνάστασιν μήτε ἄγγελον μήτε πνεῦμα· Φαρισαῖοι δὲ ὁμολογοῦσιν τὰ ἀμφότερα. 9 Ἐγένετο δὲ κραυγὴ μεγάλη· καὶ ἀναστάντες τινὲς τῶν γραμματέων τοῦ μέρους τῶν Φαρισαίων διεμάχοντο λέγοντες·

οὐδὲν κακὸν εὑρίσκομεν ἐν τῷ ἀνθρώπῳ τούτῳ· εἰ δὲ πνεῦμα ἐλάλησεν αὐτῷ ἢ ἄγγελος;

10 πολλῆς δὲ γινομένης στάσεως, φοβηθεὶς ὁ χιλίαρχος μὴ διασπασθῇ ὁ Παῦλος ὑπ' αὐτῶν ἐκέλευσεν τὸ στράτευμα καταβὰν ἁρπάσαι αὐτὸν ἐκ μέσου αὐτῶν, ἄγειν τε εἰς τὴν παρεμβολήν.

11 Τῇ δὲ ἐπιούσῃ νυκτὶ ἐπιστὰς αὐτῷ ὁ κύριος εἶπεν·

θάρσει· ὡς γὰρ διεμαρτύρω τὰ περὶ ἐμοῦ εἰς Ἰερουσαλήμ, οὕτω σε δεῖ καὶ εἰς Ῥώμην μαρτυρῆσαι.

6 Next, Paul, knowing that the one part was of the Sadducees and the other of the Pharisees, he was crying out in the council, "Fellow men, I myself am a Pharisee, a son of Pharisees. Concerning the hope and resurrection of the dead I myself am being judged!" 7 So, with him saying this, dissension occurred between the Pharisees and Sadducees, and the multitude was divided. 8 For, indeed, the Sadducees say that there is no resurrection, neither angel nor spirit; but the Pharisees profess all together. 9 Then, a great uproar occurred; and some of the scribes of the Pharisees' part standing up, were arguing pointedly, saying, "We find no evil in this person. But [what] if a spirit or angel spoke to him?!" 10 Then, with a great revolt occurring, the commanding officer, fearing that Paul would be torn in pieces by them, commanded the troops, going down, to forcibly take him from the middle of them, and at the same time to bring him into the barracks. 11 Moreover, on the following night, standing by him, the Lord said, "Take courage! For as you solemnly testified about me in Jerusalem, thus it is necessary that you testify also in Rome."

12 Γενομένης δὲ ἡμέρας ποιήσαντες συστροφὴν οἱ Ἰουδαῖοι ἀνεθεμάτισαν ἑαυτοὺς λέγοντες μήτε φαγεῖν μήτε πιεῖν ἕως οὗ ἀποκτείνωσιν τὸν Παῦλον. 13 ἦσαν δὲ πλείους τεσσεράκοντα οἱ ταύτην τὴν συνωμοσίαν ποιησάμενοι· 14 οἵτινες προσελθόντες τοῖς ἀρχιερεῦσιν καὶ τοῖς πρεσβυτέροις εἶπαν·

ἀναθέματι ἀνεθεματίσαμεν ἑαυτοὺς μηδενὸς γεύσασθαι ἕως οὗ ἀποκτείνωμεν τὸν Παῦλον. 15 νῦν οὖν ὑμεῖς ἐμφανίσατε τῷ χιλιάρχῳ σὺν τῷ συνεδρίῳ, ὅπως καταγάγῃ αὐτὸν εἰς ὑμᾶς ὡς μέλλοντας διαγινώσκειν ἀκριβέστερον τὰ περὶ αὐτοῦ· ἡμεῖς δὲ πρὸ τοῦ ἐγγίσαι αὐτὸν ἕτοιμοί ἐσμεν τοῦ ἀνελεῖν αὐτόν.

16 Ἀκούσας δὲ ὁ υἱὸς τῆς ἀδελφῆς Παύλου τὴν ἐνέδραν, παραγενόμενος καὶ εἰσελθὼν εἰς τὴν παρεμβολὴν ἀπήγγειλεν τῷ Παύλῳ.

17 προσκαλεσάμενος δὲ ὁ Παῦλος ἕνα τῶν ἑκατονταρχῶν ἔφη·

τὸν νεανίαν τοῦτον ἀπάγαγε πρὸς τὸν χιλίαρχον· ἔχει γὰρ ἀπαγγεῖλαί τι αὐτῷ.

12 So, with day coming, making a conspiracy, [some of] the Judeans bound themselves under a curse, saying that they would neither eat nor drink until they killed Paul. 13 Now, more than forty people were making this conspiracy, 14 who coming to the chief priests and the elders, said, "With a curse, we have bound ourselves under a curse to taste nothing until we killed Paul. 15 Now, therefore, you yourselves make it clear to the commanding officer with the council that he should bring him down to you as though intending to continue investigating the things about him more exactly. But we ourselves, before he draws near, are ready to kill him." 16 But Paul's sister's son, hearing about the ambush, showing up and entering into the barracks, reported [it] to Paul. 17 So, summoning one of the centurions, Paul was saying, "Take away this young man to the commanding officer, for he has something to report to him."

18 So then, taking him along, he brought him to the commanding officer and says, "The prisoner Paul, summoning, asked me to bring you this young man having something to say to you." 19 So, the commanding officer, taking him by the hand and withdrawing in private, was asking, "What is it that you are having to report to me?" 20 Then he said, "The Judeans have agreed to ask you that tomorrow you would bring Paul down into the council as though intending to inquire somewhat more accurately concerning him. 21 You, therefore, do not be won over to them! For more than forty men are lying in wait for him, who bound themselves under a curse to neither eat nor drink until they have killed him and now they are ready, awaiting the promise from you." 22 So then, the commanding officer released the young man, charging [him] to disclose [it] to no one "that you revealed these things to me."

23 And summoning two of the centurions, he said, "Prepare two hundred soldiers in order to travel as far as Caesarea, and seventy horsemen and two hundred men armed with spears, at the third hour of the night" 24 and at the same time, to provide animals in order that, setting Paul upon [one], they would bring him through safely to Felix the governor, 25 writing an epistle having this form: 26 "Claudius Lysias to the most excellent governor Felix: Greetings. 27 This man being seized by the Judeans and about to be killed by them, I, coming in with the troops, carried him away, learning that he was a Roman. 28 At the same time, wanting to understand the reason why they were accusing him, I brought him down into their council, 29 whom I found being accused concerning questions of their Law, but having no accusation worthy of death or of imprisonment. 30 So, with a plot that would occur against the man being disclosed to me, immediately I sent him to you, charging also his accusers to speak against him before you. Farewell."

31 Οἱ μὲν οὖν στρατιῶται κατὰ τὸ διατεταγμένον αὐτοῖς ἀναλαβόντες τὸν Παῦλον ἤγαγον διὰ νυκτὸς εἰς τὴν Ἀντιπατρίδα. 32 τῇ δὲ ἐπαύριον ἐάσαντες τοὺς ἱππεῖς ἀπέρχεσθαι σὺν αὐτῷ ὑπέστρεψαν εἰς τὴν παρεμβολήν· 33 οἵτινες εἰσελθόντες εἰς τὴν Καισάρειαν καὶ ἀναδόντες τὴν ἐπιστολὴν τῷ ἡγεμόνι παρέστησαν καὶ τὸν Παῦλον αὐτῷ.

34 ἀναγνοὺς δὲ καὶ ἐπερωτήσας ἐκ ποίας ἐπαρχείας ἐστὶν καὶ πυθόμενος ὅτι ἀπὸ Κιλικίας,

35 διακούσομαί σου, ἔφη, ὅταν καὶ οἱ κατήγοροί σου παραγένωνται.

κελεύσας ἐν τῷ πραιτωρίῳ τοῦ Ἡρῴδου φυλάσσεσθαι αὐτόν.

Κεφ. ΚΔ´

24:1 Μετὰ δὲ πέντε ἡμέρας κατέβη ὁ ἀρχιερεὺς Ἀνανίας μετὰ πρεσβυτέρων τινῶν καὶ ῥήτορος Τερτύλλου τινός, οἵτινες ἐνεφάνισαν τῷ ἡγεμόνι κατὰ τοῦ Παύλου. 2 κληθέντος δὲ αὐτοῦ ἤρξατο κατηγορεῖν ὁ Τέρτυλλος λέγων·

πολλῆς εἰρήνης τυγχάνοντες διὰ σοῦ καὶ διορθωμάτων γινομένων τῷ ἔθνει τούτῳ διὰ τῆς σῆς προνοίας 3 πάντῃ τε καὶ πανταχοῦ ἀποδεχόμεθα, κράτιστε Φήλιξ, μετὰ πάσης εὐχαριστίας. 4 ἵνα δὲ μὴ ἐπὶ πλεῖόν σε ἐνκόπτω, παρακαλῶ ἀκοῦσαί σε ἡμῶν συντόμως τῇ σῇ ἐπιεικείᾳ.

31 So then, the soldiers according to what had been commanded to them, taking Paul, brought him through the night into Antipatris. 32 But on the next day, permitting the horsemen to go away with him, they returned to the barracks; 33 who, entering into Caesarea and delivering the letter to the governor, they presented also Paul to him. 34 Then, he, reading and asking what province he was from and learning that he was from Cilicia, [began with] 35 "I will give you a hearing," he was saying, "whenever also your accusers arrive," commanding him to be guarded in the palace of Herod. 24:1 Now, after five days, the high priest, Ananias, went down with some elders and an orator, a certain Tertullus, who [all] reported to the governor against Paul. 2 So, being called, Tertullus began to accuse him, saying, "Attaining great peace through you and with improvements coming to this nation by your foresight, 3 both in every way and everywhere we receive [them] favorably, most excellent Felix, with all thankfulness. 4 But in order that I not delay you any more, I entreat you to hear us briefly in your clemency.

5 For, finding this man [to be] a plague and instigating riots with all the Judeans across the inhabited [Roman] world, and at the same time, a ringleader of the sect of the Nazarenes; 6 he who even attempted to profane the temple, whom also we seized. 8 From him you yourself are able, [by] examining, to fully know all these things of which we ourselves accuse him." 9 Moreover, the Judeans also were joining in the attack, affirming that these things were so. 10 At the same time, Paul answered back at the governor nodding for him to speak, "For many years knowing you to be a judge of this nation, I cheerfully am defending myself regarding the matters on my behalf, 11 you being capable to fully know that it is not more than twelve days from which I went up for worshipping at Jerusalem. 12 And neither in the temple did they find me disputing with anyone or making a hindrance of a crowd, nor in the synagogues, nor across the city. 13 Nor are they able to prove to you about the things they are now accusing me.

14 ὁμολογῶ δὲ τοῦτό σοι ὅτι κατὰ τὴν ὁδὸν ἣν λέγουσιν αἵρεσιν οὕτως λατρεύω τῷ πατρῴῳ θεῷ πιστεύων πᾶσι τοῖς κατὰ τὸν νόμον καὶ τοῖς ἐν τοῖς προφήταις γεγραμμένοις, 15 ἐλπίδα ἔχων εἰς τὸν θεὸν ἣν καὶ αὐτοὶ οὗτοι προσδέχονται, ἀνάστασιν μέλλειν ἔσεσθαι δικαίων τε καὶ ἀδίκων·

16 ἐν τούτῳ καὶ αὐτὸς ἀσκῶ ἀπρόσκοπον συνείδησιν ἔχειν πρὸς τὸν θεὸν καὶ τοὺς ἀνθρώπους διὰ παντός.

17 Δι' ἐτῶν δὲ πλειόνων ἐλεημοσύνας ποιήσων εἰς τὸ ἔθνος μου παρεγενόμην καὶ προσφοράς, 18 ἐν αἷς εὗρόν με ἡγνισμένον ἐν τῷ ἱερῷ οὐ μετὰ ὄχλου οὐδὲ μετὰ θορύβου,

19 τινὲς δὲ ἀπὸ τῆς Ἀσίας Ἰουδαῖοι, οὓς ἔδει ἐπὶ σοῦ παρεῖναι καὶ κατηγορεῖν, εἴ τι ἔχοιεν πρὸς ἐμέ. 20 ἢ αὐτοὶ οὗτοι εἰπάτωσαν τί εὗρον ἀδίκημα στάντος μου ἐπὶ τοῦ συνεδρίου,

22 Ἀνεβάλετο δὲ αὐτοὺς ὁ Φῆλιξ ἀκριβέστερον εἰδὼς τὰ περὶ τῆς ὁδοῦ εἴπας·

21 ἢ περὶ μιᾶς ταύτης φωνῆς ἧς ἐκέκραξα ἐν αὐτοῖς ἑστὼς ὅτι περὶ ἀναστάσεως νεκρῶν ἐγὼ κρίνομαι σήμερον ἐφ' ὑμῶν.

ὅταν Λυσίας ὁ χιλίαρχος καταβῇ, διαγνώσομαι τὰ καθ' ὑμᾶς.

23 διαταξάμενος τῷ ἑκατοντάρχῃ τηρεῖσθαι αὐτόν, ἔχειν τε ἄνεσιν καὶ μηδένα κωλύειν τῶν ἰδίων αὐτοῦ ὑπηρετεῖν αὐτῷ.

24 Μετὰ δὲ ἡμέρας τινὰς παραγενόμενος ὁ Φῆλιξ σὺν Δρουσίλλῃ τῇ ἰδίᾳ γυναικὶ οὔσῃ Ἰουδαίᾳ μετεπέμψατο τὸν Παῦλον καὶ ἤκουσεν αὐτοῦ περὶ τῆς εἰς χριστὸν Ἰησοῦν πίστεως. 25 διαλεγομένου δὲ αὐτοῦ περὶ δικαιοσύνης καὶ ἐγκρατείας καὶ τοῦ κρίματος τοῦ μέλλοντος ἔμφοβος γενόμενος ὁ Φῆλιξ ἀπεκρίθη·

26 ἅμα καὶ ἐλπίζων ὅτι χρήματα δοθήσεται αὐτῷ ὑπὸ τοῦ Παύλου, διὸ καὶ πυκνότερον αὐτὸν μεταπεμπόμενος ὡμίλει αὐτῷ.

τὸ νῦν ἔχον πορεύου· καιρὸν δὲ μεταλαβὼν μετακαλέσομαί σε·

14 But I confess this to you, that according to the Way, which they call a sect, thus am I serving the ancestral God believing all things according to the Law and that have been written in the Prophets, 15 having hope toward God, which these ones themselves also await, that a resurrection certainly will occur, both of the just and unjust. 16 In this I myself also am endeavoring having a conscience free of offense with God and persons in everything. 17 Now through many years, I arrived for making charitable gifts to my nation and offerings, 18 in which matters they found me having been purified in the temple, not with a crowd, nor with an uproar, 19 but some Judeans from Asia, for whom it was necessary that they be present before you and make accusation, if they had anything against me. 20 Or let these men themselves say what injustice they found with me standing before the council 21 or concerning this one statement which I shouted out standing among them, [namely] this: 'Concerning the resurrection of the dead I myself am being judged before you today!'" 22 But Felix postponed them, understanding rather accurately about the Way, saying, "Whenever Lysias, the commanding officer, comes down, I will decide the matters between you," 23 ordering carefully to the centurion for him [Paul] to be kept in custody, as well as to have leisure and for no one to prevent his own [people] from serving him. 24 But after some days, Felix, appearing with Drusilla, his own wife being a Judean, sent for Paul and heard him concerning the faith in Christ Jesus. 25 Moreover, with him discussing about righteousness and self-control and the judgment to come, Felix, becoming terrified, responded back, "For this present time, go away; then, taking opportunity afterwards, I will summon you," 26 at the same time also hoping that money would be given to him by Paul; therefore, also more frequently, summoning him, he was chatting with him.

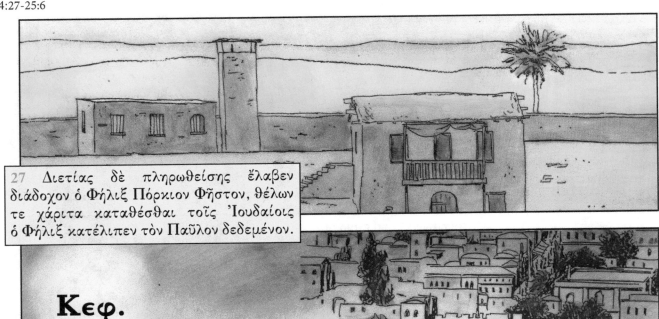

27 Διετίας δὲ πληρωθείσης ἔλαβεν διάδοχον ὁ Φῆλιξ Πόρκιον Φῆστον, θέλων τε χάριτα καταθέσθαι τοῖς Ἰουδαίοις ὁ Φῆλιξ κατέλιπεν τὸν Παῦλον δεδεμένον.

Κεφ. ΚΕ΄

25:1 Φῆστος οὖν ἐπιβὰς τῇ ἐπαρχείᾳ μετὰ τρεῖς ἡμέρας ἀνέβη εἰς Ἱεροσόλυμα ἀπὸ Καισαρείας,

2 ἐνεφάνισάν τε αὐτῷ οἱ ἀρχιερεῖς καὶ οἱ πρῶτοι τῶν Ἰουδαίων κατὰ τοῦ Παύλου καὶ παρεκάλουν αὐτὸν 3 αἰτούμενοι χάριν κατ᾽ αὐτοῦ, ὅπως μεταπέμψηται αὐτὸν εἰς Ἱερουσαλήμ, ἐνέδραν ποιοῦντες ἀνελεῖν αὐτὸν κατὰ τὴν ὁδόν. 4 Ὁ μὲν οὖν Φῆστος ἀπεκρίθη τηρεῖσθαι τὸν Παῦλον εἰς Καισάρειαν, ἑαυτὸν δὲ μέλλειν ἐν τάχει ἐκπορεύεσθαι·

5 οἱ οὖν ἐν ὑμῖν φησιν δυνατοὶ συνκαταβάντες, εἴ τι ἐστὶν ἐν τῷ ἀνδρὶ ἄτοπον, κατηγορείτωσαν αὐτοῦ.

6 διατρίψας δὲ ἐν αὐτοῖς ἡμέρας οὐ πλείους ὀκτὼ ἢ δέκα, καταβὰς εἰς Καισάρειαν, τῇ ἐπαύριον καθίσας ἐπὶ τοῦ βήματος ἐκέλευσεν τὸν Παῦλον ἀχθῆναι.

27 But, with two years completed, Felix received as successor Porcius Festus, and at the same time wanting to settle a favor with the Judeans, Felix left Paul bound up. 25:1 Therefore, Festus, having come into the province, after three days went up into Jerusalem from Caesarea, 2 and at the same time, the high priest and the principal men of the Judeans informed him against Paul and they were entreating him, 3 asking a favor against him, in order that he would summon him to Jerusalem, making a plot to kill him along the way. 4 So then, Festus answered back that Paul would be kept in custody at Caesarea, but that he himself would intend to travel out in quick order. 5 "Therefore, let the ones among you," he says, "who are in power, going down with me, accuse him if there is anything out of place in the man." 6 So, staying among them not more than eight or ten days, going down to Caesarea, on the next day sitting on the judgment seat, he commanded Paul to be brought.

7 Παραγενομένου δὲ αὐτοῦ περιέστησαν αὐτὸν οἱ ἀπὸ Ἱεροσολύμων καταβεβηκότες Ἰουδαῖοι πολλὰ καὶ βαρέα αἰτιώματα καταφέροντες, ἃ οὐκ ἴσχυον ἀποδεῖξαι,

8 τοῦ Παύλου ἀπολογουμένου ὅτι οὔτε εἰς τὸν νόμον τῶν Ἰουδαίων οὔτε εἰς τὸ ἱερὸν οὔτε εἰς Καίσαρά τι ἥμαρτον.

9 Ὁ Φῆστος δὲ θέλων τοῖς Ἰουδαίοις χάριν καταθέσθαι, ἀποκριθεὶς τῷ Παύλῳ εἶπεν· θέλεις εἰς Ἱεροσόλυμα ἀναβὰς ἐκεῖ περὶ τούτων κριθῆναι ἐπ' ἐμοῦ;

10 εἶπεν δὲ ὁ Παῦλος· ἐπὶ τοῦ βήματος Καίσαρος ἑστώς εἰμι, οὗ με δεῖ κρίνεσθαι.

Ἰουδαίους οὐδὲν ἠδίκηκα, ὡς καὶ σὺ κάλλιον ἐπιγινώσκεις· 11 εἰ μὲν οὖν ἀδικῶ καὶ ἄξιον θανάτου πέπραχά τι, οὐ παραιτοῦμαι τὸ ἀποθανεῖν· εἰ δὲ οὐδέν ἐστιν ὧν οὗτοι κατηγοροῦσίν μου, οὐδείς με δύναται αὐτοῖς χαρίσασθαι.

Καίσαρα ἐπικαλοῦμαι.

12 Τότε ὁ Φῆστος συλλαλήσας μετὰ τοῦ συμβουλίου ἀπεκρίθη· Καίσαρα ἐπικέκλησαι, ἐπὶ Καίσαρα πορεύσῃ.

7 Moreover, with him appearing, the Judeans who had come down from Jerusalem encircled him, bringing against him many and grievous charges which they were not able not prove, 8 Paul defending himself with this: "Neither against the Law of the Judeans, nor against the temple, nor against Caesar, did I sin in anything!" 9 But Festus, desiring to grant a favor to the Judeans, answering back to Paul, said, "Are you willing, going up into Jerusalem, there concerning these things to be judged by me?" 10 But Paul said, "Before Caesar's judgment seat I am standing, where it is necessary that I be judged. In no way did I wrong the Judeans, as you yourself also know rather well. 11 So then, if I am doing wrong and have committed something worthy of death, I am not refusing to die; but if there is nothing to the things that these men are accusing me of, no one is able to grant me as a 'favor' to them. I am calling upon Caesar!" 12 Then Festus, conferring with the council, answered back, "You have called upon to Caesar; to Caesar you will go!"

123

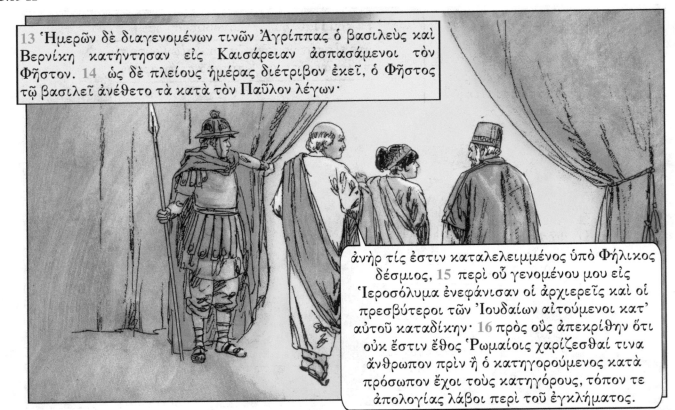

13 Ἡμερῶν δὲ διαγενομένων τινῶν Ἀγρίππας ὁ βασιλεὺς καὶ Βερνίκη κατήντησαν εἰς Καισάρειαν ἀσπασάμενοι τὸν Φῆστον. 14 ὡς δὲ πλείους ἡμέρας διέτριβον ἐκεῖ, ὁ Φῆστος τῷ βασιλεῖ ἀνέθετο τὰ κατὰ τὸν Παῦλον λέγων·

ἀνήρ τίς ἐστιν καταλελειμμένος ὑπὸ Φήλικος δέσμιος, 15 περὶ οὗ γενομένου μου εἰς Ἱεροσόλυμα ἐνεφάνισαν οἱ ἀρχιερεῖς καὶ οἱ πρεσβύτεροι τῶν Ἰουδαίων αἰτούμενοι κατ' αὐτοῦ καταδίκην· 16 πρὸς οὓς ἀπεκρίθην ὅτι οὐκ ἔστιν ἔθος Ῥωμαίοις χαρίζεσθαί τινα ἄνθρωπον πρὶν ἢ ὁ κατηγορούμενος κατὰ πρόσωπον ἔχοι τοὺς κατηγόρους, τόπον τε ἀπολογίας λάβοι περὶ τοῦ ἐγκλήματος.

17 συνελθόντων οὖν αὐτῶν ἐνθάδε ἀναβολὴν μηδεμίαν ποιησάμενος, τῇ ἑξῆς καθίσας ἐπὶ τοῦ βήματος ἐκέλευσα ἀχθῆναι τὸν ἄνδρα· 18 περὶ οὗ σταθέντες οἱ κατήγοροι οὐδεμίαν αἰτίαν ἔφερον ὧν ἐγὼ ὑπενόουν πονηράν·

19 ζητήματα δέ τινα περὶ τῆς ἰδίας δεισιδαιμονίας εἶχον πρὸς αὐτὸν καὶ περί τινος Ἰησοῦ τεθνηκότος, ὃν ἔφασκεν ὁ Παῦλος ζῆν. 20 ἀπορούμενος δὲ ἐγὼ τὴν περὶ τούτων ζήτησιν ἔλεγον εἰ βούλοιτο πορεύεσθαι εἰς Ἱεροσόλυμα κἀκεῖ κρίνεσθαι περὶ τούτων.

21 τοῦ δὲ Παύλου ἐπικαλεσαμένου τηρηθῆναι αὐτὸν εἰς τὴν τοῦ Σεβαστοῦ διάγνωσιν ἐκέλευσα τηρεῖσθαι αὐτὸν ἕως οὗ ἀναπέμψω αὐτὸν πρὸς Καίσαρα.

22 Ἀγρίππας δὲ πρὸς τὸν Φῆστον·

ἐβουλόμην καὶ αὐτὸς τοῦ ἀνθρώπου ἀκοῦσαι.

αὔριόν φησιν ἀκούσῃ αὐτοῦ.

13 Now, with some days having passed, King Agrippa and Bernice arrived at Caesarea, greeting Festus. 14 But as he was staying there many days, Festus set out the matters against Paul before the king, saying, "A certain man has been left by Felix as a prisoner. 15 about whom, with me coming into Jerusalem, the chief priests and the elders of the Judeans informed me, asking for a judgment against him; 16 to which I answered back that it is not a custom for the Romans to give up some person as a "favor" before the one being accused has met the accusers face-to-face, and at the same time has received a place of defense concerning the charge. 17 Therefore, with them coming together here, making no single postponement, on the next day sitting on the judgment seat I commanded the man to be brought; 18 concerning whom, standing, the accusers were bringing no single evil charge against him of things that I myself was suspecting. 19 But, they were having certain questions against him about their own religion and about some Jesus having died, whom Paul claimed to be living! 20 So, being perplexed about the controversy concerning these things, I was saying if he would want to travel into Jerusalem and there to be judged concerning these things. 21 But, with Paul calling out to be kept for the decision of the Emperor, I commanded him to be kept until I would send him up to Caesar." 22 So, Agrippa [said] to Festus, "I was wanting also to hear the person myself!" "Tomorrow," he says, "you will hear him."

124

23 Τῇ οὖν ἐπαύριον ἐλθόντος τοῦ Ἀγρίππα καὶ τῆς Βερνίκης μετὰ πολλῆς φαντασίας καὶ εἰσελθόντων εἰς τὸ ἀκροατήριον σύν τε χιλιάρχοις καὶ ἀνδράσιν τοῖς κατ' ἐξοχὴν τῆς πόλεως καὶ κελεύσαντος τοῦ Φήστου ἤχθη ὁ Παῦλος.

24 Καί φησιν ὁ Φῆστος·

Ἀγρίππα βασιλεῦ καὶ πάντες οἱ συνπαρόντες ἡμῖν ἄνδρες, θεωρεῖτε τοῦτον περὶ οὗ ἅπαν τὸ πλῆθος τῶν Ἰουδαίων ἐνέτυχόν μοι ἔν τε Ἱεροσολύμοις καὶ ἐνθάδε βοῶντες μὴ δεῖν αὐτὸν ζῆν μηκέτι.

25 ἐγὼ δὲ κατελαβόμην μηδὲν ἄξιον αὐτὸν θανάτου πεπραχέναι, αὐτοῦ δὲ τούτου ἐπικαλεσαμένου τὸν Σεβαστὸν ἔκρινα πέμπειν.

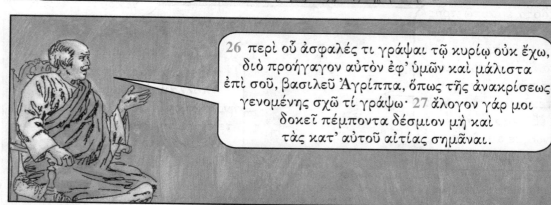

26 περὶ οὗ ἀσφαλές τι γράψαι τῷ κυρίῳ οὐκ ἔχω, διὸ προήγαγον αὐτὸν ἐφ' ὑμῶν καὶ μάλιστα ἐπὶ σοῦ, βασιλεῦ Ἀγρίππα, ὅπως τῆς ἀνακρίσεως γενομένης σχῶ τί γράψω· 27 ἄλογον γάρ μοι δοκεῖ πέμποντα δέσμιον μὴ καὶ τὰς κατ' αὐτοῦ αἰτίας σημᾶναι.

23 Therefore, on the next day, with Agrippa and Bernice coming with great pageantry and entering into the auditorium with both the commanding officers and the prominent men of the city, and Festus commanding, Paul was brought in. 24 And Festus says, "King Agrippa and all men present here with us, you are beholding this person about whom all the multitude of the Judeans entreated me, both at Jerusalem and here, shouting that it is necessary that he certainly live no longer! 25 But I myself attained that he has committed nothing worthy of death; moreover, with this one himself calling upon the Emperor, I determined to send him, 26 concerning whom I am not having anything reliable to write to my lord. Therefore, I brought him out before you and most especially before you, King Agrippa, in order that, after the examination happened, I would have what I will write. 27 For it seems to me unreasonable, in sending a prisoner, not also to signify the charges against him."

26:1 Ἀγρίππας δὲ πρὸς τὸν Παῦλον ἔφη·

ἐπιτρέπεταί σοι ὑπὲρ σεαυτοῦ λέγειν.

Κεφ. ΚΓ΄

τότε ὁ Παῦλος ἐκτείνας τὴν χεῖρα ἀπελογεῖτο·

2 περὶ πάντων ὧν ἐγκαλοῦμαι ὑπὸ Ἰουδαίων, βασιλεῦ Ἀγρίππα, ἥγημαι ἐμαυτὸν μακάριον ἐπὶ σοῦ μέλλων σήμερον ἀπολογεῖσθαι· **3** μάλιστα γνώστην ὄντα σε πάντων τῶν κατὰ Ἰουδαίους ἐθῶν τε καὶ ζητημάτων. διὸ δέομαι μακροθύμως ἀκοῦσαί μου.

4 Τὴν μὲν οὖν βίωσίν μου τὴν ἐκ νεότητος τὴν ἀπ᾽ ἀρχῆς γενομένην ἐν τῷ ἔθνει μου ἔν τε Ἱεροσολύμοις ἴσασι πάντες Ἰουδαῖοι **5** προγινώσκοντές με ἄνωθεν, ἐὰν θέλωσιν μαρτυρεῖν ὅτι κατὰ τὴν ἀκριβεστάτην αἵρεσιν τῆς ἡμετέρας θρησκείας ἔζησα Φαρισαῖος· **6** καὶ νῦν ἐπ᾽ ἐλπίδι τῆς εἰς τοὺς πατέρας ἡμῶν ἐπαγγελίας γενομένης ὑπὸ τοῦ θεοῦ ἕστηκα κρινόμενος,

7 εἰς ἣν τὸ δωδεκάφυλον ἡμῶν ἐν ἐκτενείᾳ νύκτα καὶ ἡμέραν λατρεῦον ἐλπίζει καταντῆσαι, περὶ ἧς ἐλπίδος ἐγκαλοῦμαι ὑπὸ Ἰουδαίων, βασιλεῦ, **8** τί ἄπιστον κρίνεται παρ᾽ ὑμῖν εἰ ὁ θεὸς νεκροὺς ἐγείρει;

9 Ἐγὼ μὲν οὖν ἔδοξα ἐμαυτῷ πρὸς τὸ ὄνομα Ἰησοῦ τοῦ Ναζωραίου δεῖν πολλὰ ἐναντία πρᾶξαι, **10** ὃ καὶ ἐποίησα ἐν Ἱεροσολύμοις καὶ πολλούς τε τῶν ἁγίων ἐγὼ ἐν φυλακαῖς κατέκλεισα τὴν παρὰ τῶν ἀρχιερέων ἐξουσίαν λαβών, ἀναιρουμένων τε αὐτῶν κατήνεγκα ψῆφον·

11 καὶ κατὰ πάσας τὰς συναγωγὰς πολλάκις τιμωρῶν αὐτοὺς ἠνάγκαζον βλασφημεῖν, περισσῶς τε ἐμμαινόμενος αὐτοῖς ἐδίωκον ἕως καὶ εἰς τὰς ἔξω πόλεις.

26:1 So, Agrippa was saying to Paul, "It is permitted for you to speak on your own behalf." Then Paul, stretching out his hand, defended himself. 2 "Concerning all the things that I am being accused of by the Judeans, King Agrippa, I consider myself fortunate, before you intending to defend myself today, 3 most especially with you being an expert in the matters throughout the Judeans, both customs and controversial questions. Therefore, I am begging patiently [for you] to hear me. 4 So then, my way of life from my youth up, occurring from the beginning, both in my own nation and in Jerusalem, all Judeans know, 5 knowing me in advance from the start, if they are willing to testify, that according to the strictest sect of our religion I lived as a Pharisee. 6 And now for the hope of the promise to our fathers made by God I stand here being judged, 7 for which our twelve tribe [nation], serving in earnest night and day, is hoping to attain, concerning which hope I am being accused by the Judeans, King [Agrippa]—8 why is it being judged unbelievable with you [all] if God does raise the dead ones? 9 So then, I myself decided for myself that it was necessary to do many things contrary to the name of Jesus of Nazareth, 10 which also I did in Jerusalem, and at the same time I myself shut up many of the saints in prisons, receiving authority from the chief priests, and additionally with them being put to death, I cast down a vote. 11 And across all the synagogues frequently punishing them, I was forcing them to blaspheme, and at the same time, being exceedingly enraged against them, I was persecuting [them] as far as also to the outside cities.

12 ἐν οἷς πορευόμενος εἰς τὴν Δαμασκὸν μετ' ἐξουσίας καὶ ἐπιτροπῆς τῆς τῶν ἀρχιερέων 13 ἡμέρας μέσης κατὰ τὴν ὁδὸν εἶδον, βασιλεῦ, οὐρανόθεν ὑπὲρ τὴν λαμπρότητα τοῦ ἡλίου περιλάμψαν με φῶς καὶ τοὺς σὺν ἐμοὶ πορευομένους.

14 πάντων τε καταπεσόντων ἡμῶν εἰς τὴν γῆν ἤκουσα φωνὴν λέγουσαν πρός με τῇ Ἐβραΐδι διαλέκτῳ· Σαοὺλ Σαούλ, τί με διώκεις; σκληρόν σοι πρὸς κέντρα λακτίζειν.

15 ἐγὼ δὲ εἶπα· τίς εἶ κύριε; ὁ δὲ κύριος εἶπεν· ἐγώ εἰμι Ἰησοῦς ὃν σὺ διώκεις. 16 ἀλλὰ ἀνάστηθι καὶ στῆθι ἐπὶ τοὺς πόδας σου· εἰς τοῦτο γὰρ ὤφθην σοι προχειρίσασθαί σε ὑπηρέτην καὶ μάρτυρα ὧν τε εἶδές με ὧν τε ὀφθήσομαί σοι,

17 ἐξαιρούμενός σε ἐκ τοῦ λαοῦ καὶ ἐκ τῶν ἐθνῶν, εἰς οὓς ἐγὼ ἀποστέλλω σε 18 ἀνοῖξαι ὀφθαλμοὺς αὐτῶν, τοῦ ἐπιστρέψαι ἀπὸ σκότους εἰς φῶς καὶ τῆς ἐξουσίας τοῦ σατανᾶ ἐπὶ τὸν θεόν,

τοῦ λαβεῖν αὐτοὺς ἄφεσιν ἁμαρτιῶν καὶ κλῆρον ἐν τοῖς ἡγιασμένοις πίστει τῇ εἰς ἐμέ.

12 In which circumstances, traveling into Damascus with the authority and jurisdiction from the chief priests, 13 at noon along the way I saw, King [Agrippa], from heaven beyond the brilliance of the sun a light shining around me and the ones traveling with me. 14 At the same time with us falling down to the earth, I heard a voice speaking to me in the Hebrew language, 'Saul, Saul, why are you persecuting me? It is unyielding for you to kick against the goads!' 15 But, I myself said, 'Who are you, Lord?' So, he said, 'I myself am Jesus, whom you yourself are persecuting. 16 But arise and stand on your feet; because for this I have appeared to you: that you mobilize yourself as a servant and a witness both of the things which you saw and of the things which I will show to you, 17 delivering you from the people and from the Gentiles, into whom I myself am sending you 18 to open their eyes, so that they would turn from darkness into light and from the power of Satan to God, so that they would receive deliverance from sins and an inheritance among the ones who have been sanctified by faith in me.'

19 Ὅθεν, βασιλεῦ Ἀγρίππα, οὐκ ἐγενόμην ἀπειθὴς τῇ οὐρανίῳ ὀπτασίᾳ, 20 ἀλλὰ τοῖς ἐν Δαμασκῷ πρῶτόν τε καὶ Ἱεροσολύμοις, πᾶσάν τε τὴν χώραν τῆς Ἰουδαίας, καὶ τοῖς ἔθνεσιν ἀπήγγελλον μετανοεῖν καὶ ἐπιστρέφειν ἐπὶ τὸν θεὸν ἄξια τῆς μετανοίας ἔργα πράσσοντας. 21 ἕνεκα τούτων με Ἰουδαῖοι συλλαβόμενοι ἐν τῷ ἱερῷ ἐπειρῶντο διαχειρίσασθαι.

22 ἐπικουρίας οὖν τυχὼν τῆς ἀπὸ τοῦ θεοῦ ἄχρι τῆς ἡμέρας ταύτης ἕστηκα μαρτυρόμενος μικρῷ τε καὶ μεγάλῳ, οὐδὲν ἐκτὸς λέγων ὧν τε οἱ προφῆται ἐλάλησαν μελλόντων γίνεσθαι καὶ Μωϋσῆς, 23 εἰ παθητὸς ὁ χριστός, εἰ πρῶτος ἐξ ἀναστάσεως νεκρῶν φῶς μέλλει καταγγέλλειν τῷ τε λαῷ καὶ τοῖς ἔθνεσιν.

24 Ταῦτα δὲ αὐτοῦ ἀπολογουμένου ὁ Φῆστος μεγάλῃ τῇ φωνῇ φησιν·

μαίνῃ Παῦλε· τὰ πολλά σε γράμματα εἰς μανίαν περιτρέπει.

25 ὁ δὲ Παῦλος·

οὐ μαίνομαί φησιν κράτιστε Φῆστε, ἀλλὰ ἀληθείας καὶ σωφροσύνης ῥήματα ἀποφθέγγομαι.

26 ἐπίσταται γὰρ περὶ τούτων ὁ βασιλεύς, πρὸς ὃν καὶ παρρησιαζόμενος λαλῶ· λανθάνειν γὰρ αὐτὸν τί τούτων οὐ πείθομαι οὐθέν· οὐ γάρ ἐστιν ἐν γωνίᾳ πεπραγμένον τοῦτο. 27 πιστεύεις, βασιλεῦ Ἀγρίππα, τοῖς προφήταις; οἶδα ὅτι πιστεύεις.

28 Ὁ δὲ Ἀγρίππας πρὸς τὸν Παῦλον·

ἐν ὀλίγῳ με πείθεις χριστιανὸν ποιῆσαι.

29 ὁ δὲ Παῦλος·

εὐξαίμην ἂν τῷ θεῷ καὶ ἐν ὀλίγῳ καὶ ἐν μεγάλῳ οὐ μόνον σὲ ἀλλὰ καὶ πάντας τοὺς ἀκούοντάς μου σήμερον γενέσθαι τοιούτους ὁποῖος κἀγώ εἰμι παρεκτὸς τῶν δεσμῶν τούτων.

19 Wherefore, King Agrippa, I did not become disobedient to the heavenly vision, 20 but to the ones of Damascus first as well as at Jerusalem, both all the country of Judea and also to the Gentiles, I proclaimed to be repenting and to be turning to God, doing works worthy of repentance. 21 On account of these things, the Judeans, seizing me in the temple, were attempting to lay hands to slay me. 22 Therefore, meeting with the help that is from God, to this day I stand testifying both to small and great, saying nothing outside both of which the Prophets said would happen and of Moses, 23 whether the Christ [would be] subjected to suffering, whether he, the first one from the resurrection of the dead, would intend to proclaim light both to the people and to the Gentiles." 24 So, with him thus defending himself, Festus with a loud voice says, "You are driven religiously mad, Paul! Your great learning is driving you to religious madness!" 25 But, "I am not religiously mad," Paul says, "most excellent Festus, but I am declaring openly words of truth and discretion. 26 For the king knows concerning these things, to whom also, speaking boldly, I am talking. For I am persuaded that not one item of these things escapes his notice, for this has not happened in a corner. 27 Are you believing, King Agrippa, the Prophets? I know that you believe." 28 But, Agrippa [said] to Paul, "In a short time, are you persuading to make me a Christian?" 29 So, Paul [said], "I would pray to God that, both in a short time and in a long time, not only you but also all the ones hearing me today would become the kind of persons of the sort as even I myself am except for these bonds!"

30 Ἀνέστη τε ὁ βασιλεὺς καὶ ὁ ἡγεμὼν ἥ τε Βερνίκη καὶ οἱ συνκαθήμενοι αὐτοῖς· 31 καὶ ἀναχωρήσαντες ἐλάλουν πρὸς ἀλλήλους λέγοντες ὅτι

οὐδὲν θανάτου ἢ δεσμῶν ἄξιόν τι πράσσει ὁ ἄνθρωπος οὗτος.

32 Ἀγρίππας δὲ τῷ Φήστῳ ἔφη·

ἀπολελύσθαι ἐδύνατο ὁ ἄνθρωπος οὗτος, εἰ μὴ ἐπεκέκλητο Καίσαρα.

Κεφ. ΚΖ´

27:1 Ὡς δὲ ἐκρίθη τοῦ ἀποπλεῖν ἡμᾶς εἰς τὴν Ἰταλίαν, παρεδίδουν τόν τε Παῦλον καί τινας ἑτέρους δεσμώτας ἑκατοντάρχῃ ὀνόματι Ἰουλίῳ σπείρης Σεβαστῆς.

2 ἐπιβάντες δὲ πλοίῳ Ἀδραμυττηνῷ μέλλοντι πλεῖν εἰς τοὺς κατὰ τὴν Ἀσίαν τόπους ἀνήχθημεν ὄντος σὺν ἡμῖν Ἀριστάρχου Μακεδόνος Θεσσαλονικέως.

3 τῇ τε ἑτέρᾳ κατήχθημεν εἰς Σιδῶνα, φιλανθρώπως τε ὁ Ἰούλιος τῷ Παύλῳ χρησάμενος ἐπέτρεψεν πρὸς τοὺς φίλους πορευθέντι ἐπιμελείας τυχεῖν.

30 At the same time, the king rose up and the governor, as well as Bernice and the ones sitting with them. 31 And withdrawing, they were speaking to one another, saying this: "This person is doing not any one thing worthy of death or of bonds." 32 Moreover, Agrippa was saying to Festus, "This person was able to have been released except he had called upon Caesar!" 27:1 Now, when it was determined that we should sail for Italy, they were handing over both Paul and certain other prisoners to a centurion, Julius by name, of the Augustan cohort. 2 So, embarking in a ship of Adramyttium intending to sail into places along Asia Minor, we put to sea—Aristarchus, a Macedonian of Thessalonica, being with us. 3 At the same time, on the following day, we put in at Sidon, and at the same time Julius, kindly consulting with Paul, permitted [him], going to friends, to find care.

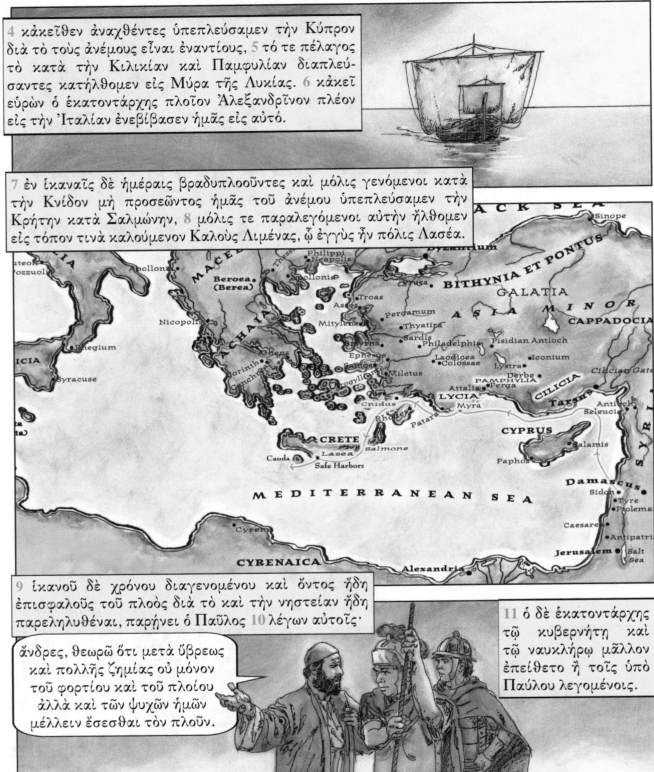

4 κἀκεῖθεν ἀναχθέντες ὑπεπλεύσαμεν τὴν Κύπρον διὰ τὸ τοὺς ἀνέμους εἶναι ἐναντίους, 5 τό τε πέλαγος τὸ κατὰ τὴν Κιλικίαν καὶ Παμφυλίαν διαπλεύσαντες κατήλθομεν εἰς Μύρα τῆς Λυκίας. 6 κἀκεῖ εὑρὼν ὁ ἑκατοντάρχης πλοῖον Ἀλεξανδρῖνον πλέον εἰς τὴν Ἰταλίαν ἐνεβίβασεν ἡμᾶς εἰς αὐτό.

7 ἐν ἱκαναῖς δὲ ἡμέραις βραδυπλοοῦντες καὶ μόλις γενόμενοι κατὰ τὴν Κνίδον μὴ προσεῶντος ἡμᾶς τοῦ ἀνέμου ὑπεπλεύσαμεν τὴν Κρήτην κατὰ Σαλμώνην, 8 μόλις τε παραλεγόμενοι αὐτὴν ἤλθομεν εἰς τόπον τινὰ καλούμενον Καλοὺς Λιμένας, ᾧ ἐγγὺς ἦν πόλις Λασέα.

9 ἱκανοῦ δὲ χρόνου διαγενομένου καὶ ὄντος ἤδη ἐπισφαλοῦς τοῦ πλοὸς διὰ τὸ καὶ τὴν νηστείαν ἤδη παρεληλυθέναι, παρῄνει ὁ Παῦλος 10 λέγων αὐτοῖς·

ἄνδρες, θεωρῶ ὅτι μετὰ ὕβρεως καὶ πολλῆς ζημίας οὐ μόνον τοῦ φορτίου καὶ τοῦ πλοίου ἀλλὰ καὶ τῶν ψυχῶν ἡμῶν μέλλειν ἔσεσθαι τὸν πλοῦν.

11 ὁ δὲ ἑκατοντάρχης τῷ κυβερνήτῃ καὶ τῷ ναυκλήρῳ μᾶλλον ἐπείθετο ἢ τοῖς ὑπὸ Παύλου λεγομένοις.

4 And from there, putting to sea, we sailed under the lee of Cyprus because the winds were contrary, 5 and at the same time sailing across the sea that is along Cilicia and Pamphylia, we came down into Myra of Lycia. 6 And there, the centurion, finding an Alexandrian ship sailing for Italy, put us on board into it. 7 Next, in a number of days, sailing slowly and coming with difficulty across from Cnidus, the wind not allowing us further, we sailed under the lee of Crete across from Salmone, 8 and at the same time with difficulty sailing along it, we came into some place called Fair Havens, near to which was the city Lasea. 9 Next, with sufficient time passing and the voyage already dangerous, because also the [day of the Atonement] Fast had already passed, Paul was strongly urging, 10 saying to them, "Men, I am perceiving that with injury and much financial loss, not only of the cargo and the ship but also of our lives, the voyage will certainly come to pass!" 11 But the centurion was giving heed more to the master and to the owner of the ship than to the things being spoken by Paul.

12 Ἀνευθέτου δὲ τοῦ λιμένος ὑπάρχοντος πρὸς παραχειμασίαν οἱ πλείονες ἔθεντο βουλὴν ἀναχθῆναι ἐκεῖθεν, εἴ πως δύναιντο καταντήσαντες εἰς Φοίνικα παραχειμάσαι λιμένα τῆς Κρήτης βλέποντα κατὰ λίβα καὶ κατὰ χῶρον.

13 Ὑποπνεύσαντος δὲ νότου δόξαντες τῆς προθέσεως κεκρατηκέναι, ἄραντες ἆσσον παρελέγοντο τὴν Κρήτην. 14 μετ᾽ οὐ πολὺ δὲ ἔβαλεν κατ᾽ αὐτῆς ἄνεμος τυφωνικὸς ὁ καλούμενος εὐρακύλων.

15 συναρπασθέντος δὲ τοῦ πλοίου καὶ μὴ δυναμένου ἀντοφθαλμεῖν τῷ ἀνέμῳ ἐπιδόντες ἐφερόμεθα.

CRETE

Cauda

Safe Harbors

16 νησίον δέ τι ὑποδραμόντες καλούμενον Κλαῦδα ἰσχύσαμεν μόλις περικρατεῖς γενέσθαι τῆς σκάφης, 17 ἣν ἄραντες βοηθείαις ἐχρῶντο ὑποζωννύντες τὸ πλοῖον· φοβούμενοί τε μὴ εἰς τὴν σύρτιν ἐκπέσωσιν χαλάσαντες τὸ σκεῦος, οὕτως ἐφέροντο.

12 Now, with the harbor in fact being unsuitable for wintering in, the majority set the plan to set sail from there, if somehow they could be able to arrive at Phoenix to winter there, a harbor of Crete looking along the southwest and along the northwest. 13 So, with the south wind blowing gently, supposing to have obtained their plan, keeping very close, they were sailing along Crete. 14 But, after not much [distance], a stormy wind called the "Northeaster" beat down from its [shore]. 15 So, with the ship being caught and not being able to face into the wind, giving in, we were being driven along. 16 But, running under the lee of a small island called Clauda, with difficulty we had power to be in control of the boat, 17 which, lifting it up, they used cables, reinforcing the ship; at the same time, fearing that they would run aground on the Syrtis sand bars, lowering the anchor, they were thus being driven along.

18 σφοδρῶς δὲ χειμαζομένων ἡμῶν τῇ ἑξῆς ἐκβολὴν ἐποιοῦντο· 19 καὶ τῇ τρίτῃ αὐτόχειρες τὴν σκευὴν τοῦ πλοίου ἔρριψαν·

20 μήτε δὲ ἡλίου μήτε ἄστρων ἐπιφαινόντων ἐπὶ πλείονας ἡμέρας, χειμῶνός τε οὐκ ὀλίγου ἐπικειμένου λοιπὸν περιηρεῖτο ἐλπὶς πᾶσα τοῦ σῴζεσθαι ἡμᾶς.

21 πολλῆς τε ἀσιτίας ὑπαρχούσης τότε σταθεὶς ὁ Παῦλος ἐν μέσῳ αὐτῶν εἶπεν·

Ἔδει μέν, ὦ ἄνδρες, πειθαρχήσαντάς μοι μὴ ἀνάγεσθαι ἀπὸ τῆς Κρήτης, κερδῆσαί τε τὴν ὕβριν ταύτην καὶ τὴν ζημίαν. 22 καὶ τὰ νῦν παραινῶ ὑμᾶς εὐθυμεῖν· ἀποβολὴ γὰρ ψυχῆς οὐδεμία ἔσται ἐξ ὑμῶν πλὴν τοῦ πλοίου.

18 So, with us being very badly tossed about by the storm, on the next day they were throwing things overboard. 19 And on the third day, with their own hands they threw out the ship's tackle. 20 Moreover, with neither sun nor stars shining for many days, and at the same time no small storm was pressing on us, beyond that, all hope that we would be saved was being taken away. 21 At the same time, with a great shortage of food in fact existing, then Paul, standing up in the middle of them, said, "It was indeed necessary, O men, having given heed to me, not to sail from Crete, and at the same time to gain this hardship and loss. 22 And with respect to the present, I am urging you to take courage; for there will be no loss of life among you, except for the ship.

23 For by me on this night stood an angel of God, to whom I belong, for whom also I serve, 24 saying, 'Do not be afraid, Paul; it is necessary that you stand before Caesar, and behold, God has shown favor to you [regarding] all the ones sailing with you. 25 Therefore, take courage, men! For I believe God, that it will be thus in like manner as has been spoken to me. 26 But it is necessary that we run aground on some island." 27 But when the fourteenth night had come, with us being tossed about in the Adriatic Sea, about the middle of the night the sailors were suspecting some land was approaching them. 28 And taking soundings, they found twenty fathoms, then setting short intervals and sounding again, they found fifteen fathoms. 29 At the same time, fearing that we would run aground somewhere along rocky places, ripping the four anchors from the stern, they were praying that day would come.

30 But, with the sailors seeking to flee out of the ship and lowering the boat into the sea with a pretense of intending to lay out anchors from the bow, 31 Paul said to the centurion and to the soldiers, "Unless these men stay in the ship, you yourselves are not able to be saved!" 32 Then the soldiers cut away the ropes of the boat and let it fall off. 33 So, up until the time that day was about to come, Paul was urging all of them to take some food, saying, "Today, waiting for the fourteenth day, you are continuing without food, having taken nothing. 34 Therefore, I urge you to take food! For this is in fact for your safety; for a hair from the head of not a single one of you will perish!" 35 Now, saying these things and taking bread, he gave thanks to God in the sight of all, and breaking it, he began to eat. 36 Then, all becoming encouraged, they also took food. 37 So, we were two hundred seventy-six souls on the ship.

38 κορεσθέντες δὲ τροφῆς ἐκούφιζον τὸ πλοῖον ἐκβαλλό-μενοι τὸν σῖτον εἰς τὴν θάλασσαν.

39 ὅτε δὲ ἡμέρα ἐγένετο, τὴν γῆν οὐκ ἐπεγίνωσκον, κόλπον δέ τινα κατενόουν ἔχοντα αἰγιαλόν, εἰς ὃν ἐβουλεύοντο, εἰ δύναιντο, ἐξῶσαι τὸ πλοῖον. 40 καὶ τὰς ἀγκύρας περιελόντες εἴων εἰς τὴν θάλασσαν, ἅμα ἀνέντες τὰς ζευκτηρίας τῶν πηδαλίων καὶ ἐπάραντες τὸν ἀρτέμωνα τῇ πνεούσῃ κατεῖχον εἰς τὸν αἰγιαλόν.

41 περιπεσόντες δὲ εἰς τόπον διθάλασσον ἐπέκειλαν τὴν ναῦν· καὶ ἡ μὲν πρῷρα ἐρείσασα ἔμεινεν ἀσάλευτος, ἡ δὲ πρύμνα ἐλύετο ὑπὸ τῆς βίας τῶν κυμάτων. 42 τῶν δὲ στρατιωτῶν βουλὴ ἐγένετο ἵνα τοὺς δεσμώτας ἀποκτείνωσιν, μή τις ἐκκολυμβήσας διαφύγῃ.

43 ὁ δὲ ἑκατοντάρχης βουλόμενος διασῶσαι τὸν Παῦλον ἐκώλυσεν αὐτοὺς τοῦ βουλήματος, ἐκέλευσέν τε τοὺς δυναμένους κολυμβᾶν ἀπορίψαντας πρώτους ἐπὶ τὴν γῆν ἐξιέναι, 44 καὶ τοὺς λοιποὺς οὓς μὲν ἐπὶ σανίσιν, οὓς δὲ ἐπί τινων τῶν ἀπὸ τοῦ πλοίου. καὶ οὕτως ἐγένετο πάντας διασωθῆναι ἐπὶ τὴν γῆν.

38 Moreover, being satisfied with the food, they were lightening the ship, throwing out the wheat into the sea. 39 But, when it became day, they were not recognizing the land, but they were noticing some bay having a beach, into which they were considering, if they were able, to drive the ship. 40 And casting off the anchors, leaving them in the sea, simultaneously untying the rudder ropes and hoisting up the foresail to the wind, they were making for the beach. 41 But falling between a place where two seas met, they ran the ship aground. And, on the one hand, the bow, striking, remained immovable, but, on the other hand, the stern was being broken by the force of the waves. 42 Then, a plan of the soldiers was in order that they kill the prisoners, so that someone, swimming out, would not escape. 43 But the centurion, wanting to bring Paul to safety, stopped them from their plan, and at the same time commanded that the ones being able to swim, throwing themselves overboard first, should depart for the land, 44 and [then] the rest, some on planks and some on other things from the ship. And in this way, it happened that all were brought to safety on land.

Κεφ. ΚΗ΄

28:1 καὶ διασωθέντες τότε ἐπέγνωμεν ὅτι Μελίτη ἡ νῆσος καλεῖται· 2 οἵ τε βάρβαροι παρεῖχαν οὐ τὴν τυχοῦσαν φιλανθρωπίαν ἡμῖν· ἅψαντες γὰρ πυρὰν προσελάβοντο πάντας ἡμᾶς διὰ τὸν ὑετὸν τὸν ἐφεστῶτα καὶ διὰ τὸ ψῦχος.

3 συστρέψαντος δὲ τοῦ Παύλου φρυγάνων τι πλῆθος καὶ ἐπιθέντος ἐπὶ τὴν πυρὰν ἔχιδνα ἀπὸ τῆς θέρμης ἐξελθοῦσα καθῆψε τῆς χειρὸς αὐτοῦ.

4 Ὡς δὲ εἶδον οἱ βάρβαροι κρεμάμενον τὸ θηρίον ἐκ τῆς χειρὸς αὐτοῦ, πρὸς ἀλλήλους ἔλεγον·

πάντως φονεύς ἐστιν ὁ ἄνθρωπος οὗτος, ὃν διασωθέντα ἐκ τῆς θαλάσσης ἡ δίκη ζῆν οὐκ εἴασεν.

5 Ὁ μὲν οὖν ἀποτινάξας τὸ θηρίον εἰς τὸ πῦρ ἔπαθεν οὐδὲν κακόν. 6 οἱ δὲ προσεδόκων αὐτὸν μέλλειν πίμπρασθαι ἢ καταπίπτειν ἄφνω νεκρόν·

ἐπὶ πολὺ δὲ αὐτῶν προσδοκώντων καὶ θεωρούντων μηδὲν ἄτοπον εἰς αὐτὸν γινόμενον μεταβαλόμενοι ἔλεγον αὐτὸν εἶναι θεόν.

28:1 And being brought to safety, then they discovered that the island was called Malta. 2 At the same time, the [foreign] natives were offering us unexpected kindness; for all of them kindled a fire for all of us because of the present rain and because of the cold. 3 But with Paul gathering a large bundle of sticks and setting it on the fire, a viper, coming out from the heat, fastened on his hand! 4 So, when the natives saw the creature hanging from his hand, they were saying to one another, "Certainly, this person is a murderer, whom, [although] being brought to safety from the sea, Justice has not allowed to live!" 5 So then, he, shaking off the creature into the fire, suffered nothing bad. 6 But they were expecting that he would be swelling or falling down suddenly dead; so, for a long time waiting and seeing nothing untypical happening to him, thinking differently, they were saying that he was a god.

7 Ἐν δὲ τοῖς περὶ τὸν τόπον ἐκεῖνον ὑπῆρχεν χωρία τῷ πρώτῳ τῆς νήσου, ὀνόματι Ποπλίῳ, ὃς ἀναδεξάμενος ἡμᾶς τρεῖς ἡμέρας φιλοφρόνως ἐξένισεν.

8 Ἐγένετο δὲ τὸν πατέρα τοῦ Ποπλίου πυρετοῖς καὶ δυσεντερίῳ συνεχόμενον κατακεῖσθαι· πρὸς ὃν ὁ Παῦλος εἰσελθὼν καὶ προσευξάμενος, ἐπιθεὶς τὰς χεῖρας αὐτῷ, ἰάσατο αὐτόν.

9 Τούτου δὲ γενομένου καὶ οἱ λοιποὶ οἱ ἐν τῇ νήσῳ ἔχοντες ἀσθενείας προσήρχοντο καὶ ἐθεραπεύοντο· 10 οἳ καὶ πολλαῖς τιμαῖς ἐτίμησαν ἡμᾶς, καὶ ἀναγομένοις ἐπέθεντο τὰ πρὸς τὰς χρείας.

7 Now in the [areas] around that place were fields belonging in fact to the chief person of the island, Publius by name, who, receiving us for three days, kindly offered hospitality. 8 So, it happened that the father of Publius, being afflicted with fevers and dysentery, was lying down, to whom Paul, entering and praying—laying his hands on him—healed him. 9 Then, with this occurring, also the remaining ones on the island having illnesses were coming and being healed; 10 who also with many honors gave us honor, and, for [us] setting sail they provided the things needed.

11 Μετὰ δὲ τρεῖς μῆνας ἀνήχθημεν ἐν πλοίῳ παρακεχειμακότι ἐν τῇ νήσῳ, Ἀλεξανδρίνῳ, παρασήμῳ Διοσκούροις· 12 καὶ καταχθέντες εἰς Συρακούσας ἐπεμείναμεν ἡμέρας τρεῖς, 13 ὅθεν περιελθόντες κατηντήσαμεν εἰς Ῥήγιον καὶ μετὰ μίαν ἡμέραν ἐπιγενομένου νότου δευτεραῖοι ἤλθομεν εἰς Ποτιόλους· 14a οὗ εὑρόντες ἀδελφοὺς παρεκλήθημεν παρ᾽ αὐτοῖς ἐπιμεῖναι ἡμέρας ἑπτά·

14b καὶ οὕτως εἰς τὴν Ῥώμην ἤλθαμεν. 15 κἀκεῖθεν οἱ ἀδελφοὶ ἀκούσαντες τὰ περὶ ἡμῶν ἦλθαν εἰς ἀπάντησιν ἡμῖν ἄχρι Ἀππίου Φόρου καὶ Τριῶν Ταβερνῶν, οὓς ἰδὼν ὁ Παῦλος εὐχαριστήσας τῷ θεῷ ἔλαβε θάρσος.

16 Ὅτε δὲ εἰσήλθομεν εἰς Ῥώμην, ἐπετράπη τῷ Παύλῳ μένειν καθ᾽ ἑαυτὸν σὺν τῷ φυλάσσοντι αὐτὸν στρατιώτῃ.

11 So, after three months, we set sail in a ship having wintered in the island, an Alexandrian one with the emblem "The Twin Brothers." 12 And putting in at Syracuse, we stayed three days, 13 from there, circling around, we arrived at Rhegium and after one day, with a south wind springing up, on the second day we came into Puteoli, 14 where, finding brothers, we were encouraged to remain with them for seven days. And in this way, we came into Rome. 15 And from there, the brothers, hearing about our circumstances, came to meet us as far as The Market of Appius and The Three Taverns, whom Paul seeing—giving thanks to God— took courage. 16 Then, when we entered into Rome, the centurion allowed for Paul to stay by himself with the soldier guarding him.

17 Ἐγένετο δὲ μετὰ ἡμέρας τρεῖς συγκαλέσασθαι αὐτὸν τοὺς ὄντας τῶν Ἰουδαίων πρώτους· συνελθόντων δὲ αὐτῶν ἔλεγεν πρὸς αὐτούς·

ἐγώ, ἄνδρες ἀδελφοί, οὐδὲν ἐναντίον ποιήσας τῷ λαῷ ἢ τοῖς ἔθεσι τοῖς πατρῴοις, δέσμιος ἐξ Ἱεροσολύμων παρεδόθην εἰς τὰς χεῖρας τῶν Ῥωμαίων, **18** οἵτινες ἀνακρίναντές με ἐβούλοντο ἀπολῦσαι διὰ τὸ μηδεμίαν αἰτίαν θανάτου ὑπάρχειν ἐν ἐμοί·

19 ἀντιλεγόντων δὲ τῶν Ἰουδαίων ἠναγκάσθην ἐπικαλέσασθαι Καίσαρα οὐχ ὡς τοῦ ἔθνους μου ἔχων τί κατηγορεῖν.

20 διὰ ταύτην οὖν τὴν αἰτίαν παρεκάλεσα ὑμᾶς ἰδεῖν καὶ προσλαλῆσαι· ἕνεκεν γὰρ τῆς ἐλπίδος τοῦ Ἰσραὴλ τὴν ἅλυσιν ταύτην περίκειμαι.

21 οἱ δὲ πρὸς αὐτὸν εἶπαν·

ἡμεῖς οὔτε γράμματα περὶ σοῦ ἐδεξάμεθα ἀπὸ τῆς Ἰουδαίας, οὔτε παραγενόμενός τις τῶν ἀδελφῶν ἀπήγγειλεν ἢ ἐλάλησέν τι περὶ σοῦ πονηρόν.

22 ἀξιοῦμεν δὲ παρὰ σοῦ ἀκοῦσαι ἃ φρονεῖς· περὶ μὲν γὰρ τῆς αἱρέσεως ταύτης γνωστὸν ἡμῖν ἐστιν ὅτι πανταχοῦ ἀντιλέγεται.

17 So, after three days it happened that he called together the prominent men of the Judeans. Then, with them coming together, he said to them, "I, fellow brothers, [although] doing nothing against the people or the ancestral customs, was delivered prisoner from Jerusalem into the hands of the Romans, 18 who, examining me, were wanting to release me because there was in fact not one reason for death in me. 19 But with the Judeans speaking against it, I was forced to call upon Caesar, not as though having something to accuse my nation. 20 For this reason, therefore, I asked to see you and to speak with you. For because of the hope of Israel I am wearing this chain." 21 But they said to him, "We ourselves neither received letters from Judea concerning you, nor did anyone of the brothers, arriving, report or speak anything evil about you. 22 But we consider it worthy to hear from you what things you have in mind. For, concerning this sect, it is known to us that everywhere it is being spoken against."

23 Ταξάμενοι δὲ αὐτῷ ἡμέραν ἦλθον πρὸς αὐτὸν εἰς τὴν ξενίαν πλείονες, οἷς ἐξετίθετο διαμαρτυρόμενος τὴν βασιλείαν τοῦ θεοῦ, πείθων τε αὐτοὺς περὶ τοῦ Ἰησοῦ, ἀπό τε τοῦ νόμου Μωϋσέως καὶ τῶν προφητῶν ἀπὸ πρωῒ ἕως ἑσπέρας. 24 καὶ οἱ μὲν ἐπείθοντο τοῖς λεγομένοις, οἱ δὲ ἠπίστουν. 25 ἀσύμφωνοι δὲ ὄντες πρὸς ἀλλήλους ἀπελύοντο εἰπόντος τοῦ Παύλου ῥῆμα ἕν, ὅτι

καλῶς τὸ πνεῦμα τὸ ἅγιον ἐλάλησεν διὰ Ἡσαΐου τοῦ προφήτου πρὸς τοὺς πατέρας ὑμῶν 26 λέγων·

πορεύθητι πρὸς τὸν λαὸν τοῦτον καὶ εἰπόν· ἀκοῇ ἀκούσετε καὶ οὐ μὴ συνῆτε, καὶ βλέποντες βλέψετε καὶ οὐ μὴ ἴδητε· 27 ἐπαχύνθη γὰρ ἡ καρδία τοῦ λαοῦ τούτου, καὶ τοῖς ὠσὶν βαρέως ἤκουσαν καὶ τοὺς ὀφθαλμοὺς αὐτῶν ἐκάμμυσαν· μή ποτε ἴδωσιν τοῖς ὀφθαλμοῖς καὶ τοῖς ὠσὶν ἀκούσωσιν καὶ τῇ καρδίᾳ συνῶσιν καὶ ἐπιστρέψωσιν καὶ ἰάσομαι αὐτούς.

28 Γνωστὸν οὖν ἔστω ὑμῖν ὅτι τοῖς ἔθνεσιν ἀπεστάλη τοῦτο τὸ σωτήριον τοῦ θεοῦ, αὐτοὶ καὶ ἀκούσονται.

30* Ἐνέμεινεν δὲ διετίαν ὅλην ἐν ἰδίῳ μισθώματι καὶ ἀπεδέχετο πάντας τοὺς εἰσπορευομένους πρὸς αὐτὸν 31 κηρύσσων τὴν βασιλείαν τοῦ θεοῦ καὶ διδάσκων τὰ περὶ τοῦ κυρίου Ἰησοῦ χριστοῦ μετὰ πάσης παρρησίας ἀκωλύτως.

23 So, appointing a day for him, many came to him at his lodging, to whom he was setting forth, testifying about the kingdom of God, at the same time persuading them concerning Jesus, both from the Law of Moses and from the Prophets, from morning until evening. 24 And some were being persuaded by the things being spoken, but some were disbelieving. 25 Moreover, with a disagreement existing with one another, they departed with Paul speaking one word, [saying] this: "Well did the Holy Spirit speak through Isaiah the prophet to our fathers, 26 saying, 'Go to this people and say, 'With hearing, you will hear and will never understand. Seeing, you will see and will never perceive. 27 For this people's heart has become thick, and with ears they hear with difficulty and they closed their eyes; so that never they would see with their eyes and with their ears would they hear and with their heart would they understand and would turn again and I will heal them.'' 28 Therefore, let it be known to you that to the Gentiles this salvation of God has been sent, and they themselves will listen!" 30 So, Paul remained two whole years in his own rented house and he was receiving all coming to him, 31 preaching the kingdom of God and teaching the things concerning the Lord, Jesus Christ, with all boldness unhindered.

CPSIA information can be obtained
at www.ICGtesting.com
Printed in the USA
FFHW012309300319
51316573-56795FF